EPHESIANS

THE NEW TESTAMENT LIBRARY
Current and Forthcoming Titles

Editorial Advisory Board

COMMENTARY SERIES

MATTHEW. BY R. ALAN CULPEPPER, MCAFEE SCHOOL OF THEOLOGY, MERCER UNIVERSITY

MARK. BY M. EUGENE BORING, BRITE DIVINITY SCHOOL, TEXAS CHRISTIAN UNIVERSITY

LUKE. BY JOHN T. CARROLL, UNION PRESBYTERIAN SEMINARY

JOHN. BY MARIANNE MEYE THOMPSON, FULLER THEOLOGICAL SEMINARY

ACTS. BY CARL R. HOLLADAY, CANDLER SCHOOL OF THEOLOGY, EMORY UNIVERSITY

ROMANS. BY BEVERLY ROBERTS GAVENTA, PRINCETON THEOLOGICAL SEMINARY

I CORINTHIANS. BY ALEXANDRA R. BROWN, WASHINGTON & LEE UNIVERSITY

II CORINTHIANS. BY FRANK J. MATERA, THE CATHOLIC UNIVERSITY OF AMERICA

GALATIANS. BY MARTINUS C. DE BOER, VU UNIVERSITY AMSTERDAM

EPHESIANS. BY STEPHEN E. FOWL, LOYOLA COLLEGE

PHILIPPIANS AND PHILEMON. BY CHARLES B. COUSAR, COLUMBIA THEOLOGICAL SEMINARY

COLOSSIANS. BY JERRY L. SUMNEY, LEXINGTON THEOLOGICAL SEMINARY

I & II THESSALONIANS. BY SUSAN EASTMAN, DUKE DIVINITY SCHOOL

I & II TIMOTHY AND TITUS. BY RAYMOND F. COLLINS, THE CATHOLIC UNIVERSITY OF AMERICA

HEBREWS. BY LUKE TIMOTHY JOHNSON, CANDLER SCHOOL OF THEOLOGY, EMORY UNIVERSITY

JAMES. BY REINHARD FELDMEIER, UNIVERSITY OF GÖTTINGEN

I & II PETER AND JUDE. BY LEWIS R. DONELSON, AUSTIN PRESBYTERIAN THEOLOGICAL SEMINARY

I, II, & III JOHN. BY JUDITH M. LIEU, UNIVERSITY OF CAMBRIDGE

REVELATION. BY BRIAN K. BLOUNT, UNION PRESBYTERIAN SEMINARY

CLASSICS

HISTORY AND THEOLOGY IN THE FOURTH GOSPEL. BY J. LOUIS MARTYN, UNION THEOLOGICAL SEMINARY, NEW YORK

IMAGES OF THE CHURCH IN THE NEW TESTAMENT. BY PAUL S. MINEAR, YALE DIVINITY SCHOOL

PAUL AND THE ANATOMY OF APOSTOLIC AUTHORITY. BY JOHN HOWARD SCHÜTZ, UNIVERSITY OF NORTH CAROLINA, CHAPEL HILL

THEOLOGY AND ETHICS IN PAUL. BY VICTOR PAUL FURNISH, PERKINS SCHOOL OF THEOLOGY, SOUTHERN METHODIST UNIVERSITY

THE WORD IN THIS WORLD: ESSAYS IN NEW TESTAMENT EXEGESIS AND THEOLOGY. BY PAUL W. MEYER, PRINCETON THEOLOGICAL SEMINARY

GENERAL STUDIES

THE LAW AND THE PROPHETS BEAR WITNESS: THE OLD TESTAMENT IN THE NEW. BY J. ROSS WAGNER, PRINCETON THEOLOGICAL SEMINARY

METHODS FOR NEW TESTAMENT STUDY. BY A. K. M. ADAM, UNIVERSITY OF GLASGOW

NEW TESTAMENT BACKGROUNDS. BY CARL R. HOLLADAY, CANDLER SCHOOL OF THEOLOGY, EMORY UNIVERSITY

Stephen E. Fowl

Ephesians

A Commentary

WESTMINSTER
JOHN KNOX PRESS
LOUISVILLE • KENTUCKY

© 2012 Stephen E. Fowl

2012 paperback edition
Originally published in hardback in the United States
by Westminster John Knox Press
Louisville, Kentucky

12 13 14 15 16 17 18 19 20 21—10 9 8 7 6 5 4 3 2 1

The translation of Ephesians is by the author. Except as indicated, other Scripture quotations are from the New Revised Standard Version of the Bible, copyright © 1989 by the Division of Christian Education of the National Council of the Churches of Christ in the U.S.A., and used by permission. AT = author's translation.

Book design by Jennifer K. Cox

Library of Congress Cataloging-in-Publication Data

Fowl, Stephen E.
    Ephesians : a commentary / Stephen E. Fowl.
        pages cm—(The New Testament library)
    Includes bibliographical references and indexes.
    ISBN 978-0-664-22125-6 (hardback)
    1. Bible. N.T. Ephesians—Commentaries.   I. Title.
    BS2695.53.F69   2012
    227'.507—dc23

                                        2012010949

ISBN: 978-0-664-23944-2 (paperback)

♾ The paper used in this publication meets the minimum requirements of the American National Standard for Information Sciences—Permanence of Paper for Printed Library Materials, ANSI Z39.48-1992.

CONTENTS

PREFACE

This volume is long overdue. As a result, I have accumulated many debts in relation to this project, and I want to acknowledge them with gratitude. Unfortunately, the passage of time has ensured that I will probably forget to mention several people. I began working on this commentary during a sabbatical year in 2004–5 spent at The Center of Theological Inquiry in Princeton. Robert Jenson and Wallace Alston, and the members of the Center, especially Beverly Gaventa, were extremely helpful as I got this project off the ground.

My colleagues at Loyola, including our dean, Jim Buckley, have always known how to mingle the rigors and trials of work with the joys of friendship in ways that mitigated the burdens of being chair of the department. Moreover, I have received very generous institutional support from Loyola's faculty development program. They provided both sabbatical support as well as grants for summer research.

Over the years I have worked on this commentary, I have made numerous presentations on Ephesians to various groups. This allowed me to test ideas, clarify my own thinking, and engage in stimulating conversation with a host of gracious people. In particular I want to thank Mark Gornik and the students of City Seminary of New York. At Mark's invitation I was able to try out some ideas about Ephesians and reconciliation in one of the most vibrant classroom settings I have known. My dear friends at the Church of the Servant King in Eugene always challenge me to speak clearly and walk worthily. During this time I also taught a class on Ephesians at the Ecumenical Institute of St. Mary's Seminary and University in Baltimore. The students in that class also challenged and encouraged me throughout the term.

Many people have read and commented on parts of this manuscript. I am especially grateful to Mike Gorman for some keen insight and encouraging conversation. The members of the Christology and Scripture Symposium that met at the University of Gloucestershire in 2005 read and engaged my ideas about Ephesians 2, and I am very grateful to have been a part of that group. These people all read pieces of this commentary. Gene Boring has read the whole thing, and more than once. He has offered superb editorial, exegetical, and theological advice. This work is far better than it would have been without his help. In addition, a former student, Kate Gerwin, helped to prepare the bibliography and footnotes. Daniel Braden and the staff at Westminster John Knox have done a superb job with my work. I am very grateful for their care and patience. All of these people have contributed to the betterment of this commentary. I must take full responsibility for its remaining shortcomings and errors.

When I started this project, Brendan and Liam were boys. Now they are young men. It is hard to figure out how that has happened so fast. My wife Melinda deserves a great deal of credit for this. Moreover, she has been a ready source of support and editorial advice for me.

Just as I was completing the final draft of this commentary, one of the great saints of Baltimore, Allan Tibbels, died far too young. God gave Allan a host of gifts to "equip the saints for the work of ministry, for building up the body of Christ" (Eph 4:12). He shared those gifts with his neighbors and with those of us who were fortunate enough to cross his path on the streets of Sandtown. This commentary is dedicated to his memory.

ABBREVIATIONS

ANTC	Abingdon New Testament Commentaries
BDAG	Bauer, W., F. W. Danker, W. F. Arndt, and F. W. Gingrich. *A Greek-English Lexicon of the New Testament and Other Early Christian Literature.* 3rd ed. Chicago, 2000
BCBC	Believers Church Bible Commentary
BDF	Blass, R., A. Debrunner, and R. W. Funk. *A Greek Grammar of the New Testament and Other Early Christian Literature.* Chicago, 1961
Bib	*Biblica*
BibInt	*Biblical Interpretation*
CBQ	*Catholic Biblical Quarterly*
EKKNT	Evangelisch-katholischer Kommentar zum Neuen Testament
ExpTim	*Expository Times*
HNT	Handbuch zum Neuen Testament
ICC	International Critical Commentary
JB	Jerusalem Bible
JBL	*Journal of Biblical Literature*
JETS	*Journal of the Evangelical Theological Society*
JSNT	*Journal for the Study of the New Testament*
JSNTSup	Journal for the Study of the New Testament: Supplement Series
JSOT	*Journal for the Study of the Old Testament*
JTS	*Journal of Theological Studies*
LSJ	Liddell, H. G., R. Scott, and H. S. Jones. *A Greek-English Lexicon.* 9th ed. with revised supplement. Oxford, 1996
MM	Moulton, J. H., and G. Milligan. *The Vocabulary of the Greek Testament.* London, 1930. Reprint, Peabody, MA, 1997
NABPR	National Association of Baptist Professors of Religion
NovT	*Novum Testamentum*
NovTSup	Supplements to Novum Testamentum
NTS	*New Testament Studies*
NTTS	New Testament Tools and Studies

SNT	Studien zum Neuen Testament
SNTSMS	Society for New Testament Studies Monograph Series
UBS[3]	*The Greek New Testament,* United Bible Societies, 3rd ed.
UBS[4]	*The Greek New Testament,* United Bible Societies, 4th ed.
WBC	Word Biblical Commentary
WTJ	*Westminster Theological Journal*
ZNW	*Zeitschrift für die neutestamentliche Wissenschaft und die Kunde der älteren Kirche*

BIBLIOGRAPHY

Cited by author, plus short title if necessary

Abbott, T. K. [Thomas Kingsmill]. *Ephesians and Colossians*. ICC. Edinburgh: T&T Clark, 1897.

Allan, John A. "The 'In Christ' Formula in Ephesians." *NTS* 5 (1958): 54–62.

Allen, Thomas G. "Exaltation and Solidarity with Christ: Ephesians 1.20 and 2.6." *JSNT* 28 (1986): 103–20.

Arnold, Clinton E. *Power and Magic: The Concept of Power in Ephesians*. Grand Rapids: Baker, 1989.

Balch, David L. *Let Wives Be Submissive: The Domestic Code in 1 Peter*. Chico, CA: Scholars Press, 1981.

Balch, David L., and Carolyn Osiek, eds. *Early Christian Families in Context*. Grand Rapids: Eerdmans, 2003.

Balthasar, Hans Urs von. *Dare We Hope "That All Men Be Saved"? With a Short Discourse on Hell*. Translated by David Kipp and Lothar Krauth. San Francisco: Ignatius Press, 1987.

Barclay, John M. G. "Mirror-Reading a Polemical Letter: Galatians as a Test Case." *JSNT* 31 (1987): 79–93.

Barth, Marcus. *Ephesians*. 2 vols. New York: Doubleday, 1974.

Bassler, Jouette M. *Divine Impartiality: Paul and a Theological Axiom*. Chico, CA: Scholars Press, 1982.

Bauckham, Richard. *God Crucified: Monotheism and Christology in the New Testament*. Grand Rapids: Eerdmans, 1998.

Benoit, Pierre. "Head, Body, and *Plērōma* in the Epistles of Captivity." Pages 51–92 in vol. 2 of *Jesus and the Gospel*. Translated by B. Weatherhead. New York: Crossroad, 1974.

Best, Ernest. *Ephesians*. Edinburgh: T&T Clark, 2001.

———. "Who Used Whom? The Relationship of Ephesians and Colossians." *NTS* 43 (1997): 72–96.

Bjerkelund, Carl J. *Parakalō: Form, Funktion und Sinn der parakalō-Sätze in den paulinischen Briefen*. Oslo: Universitetsforlaget, 1967.

Brett, Mark G. "Motives and Intentions in Genesis 1." *JTS* 42 (1991): 1–16.

Bruce, F. F. [Frederick Fyvie]. *The Epistle to the Ephesians*. London: Pickering & Inglis, 1961.

Budde, Michael L. *The Magic Kingdom of God*. Boulder, CO: Westview, 1997.

Caird, George B. "The Descent of Christ in Ephesians 4:7–11." Pages 535–45 in *Studia evangelica*. Vol. 2. Edited by Frank L. Cross. Berlin: Akademie, 1964.

Calvin, John. *The Epistles of Paul the Apostle to the Galatians, Ephesians, Philippians and Colossians*. Translated by Thomas H. L. Parker. Edited by David W. Torrance and Thomas F. Torrance. Grand Rapids: Eerdmans, 1996.

Caragounis, Chrys C. *The Ephesian* Mystērion: *Meaning and Content*. Lund: Gleerup, 1977.

Carr, Wesley. *Angels and Principalities: The Background, Meaning and Development of the Pauline Phrase* hai archai kai exousiai. Cambridge: Cambridge University Press, 1981.

Cassidy, Richard J. *Paul in Chains: Roman Imprisonment and the Letters of St. Paul*. New York: Herder & Herder, 2001.

Catherine of Siena. *Selected Writings*. Edited and introduced by Mary O'Driscoll, OP. Hyde Park, NY: New City Press, 1993.

Dahl, Nils A. "Christ, Creation and the Church." Pages 422–44 in *The Background to the New Testament and Its Eschatology*. Edited by W. D. Davies and David Daube. Cambridge: Cambridge University Press, 1956.

— — —. "Cosmic Dimensions and Religious Knowledge." Pages 365–88 in *Studies in Ephesians*. Tübingen: Mohr, 2000.

Darko, Daniel K. *No Longer Living as the Gentiles: Differentiation and Shared Ethical Values in Ephesians 4.17–6.9*. Edinburgh: Continuum, 2008.

Dawes, Gregory W. *The Body in Question: Metaphor and Meaning in the Interpretation of Ephesians 5:21–33*. Leiden: Brill, 1998.

Deichgräber, Reinhard. *Gotteshymnus und Christushymnus in der frühen Christenheit: Untersuchungen zu Form, Sprache und Stil der frühchristlichen Hymnen*. Göttingen: Vandenhoeck & Ruprecht, 1967.

Dibelius, Martin. *An die Kolosser; Epheser; An Philemon*. HNT 3, Die Briefe des Apostels Paulus 2. Tübingen: Mohr, 1912.

Dixon, Suzanne. "Sex and the Married Woman in Ancient Rome." Pages 111–29 in *Early Christian Families in Context*. Edited by David L. Balch and Carolyn Osiek. Grand Rapids: Eerdmans, 2003.

Donaldson, Terence L. *Paul and the Gentiles: Remapping the Apostle's Convictional World*. Minneapolis: Fortress, 1997.

Donelson, Lewis R. *1 & II Peter and Jude: A Commentary*. NTL. Louisville: Westminster John Knox, 2010.

Dunn, James D. G. *Theology of Paul the Apostle*. Grand Rapids: Eerdmans, 1998.

Elliott, John H. "1 Peter, Its Situation and Strategy." Pages 61–78 in *Perspectives on 1 Peter*. Edited by Charles H. Talbert. NABPR Special Studies 9. Macon, GA: Mercer University Press, 1986.

Engberg-Pedersen, Troels. "Ephesians 5,12–13: ἐλέγχειν and Conversion in the New Testament." *ZNW* 80 (1989): 89–110.

Fee, Gordon D. *God's Empowering Presence.* Peabody, MA: Hendrickson, 1994.

Findlay, James Alexander. "Ephesians vi.29." *ExpTim* 46 (1934–35): 429.

Fowl, Stephen N. *Engaging Scripture: A Model for Theological Interpretation.* Oxford: Blackwell, 1998.

———. *The Story of Christ in the Ethics of Paul: An Analysis of the Function of the Hymnic Material in the Pauline Corpus.* Sheffield: JSNT Press, 1990.

———. *Theological Interpretation of Scripture.* Eugene, OR: Cascade Books, 2009.

Gnilka, Joachim. *Der Brief an die Epheser.* EKKNT 10. Freiburg: Herder, 1971.

Gombis, Timothy G. "Cosmic Lordship and Divine Gift Giving: Psalm 68 in Ephesians 4:8." *NovT* 47 (2005): 367–80.

———. "Ephesians 2 as Narrative of Divine Warfare." *JSNT* 26 (2004): 403–18.

———. "Ephesians 3:2–13: Pointless Digression, or Epitome of the Triumph of God in Christ?" *WTJ* 66 (2004): 313–23.

Gorman, Michael J. *Reading Paul.* Eugene, OR: Cascade Books, 2008.

Gudorf, Michael E. "The Use of πάλη in Ephesians 6:12." *JBL* 117 (1998): 331–35.

Harris, W. Hall, III. *The Descent of Christ in Ephesians 4:7–11 and Traditional Hebrew Imagery.* Leiden: Brill, 1996.

Hay, David M. *Glory at the Right Hand: Psalm 110 in Early Christianity.* Nashville: Abingdon, 1973.

Heil, John Paul. *Ephesians: Empowerment to Walk in Love for the Unity of All in Christ.* Atlanta: Society of Biblical Literature, 2007.

———. "Ephesians 5:18b: 'But be filled in the Spirit.'" *CBQ* 69 (2007): 506–16.

Heine, Ronald E., ed. *The Commentaries of Origen and Jerome on St. Paul's Epistle to the Ephesians.* Introduced and translated by Ronald E. Heine. Oxford: Oxford University Press, 2002.

Hoehner, Harold W. *Ephesians: An Exegetical Commentary.* Grand Rapids: Baker Academic, 2002.

Hurtado, Larry W. *Lord Jesus Christ.* Grand Rapids: Eerdmans, 2003.

Jeal, Roy R. *Integrating Theology and Ethics in Ephesians: The Ethos of Communication.* Lewiston, NY: Edwin Mellen, 2000.

Käsemann, Ernst. "On the Subject of Primitive Christian Apocalyptic." Pages 108–37 in *New Testament Questions of Today.* Translated by W. J. Montague. London: SCM, 1969.

———. "Paul and Early Catholicism." Pages 236–51 in *New Testament Questions of Today.* Translated by W. J. Montague. London: SCM, 1969.

Kirby, John C. *Ephesians: Baptism and Pentecost; An Inquiry into the Structure and Purpose of the Epistle to the Ephesians.* Montreal: McGill University Press, 1968.

Kreitzer, Larry J. *Hierapolis in the Heavens*. Edinburgh: T&T Clark, 2007.

La Potterie, Ignace de. "Le Christ, Plērōme de l'Église (Ep 1,22–23)." *Bib* 58 (1977): 500–524.

Lampe, G. W. H. [Geoffrey William Hugo], ed. *A Patristic Lexicon*. Oxford: Oxford University Press, 1961.

Lemcio, Eugene E. "Ephesus and the New Testament Canon." Pages 335–60 in *The New Testament as Canon*. Edited by R. Wall and E. Lemcio. Sheffield: JSOT Press, 1992.

Levenson, Jon Douglas. *Creation and the Persistence of Evil*. Princeton: Princeton University Press, 1994.

Levering, Matthew. *Christ's Fulfillment of Torah and Temple: Salvation according to Thomas Aquinas*. Notre Dame, IN: University of Notre Dame Press, 2002.

———. *Scripture and Metaphysics: Aquinas and the Renewal of Trinitarian Theology*. Oxford: Blackwell, 2004.

Lincoln, Andrew T. *Ephesians*. WBC 42. Waco, TX: Word, 1990.

———. *Paradise Now and Not Yet: Studies in the Role of the Heavenly Dimension in Paul's Thought with Special Reference to His Eschatology*. Cambridge: Cambridge University Press, 1981.

———. "'Stand, Therefore . . .': Ephesians 6:10 as *Peroratio*." *BibInt* 3 (1995): 99–114.

———. "The Use of the OT in Ephesians." *JSNT* 14 (1982): 16–57.

Lohfink, Gerhard. *Jesus and Community*. Translated by John P. Galvin. Philadelphia: Fortress, 1984.

Lyall, Francis. *Slaves, Citizens, and Sons: Legal Metaphors in the Epistles*. Grand Rapids: Academie Books, 1984.

Lyonnet, Stanislaus, and Léopold Sabourin. *Sin, Redemption, and Sacrifice: A Biblical and Patristic Study*. Rome: Biblical Institute Press, 1970.

MacDonald, Margaret Y. *Colossians, Ephesians*. Collegeville, MN: Liturgical Press, 2000.

———. *The Pauline Churches: A Sociohistorical Study of Institutionalization in Pauline and Deutero-Pauline Writings*. Cambridge: Cambridge University Press, 1984.

———. "The Politics of Identity." *JSNT* 26:4 (2004): 419–44.

Malherbe, Abraham J. *Moral Exhortation: A Greco-Roman Sourcebook*. Philadelphia: Westminster, 1986. Reprint, 1989.

Martin, Dale B. "Slave Families and Slaves in Families." Pages 207–30 in *Early Christian Families in Context*. Edited by David L. Balch and Carolyn Osiek. Grand Rapids: Eerdmans, 2003.

Martin, Ralph P. *Reconciliation*. Atlanta: John Knox Press, 1981.

Martyn, J. Louis. "Apocalyptic Antinomies." Pages 111–24 in *Theological Issues in the Letters of Paul*. Edinburgh: T&T Clark, 1997.

McHugh, John. "A Reconsideration of Ephesians 1:10b in the Light of Ire-naeus." Pages 302–9 in *Paul and Paulinism: Essays in Honour of C. K. Barrett*. Edited by Morna D. Hooker and S. G. Wilson. London: SPCK, 1982.

McKelvey, Robert J. *The New Temple: A Study in New Testament Imagery.* Oxford: Oxford University Press, 1969.

Metzger, Bruce M. *A Textual Commentary on the Greek New Testament.* 2nd ed. Stuttgart: Deutsche Bibelgesellschaft, 1994.

Morgenthaler, Robert. *Statistik der neutestamentlichen Wortschatzes.* 4th ed. Zurich: Gotthelf, 1992.

Moritz, Thorsten. *A Profound Mystery: The Use of the Old Testament in Ephesians.* Leiden: Brill, 1996.

Moule, C. F. D. [Charles Francis Digby]. *Idiom Book of New Testament Greek.* Cambridge: Cambridge University Press, 1953.

Muddiman, John. *The Epistle to the Ephesians.* Peabody, MA: Hendrickson, 2004.

Mussner, F. "Contributions Made by Qumran to the Understanding of the Epistle to the Ephesians." Pages 159–78 in *Paul and Qumran*. Edited by J. Murphy-O'Connor. Chicago: Priory Press, 1968.

O'Brien, Peter Thomas. "Ephesians 1: An Unusual Introduction to a Pauline Letter." *NTS* 25 (1979): 504–16.

— — —. "Principalities and Powers: Opponents of the Church." Pages 111–49 in *Biblical Interpretation and the Church*. Edited by Don A. Carson. Exeter: Paternoster, 1984.

Osiek, Carolyn. "Female Slaves, *Porneia*, and the Limits of Obedience." Pages 255–74 in *Early Christian Families in Context*. Edited by David L. Balch and Carolyn Osiek. Grand Rapids: Eerdmans, 2003.

Page, Sydney H. T. "Whose Ministry? A Re-Appraisal of Ephesians 4:12." *NovT* 47 (2005): 26–46.

Percy, Ernst. *Die Probleme der Kolosser- und Epheserbriefe.* Gleerup: Lund, 1946.

Perkins, Pheme. *Ephesians.* ANTC 10. Nashville: Abingdon, 1997.

Porter, Stanley E. *Verbal Aspect in the Greek of the New Testament with Reference to Tense and Mood.* Studies in Biblical Greek. New York: Peter Lang, 1989.

Rader, William. *The Church and Racial Hostility: A History of Interpretation of Ephesians 2, 11–22.* Tübingen: Mohr, 1978.

Radner, Ephraim. *The End of the Church: A Pneumatology of Christian Division in the West.* Grand Rapids: Eerdmans, 1998.

Reinhard, Donna B. "Ephesians 6:10–20: A Call to Personal Piety or Another Way of Describing Union with Christ?" *JETS* 48 (2005): 521–32.

Reumann, John. "OIKONOMIA-Terms in Paul in Comparison with Lucan *Heilsgeschichte*." *NTS* 13 (1967): 144–64.

Robinson, J. Armitage. *Commentary on Ephesians*. Grand Rapids: Kregel, 1979.

Roon, Aart van. *The Authenticity of Ephesians*. Translated by S. Prescod-Jokel. NovTSup 39. Leiden: Brill, 1974.

Root, Michael. "Why Care about the Unity of the Church?" Pages 98–111 in *Why Are We Here? Everyday Questions and the Christian Life*. Edited by Ronald F. Thiemann and William C. Placher. Harrisburg, PA: Trinity Press International, 1998.

Saller, Richard. "Women, Slaves, and the Economy of the Roman Household." Pages 185–204 in *Early Christian Families in Context*. Edited by David L. Balch and Carolyn Osiek. Grand Rapids: Eerdmans, 2003.

Sampley, J. Paul. *And the Two Shall Become One Flesh: A Study of Traditions in Ephesians 5:21–33*. Cambridge: Cambridge University Press, 1971.

Sanders, Jack T. *The New Testament Christological Hymns: Their Historical Religious Background*. Cambridge: Cambridge University Press, 1971.

Schlier, Heinrich. *Der Brief an die Epheser*. Düsseldorf: Patmos, 1957.

Schnackenburg, Rudolf. *The Epistle to the Ephesians*. Translated by Helen Heron. Edinburgh: T&T Clark, 1991.

Schubert, Paul. *Form and Function of the Pauline Thanksgivings*. Berlin: A. Töpelmann, 1939.

Scott, James M. *Adoption as Sons of God: An Exegetical Investigation into the Background of* υἱοθεσία *in the Pauline Corpus*. Tübingen: Mohr, 1992.

Skinner, Quentin. "Motives, Intentions and the Interpretation of Texts." *New Literary History* 3 (1971): 393–408.

Stuhlmacher, Peter. *Reconciliation, Law, and Righteousness: Essays in Biblical Theology*. Philadelphia: Fortress, 1986.

Thomas Aquinas. *Commentary on Saint Paul's Epistle to the Ephesians*. Translated by M. Lamb. Albany, NY: Magi Books, 1966.

Thrall, Margaret E. *Greek Particles in the New Testament: Linguistic and Exegetical Studies*. NTTS 3. Grand Rapids: Eerdmans, 1962.

Wallace-Hadrill, Andrew. "*Domus* and *Insulae* in Rome: Families and Households." Pages 3–18 in *Early Christian Families in Context*. Edited by David L. Balch and Carolyn Osiek. Grand Rapids: Eerdmans, 2003.

Walters, James C. "Paul, Adoption and Inheritance." Pages 43–76 in *Paul in the Greco-Roman World*. Edited by J. Paul Sampley. Harrisburg, PA: Trinity Press International, 2003.

Wedderburn, Alexander J. M. "Some Observations on Paul's Use of the Phrases 'In Christ' and 'With Christ.'" *JSNT* 25 (1985): 83–97.

Wengst, Klaus. *Christologische Formeln und Lieder des Urchristentums*. SNT 7. Gütersloh: Mohn, 1972

Westcott, Brooke Foss. *Saint Paul's Epistle to the Ephesians: The Greek Text, with Notes and Addenda*. London: Macmillan, 1906.

Wild, Robert A. "'Be Imitators of God': Discipleship in the Letter to the Ephesians." Pages 127–43 in *Discipleship in the New Testament*. Edited by Fernando F. Segovia. Philadelphia: Fortress, 1985.

Wink, Walter. *Naming the Powers*. Philadelphia: Fortress, 1984.

Yee, Tet-Lim N. *Jews, Gentiles and Ethnic Reconciliation: Paul's Jewish Identity and Ephesians*. SNTSMS 130. Cambridge: Cambridge University Press, 2005.

Yoder Neufeld, Thomas R. *Ephesians*. BCBC. Scottdale, PA: Herald Press, 2002.

— — —. *"Put On the Armour of God": The Divine Warrior From Isaiah to Ephesians*. JSNTSup 140. Sheffield: Sheffield Academic Press, 1997.

Yorke, Gosnell L. "Hearing the Politics of Peace in Ephesians: A Proposal from an African Postcolonial Perspective." *JSNT* 30 (2007): 112–27.

INTRODUCTION

The introduction to a commentary generally provides the author with an occasion to speak about a variety of critical issues surrounding the text in question. In the course of examining such issues, a reader can begin to gather a sense of what the commentator thinks about the text and what the commentator's overall aims might be. Before moving to discuss issues about the overall argument of Ephesians, the addressees and authorship questions, I will say a few words about the aims of this commentary.

There are a variety of approaches to take in writing a commentary. One way to think of this variety is to imagine a continuum. On one end are those who seek to explicate the text in a fairly straightforward way, paying little if any overt attention to scholarly debates, technical problems, or textual ambiguities. Reading these commentaries gives one a clear and unobstructed view of what the commentator takes to be the central argument of the epistle. This approach tends to obscure all of the heavy interpretive work that the commentator is doing. All sorts of interpretive decisions are being made without being justified or subjected to the judgment of readers.

At the other end of the continuum are those commentators who clearly and diligently display a wide variety of scholarly opinions regarding any word, phrase, or clause in Ephesians that has generated attention. Readers can gain a great deal of knowledge about the state of the scholarly discussion on any issue by studying these commentaries. It is much more common in these cases, however, to find that the commentator's own interpretive voice gets lost in the details of others' positions. In addition, this wealth of detail can obscure the lively flow of the text as it moves from point to point.

Of course, no commentary occupies either end of the continuum. Yet it is possible to locate commentators relative to these two poles. For example, the commentaries of Andrew Lincoln (*Ephesians*), Ernest Best (*Ephesians*), and Harold Hoehner are all excellent resources for finding out what a number of other scholars think about any particular issue in Ephesians.[1] They are invaluable to every other commentator writing in English. Because these

---

1. See the bibliography for these authors (here and below), for Gnilka, and for Schlier.

commentaries are both well done and relatively recent, I have to some extent risked a lesser degree of attention to scholarly disputes around aspects of Ephesians in favor of keeping my attention focused more closely on displaying the argument of Ephesians.

When I thought it was appropriate, I have made reference to premodern commentators on Ephesians. In particular, I have regularly engaged John Chrysostom's *Homilies* and the commentaries of Thomas Aquinas and John Calvin. I have no doubt that I could have engaged these three much more and others besides. I hope that readers will find that in many cases these premodern interpreters were able to discern and address the theological crux of a passage in ways that modern interpreters do not.

In addition, I have tried to keep in mind the fact that most of the people who will read this commentary are studying Ephesians because they are Christians and read Ephesians in ways that both shape and are shaped by their Christian faith and practice. With this in mind, I have tried to keep my comments relevant to such concerns, nonetheless hoping to make sure that my comments are disciplined by the text of Ephesians. For many years, I have been concerned with reinvigorating and reforming the practice of reading Scripture theologically. Commentary writing and the aims of this series in particular do not invite a large-scale theoretical discussion about theological interpretation. Moreover, I have written a good deal on this elsewhere (*Engaging Scripture* and *Theological Interpretation*). Christians are called to read, interpret, and embody Scripture in ways that deepen their love for God, for each other, and for the world. A commentary can aid that practice in a variety of ways. For example, it can clarify obscure phrases and terms by setting them in a plausible historical context, thus disciplining our thinking about a text. A commentary can explicate a passage of Scripture in ways that might illumine a contemporary context or concern of Christians, thus opening up interpretive possibilities in the present. A commentary may indicate how specific passages, in connection with other passages and in the light of larger convictions about God and world, cohere with and regulate one another, thus helping Christians speak about their faith and practice with greater precision and clarity. My hope is that this commentary will do all of these things when and as it is appropriate to do so.

Yet in all of this my aim is not to say the last word on Ephesians, but to offer my comments as part of an ongoing conversation with interpreters past, present, and future. In this light, it seems best to move on to matters more directly related to Ephesians. Thus I will make some comments about the overall argument of Ephesians and about relationships between the text of Ephesians and the Acts narratives of the church's founding in Ephesus. In addition, I will address, but by no means resolve, some of the questions surrounding the author and the initial recipients of Ephesians.

Argument of Ephesians

In the body of this commentary, the text of Ephesians is divided into discrete units, each composed of several verses. Sometimes these units are divided into subunits. This sort of division aids one in digging deeply into the text of Ephesians. It also brings with it the possibility that one examines the discrete details of the text so closely that one loses the sense of the whole. To counter that possibility, there are remarks at the beginning and end of each section explaining how each piece of the text fits with what precedes and anticipates what follows. In addition, I will here offer a narrative summary of how the argument of Ephesians unfolds and provide an outline of that argument:

Following the opening greeting, Paul[2] offers a blessing to the "God and Father of our Lord Jesus Christ." On the one hand, this directs praise to God and invites the Ephesians to likewise praise God. Moreover, this blessing also allows Paul to narrate God's drama of salvation, a drama that was initiated before the foundation of the world and that reaches its climax as everything is brought to its proper end in Christ. This drama is cosmic in its scope and consequences. In addition, God has graciously incorporated the Ephesians into this drama. Indeed, the presence of the Spirit in the Ephesians' midst confirms their incorporation into God's drama of salvation (1:3–14).

This leads Paul to offer a prayer on the Ephesians' behalf. The hope of this prayer is that the Ephesians will come to understand the significance of God's drama of salvation and Christ's particular place in this drama (1:15–23).

Paul then goes on to discuss the Ephesians' incorporation into God's drama of salvation from two different, though related, perspectives. First, Paul discusses how the Ephesians' sin had alienated them from God. Though their sin alienated them from God, God graciously acted to redeem them through Christ (2:1–10). Second, Paul narrates how the Ephesians were also alienated from God's chosen people. This too resulted in alienation from God. Astonishingly, God's plan to draw all the nations to God through the life of redeemed Israel is revealed to have its locus in the life, death, and resurrection of Christ. Christ is the one who brings about the reconciliation of Jews and Gentiles to God and to one another in the church. Coming to see God's drama of salvation in this way will require the Gentile Christians in Ephesus to learn to think of themselves as Gentiles, both before and after becoming Christians (2:11–22).

In chapter 2 Paul has interpreted both God's drama of salvation and the Ephesians' place in that drama in some rather bold ways, in ways that even Paul himself could not have anticipated before the time when God revealed the surprising movements of this drama to him. Thus in chapter 3 Paul both asserts

---

2. See my comments below about why I will retain the name "Paul" for the author of this letter and my ambivalence about the purposes, methods, and results of discussions about the authorship of Ephesians.

the divine source for his views and claims that God has commissioned him to proclaim this particular understanding of God's drama to the Ephesians and others. As recipients of this message, the church in Ephesus (and elsewhere) has a particular role to play in that drama, and Paul begins to articulate that for them. Paul also recognizes that for the Ephesians (or any other body of believers) to inhabit God's drama of salvation appropriately in any particular context, they will need a form of practical wisdom that comes from God. Hence he concludes chapter 3 with a prayer that God will grant this sort of wisdom to the Ephesians.

In the light of this prayer at the end of chapter 3, Paul begins chapter 4 with the admonition to the Ephesians to walk in a manner worthy of their calling. Based on this general admonition, Paul urges the Ephesians to adopt certain habits, practices, and dispositions and to avoid others. Initially he presents habits and dispositions essential to maintaining "the unity of the Spirit in the bond of peace" (4:1–16). Then he commands the Ephesians to make a clean break with their past, abjuring practices and dispositions characteristic of Gentile existence outside of Christ (4:17–24). Next he focuses on the common life of the Ephesian church and the things they can do to enhance or frustrate their life together (4:25–5:2). Having already encouraged the Ephesians to continue turning away from their past corrupt practices, Paul speaks about the boundary between the congregation and the community at large, focusing on how he wants that larger community to perceive the body of Christ (5:3–14). This leads to a brief discussion of living wisely and the connections between worship and wise living (5:15–20). Paul then moves on to discuss wise living in the context of the patriarchal household. Apparently Paul does not imagine this as the only form of household arrangement that is pleasing to God, but it is the form he and the Ephesians know (5:21–6:9). Finally, in a passage that draws on elements from many parts of the epistle, Paul urges the Ephesians to take on the armor of God in order to stand fast in the faith amid all the spiritual forces arrayed against them, forces that Christ ultimately will subject to himself but that have yet to be subdued (6:10–20).

Outline of Ephesians

One should be aware that there is a variety of ways to organize and outline the text of Ephesians. Readers will find works dividing Ephesians into a series of complex chiastic structures (e.g., Heil, *Ephesians*) and others that divide the text according to conventions of Greco-Roman rhetoric (e.g., Lincoln, *Ephesians*). At their best, such structures can help to remind readers what has already transpired and to anticipate where the argument might be moving. Sometimes an author will rely on a structure to resolve a difficulty in the text or to make a historical point. At such points readers need to be wary. Any and all structures and outlines of Ephesians or any other text should only be deployed in the light of prior close textual analysis. That is, structures and outlines presume decisions and judgments about how to interpret specific passages or verses. It is crucial for readers to remember that outlines are summaries of understanding already achieved on other grounds. Thus, since such structures already presume that the text has been analyzed and understood, the structure cannot be used to resolve difficulties in the text.

Ephesus and Paul in Acts

In Acts 18–20 we read a good deal about the church in Ephesus and how Paul is portrayed in relation to that church. It will be useful to review the account in Acts before trying to see how it might relate to the Epistle to the Ephesians.[3]

Toward the end of his second missionary journey, on his way from Corinth to Jerusalem and before heading to Antioch, Paul and his coworkers Priscilla and Aquila stop in Ephesus. As is his custom, Paul speaks in the synagogue. His initial encounter here seems relatively positive. The Jews there ask him to stay so they can discuss things further with him. Paul, however, is intent on reaching Jerusalem. He promises to return to Ephesus if God is willing (18:18–21).

Paul appears to leave Priscilla and Aquila behind in Ephesus. As a result we next learn that they encounter Apollos, an educated and articulate Jew, originally from Alexandria. He is well versed in "the Way of the Lord" and speaks accurately about Jesus in the synagogue. Yet he knows only of the baptism of John and welcomes further instruction from Priscilla and Aquila. Apollos then goes on to Corinth with the blessing of believers in Ephesus (18:24–28).

While Apollos is in Corinth, Paul returns to Ephesus. He encounters a small group of believers (about twelve) whose formation in the gospel is incomplete.

---

3. Readers may already be aware of some dispute about the originality of the phrase "in Ephesus" in 1:1. This issue is addressed below.

They know only the baptism of John and have not heard of the Holy Spirit. Paul rectifies these deficiencies (19:1–7).

In 19:8–10 Paul returns to the synagogue. Now, however, he faces the sort of hostility that typifies Paul's mission to the synagogue. He and his followers leave the synagogue, and for the next two years he teaches in the "hall of Tyrannus" (19:8–10), a place otherwise unattested. Luke tells us that through this activity all of Asia learns of the gospel.

We then read that Paul's ministry in Ephesus is marked by great signs of power and of healings. Some even try to copy his exorcisms, with unpleasant results. These signs of power draw many residents of Ephesus, both Jews and Gentiles. We learn that the name of Jesus is praised, but we are also left with the impression that only a portion of those who are amazed by Paul's acts of power actually become believers. Those who do become believers give up their magical practices and books of spells (19:11–20).

After a brief aside telling us of Paul's intention to move on to Macedonia, Achaia, and then Jerusalem, we read of the conflict between the believers in Ephesus and their neighbors. This conflict is stirred up by Demetrius the silversmith. He fears that if the Christian movement continues to grow in Ephesus, his business, which is tied to the great temple of Artemis, is likely to suffer. He and his colleagues instigate a demonstration in the magnificent theater of Ephesus, which threatens to get out of hand. Although Paul seeks to address this crowd, he is prevented from doing so. Ultimately a civic official is able to quiet the crowd and send them home (19:23–41).

Finally, as Paul is on his way to Jerusalem, in Acts 20 he stops in Miletus, to the south of Ephesus, and calls for the "elders of the church" to come to him. Paul's speech to the Ephesian elders is cast very much as a final testament or farewell to them, reviewing the past and anticipating the future with the aim of helping these elders keep the church in Ephesus in good working order.

The speech begins with a defense of Paul's ministry among the Ephesians, noting his diligence and courage in the face of opposition. Despite these trials, Paul has proclaimed to both Jews and Greeks the message of "repentance toward God and faith toward our Lord Jesus" (20:21). Paul reveals to them that under the Spirit's compulsion he is moving toward the completion of his ministry and that he will not see them again.

Because Paul has made known to them "the whole purpose of God," he cannot be held responsible for any of their failures to adhere to the gospel (20:25–26; cf. *T. Sim.* 6.1; *T. Levi* 10.1). They have been given all that they will need. They have only to remain watchful and attentive, protecting the church from internal and external threats. Paul promises that God will provide them with the grace they need to accomplish this. He also comments that he did not take any money from the Ephesians while he worked among them and indicates that this should provide the elders with an example for their own ministry (20:28–35).

At this point Paul leaves Miletus, eventually arriving in Jerusalem, where he is arrested and sent on to Rome. Acts ends with Paul in Rome.

Many contemporary scholars do not think that the Letter to the Ephesians was written to a Christian community in Ephesus. An even larger number of scholars doubt that the letter was written by Paul the apostle. In the course of this introduction, we need to address these historical points. Nevertheless, if one is a Christian committed to treating all of the NT as Scripture, one might want to know if the story of the church in Ephesus related in Acts is relevant to interpreting the Letter to the Ephesians, or if the letter sheds light on Acts.[4]

Here are some, but by no means the only, ways this might be so: First, in Acts we read of Paul's typical pattern of preaching first in the synagogue in Ephesus before moving out from there in the face of Jewish hostility to his gospel. Paul also asserts in Acts that he has proclaimed his gospel to both Jews and Gentiles. On the one hand, this fits with the epistle's emphasis on the reconciliation of Jew and Gentile in Christ. On the other hand, the letter gives the clear impression that the church in Ephesus is overwhelmingly Gentile and that it seems to have little direct conflict with either Jews or Jewish Christians. For that matter, the epistle does not reflect the situation of hostility narrated in the story of Demetrius the silversmith (Acts 19:23–41). Although Paul in the epistle is critical of aspects of Ephesian culture, he has a concern about how the church will be viewed by outsiders and how the church in Ephesus will engage the wider populace in ways that do not reflect a situation of active hostility to the church. Alternatively, Paul is in chains when he writes Ephesians. Indeed, in 6:20 he refers to himself as an ambassador of the gospel in chains. All of this indicates that those addressed in the epistle understand that walking in a manner worthy of their calling might bring them into conflict with the civil authorities.

Paul's strong defense of his ministry in Acts 20:17–35 may find an analogue in Paul's account of his apostolic ministry in Eph 3. Moreover, Paul's assertion that he has made known "the whole purpose of God" to the Ephesians may also fit with Paul's account of making known the mystery of Christ in Eph 3. The internal and external threats Paul anticipates in Acts 20, however, seem to have a much more direct connection to 1 Timothy, which also has a connection to Ephesus, than to anything found in the epistle.[5]

Certainly the emphasis on the Holy Spirit throughout the epistle is consistent with Paul's making known the work of the Spirit to believers in Ephesus (Acts 19:1–7), but it is not clear that either text directly informs the other.

---

4. Lemcio (335–60) nicely examines the impressive number of NT texts and NT characters that have a connection to Ephesus.

5. According to 1 Tim 1:3, Paul left Timothy behind in Ephesus to instruct and direct the congregation while he went to Macedonia.

Acts 19 indicates that there is a great emphasis on magic and spiritual powers in Ephesus. Certainly the epistle emphasizes both Christ's superiority to all other spiritual powers or forces (1:15–23), the church's ministry of witnessing to these powers (3:8–13), and the church's struggle with them (6:14–17). This connection is probably not sufficient, however, to sustain a great deal of historical reconstruction regarding the recipients of the letter (contra Arnold, *Power and Magic*) since the interest in magic and power that the citizens of Ephesus manifest was probably widespread throughout the empire (Best, *Ephesians* 5–6).

It appears, then, that there are some mutually informative overlaps between Ephesians and Acts. Moreover, the two texts do not present incompatible pictures of the church in Ephesus or of Paul's ministry. Even so, it is also not clear that these points of overlap are sufficient to render either text of much benefit when it comes to explicating obscure parts of the other.

Authorship

Anyone who has studied modern scholarship on Ephesians realizes that there is a sharp dispute over the authorship of the epistle. It is also clear, however, that scholars often bundle together a great number of discrete and often separable interpretive concerns under their consideration of authorship. As a way of taking some of the heat out of this issue, and with the hope of shedding some light on the matter, it may be useful to try to separate some of the interpretive issues at stake in addressing the question of the authorship of Ephesians.

The Authorship of Ephesians and Reading Theologically

The overwhelming majority of people read Ephesians for broadly theological reasons. That is, they read Ephesians because it is indisputably a part of Christian Scripture, and Christians by virtue of their identity are called to a lifelong engagement with Scripture as part of their ongoing struggle to live and worship faithfully before the triune God. Christians read Scripture in a variety of ways and in a variety of contexts to deepen their love of God and love of neighbor. Given the ends for which Christians engage Scripture theologically, the issue of authorship is not particularly relevant. Ephesians plays the role it does in the life and worship of Christians because it is part of the canon, not because it is written by Paul or not written by Paul. The text is canonical, Paul is not.

At the same time, we have every reason to think that those involved in the formation of the NT canon took Ephesians to be authentically Pauline.[6] Thus,

---

6. Thus *1 Clem.* 46.6; Ign. *Eph.* 1.1–2; and Pol. *Phil.* 12.1, all from the late first or early second century, seem to allude to Ephesians. In the late second century Irenaeus explicitly cites Ephesians and attributes the letter to Paul (*Haer.* 5.2.3; 5.8.1; etc.). Clement of Alexandria, *Strom.* 4.8 does likewise.

one might ask whether texts should remain canonical if they are not written by those assumed by the fathers of the church to have written them. Answering such a question involves a number of issues that could be the subject of distinct monographs. This introduction can only summarize these matters. Most important, it is simply a matter of sociological fact that (debates about the Apocrypha aside) the Christian churches are not likely to alter the canon of Scripture in the foreseeable future.

Further, one should recognize that the issue of authorship has its most direct impact on attempts to read Ephesians theologically (broadly conceived) only if one holds a very particular view of Scripture's inerrancy, whose proponents would argue something like this: If the text claims to be written by Paul the apostle and can be shown to have been written by someone else, then this fact throws into doubt everything else the text asserts about God, Christ, reconciliation, and salvation. In short, the truthfulness of any of the text's assertions — and therefore its theological authority — depends on the truthfulness of the assertion of Pauline authorship.

Several things might be said about this. First, although ancient people were familiar with the idea of forgery and other types of deception, they were also familiar with conventions and practices related to writing in the name of other, more prominent people in order to properly locate one's thoughts in a relationship to those other more prominent people. It is not exactly clear how widespread this practice, known as pseudepigraphy, was.[7] Yet there are numerous examples of such writing among Christians (from at least the second century), Jews (from at least the second century B.C.E.), and pagans. Most scholars who do not think Paul wrote Ephesians think that the letter was written by a disciple of Paul who was hoping faithfully to further or enhance Paul's teaching rather than to confuse or deceive.

Second, and more important, it is essential to understand that the linking of authorship to authority reflects a modern set of concerns. Theologians from at least the days of Origen, if not Paul's own day, understood that some events described in Scripture probably did not or could not have occurred in quite the ways Scripture records. This recognition neither threatened the integrity of such people's faith nor caused them to stop treating Scripture as authoritative. Indeed as Origen understands it, God placed those accounts into Scripture to invite us to dig deeper into the text. Moreover, if one's theology is going to be undermined by threats to this particular way of understanding inerrancy, then issues around the authorship of Ephesians might not be the most pressing set of concerns for such an outlook. The authorship of much of the OT, as well as divergences among the Gospels, would prove to be equal if not greater problems.

---

7. The issue of pseudepigraphy and how it was understood is a matter of complex historical argument. Best (*Ephesians* 10–13) gives a very good introduction to the central issues.

Thus in contrast, for the great bulk of the Christian tradition, the question of the authorship of Ephesians did not affect the text's authority. Apart from any strong views either pro or con about Pauline authorship, Christians can and have engaged Ephesians and the rest of Scripture in the manner in which they are called to do by virtue of their identity.

Even though this particular historical question does not impinge directly on bringing theological concerns to bear on one's reading of Ephesians, it does not mean that readers should always be indifferent to such historical matters. In several other works I have explained in some detail the ways in which Christians interested in interpreting Scripture theologically should engage the historically focused works of biblical scholars. I do not intend to rehearse those arguments here. Instead, I hope that my comments both here and in the body of the commentary display the type of ad hoc engagement with historical criticism that I have advocated elsewhere.[8]

Authorship and Interpretation

On the one hand, it might seem that precise identification of an author is essential to interpreting any text.[9] On the other hand, although this may seem to be self-evidently true, it is less easy to say why and how it is true. According to one view, knowing that Paul, as opposed to someone else, used a certain word or phrase is important because Paul typically used that word or phrase in a particular way, with particular shades of meaning and inference. Thus knowing that Paul did or did not write Ephesians might be significant for understanding particular words or phrases in Ephesians.[10]

Although I am willing to grant the theoretical plausibility of such a claim, and I will explore passages where issues of authorship might affect interpretation, I want to add some significant qualifications. These qualifications are practical and theoretical. First, practically speaking, it is not immediately evident that there are actual instances in Ephesians where one would interpret a word or phrase differently based on the judgment that Paul did or did not write Ephesians. If one examines a variety of commentaries written over the past fifty years, one can find both those strongly defending Pauline authorship as well as those who reject Pauline authorship. These generally ascribe Ephesians to a Pauline "disciple," or a "second-generation Paulinist," or some

---

8. See in particular, *Engaging Scripture* and *Theological Interpretation of Scripture*.

9. Muddiman (2–3) firmly holds to this view. I will try to show that this is due to a confusion of interpretive aims.

10. Lincoln (*Ephesians* lx–lxi) in particular addresses this issue in terms of Paul's being the undisputed "implied author" of Ephesians. Although his view may be helpful in showing how little the question of authorship matters to interpretation, I believe that the distinction between motive and communicative intention described below gets at this issue a bit more clearly.

similar term. Thus, despite the sometimes strenuous arguments over authorship, the overwhelming majority of recent scholarship places Ephesians somewhere within a fifteen- to twenty-year period beginning toward the end of Paul's life in the middle of the 60s C.E. As a result, the overwhelming majority of the data regarding the social and linguistic conventions, as well as the general historical background information that one might bring to the interpretation of Ephesians, is very similar whether one attributes the text to Paul or a Pauline disciple. Thus, and most important, although these commentators do not always agree with one another about how to interpret any given verse or phrase in Ephesians, their interpretive disagreements never seem to hang on how they have resolved the question of authorship.[11]

Moreover, there are several theoretical concerns that lead me to argue that in the case of Ephesians, the question of authorship is less significant than one might think for the type of interpretive work I and most other modern commentators do in our commentaries. First, it is crucial to recognize that a word's use in specific contexts should override any presumptions about what a word must mean based on its authorship. Paul and anyone else writing during this time period were obliged for the most part to follow the linguistic conventions in place at the time. Failure to do so in any sort of comprehensive way would risk lapsing into unintelligibility. This is not to deny that we may have difficulties, debates, and arguments about how to identify the linguistic conventions operative at any point in time. In addition, we may also have difficulty situating a text within the linguistic conventions of a relatively specific period of time. In such circumstances, one will at least need to make and defend judgments about how and why one situates a text within the linguistic conventions of a specific period rather than another even if one cannot precisely identify a text's author. Yet in the case of Ephesians, as far as we can tell, the basic linguistic conventions operative in 60 C.E. were also operative in 80 or even 90.

Those who read a variety of commentaries on Ephesians will note that from time to time scholars do argue that words, phrases, assertions, and convictions expressed in Ephesians are used in ways that are so different from how similar words and phrases are used in the undisputed Pauline Letters[12] that it becomes highly unlikely that the same person wrote Ephesians and the undisputed Letters. Whether or not one agrees with this claim, it is not an example of authorship's making a difference in interpreting Ephesians. Rather, the claim presumes that one has already understood both the relevant passages in Ephesians and the

---

11. A possible exception to this is that in a few cases interpretive differences do seem to hang on how scholars understand the relationship between Ephesians and Colossians. In these cases, however, I still argue that the question of authorship does not determine or even significantly influence interpretation.

12. These are Romans, 1–2 Corinthians, Galatians, 1 Thessalonians, Philippians, and Philemon.

undisputed Letters sufficiently well to assert that there is too much discontinuity between Ephesians and the other Letters to claim that Ephesians is Pauline. Because interpretation might shape judgments about authorship is not a reason to think that judgments about authorship must influence interpretation.

As a further theoretical observation and qualification, it is important to distinguish between interpretation that aims to elucidate a text's communicative intention on the one hand, and on the other hand interpretation that seeks to uncover an author's motives. Even though they might not think of matters in quite this way, most modern commentaries, this one included, interpret both Ephesians and the undisputed Paulines with the aim of illuminating the author's communicative intention. Such an aim requires one to distinguish authorial motives from an author's communicative intentions.[13] "That is to say, one ought to distinguish between *what* an author is trying to say (which might be called a 'communicative intention') and *why* it is being said (which might be called a motive)" (Brett 5). An author might write from any number of motives. He or she might have a desire for fame and fortune, or failing that, tenure. Some authors might have a deep psychological need to share their thoughts with a wider public. There might be (and probably are) motives at work of which an author is not fully conscious. Alternatively, in the case of lying, an author may be conscious of one's motives but wish to conceal them from others. As Mark Brett (5) observes, "Any single motive can give rise to a vast range of quite different communicative intentions." In order to reveal an author's motives, semantic and historical analysis of that writer's texts is never enough. A desire to discover an author's motives is quite hard to fulfill in almost all cases. Moreover, in the case of ancient authors an interest in motives will tend to be frustrated by our lack of knowledge about these characters.[14]

In the case of Ephesians, for example, one might seek to demonstrate that the motive of the letter's author was to combat or modify certain aspects of Paul's teaching by recasting that teaching under the guise of a letter from Paul. This would be an extremely interesting and important case to make. It might even lead one to argue that certain passages should be read very differently from the way they are currently read. This perfectly valid interest in the motives of the author of Ephesians faces some fairly significant obstacles. First, demonstrating the motives of a person who is otherwise unknown apart from the text of Ephesians is going to be very difficult. Other evidence would need to be marshaled. Even if such evidence were found, one might face another obstacle:

---

13. This distinction is initially made by Skinner. For biblical scholars this notion is expertly articulated by Brett. In what follows I am largely following Brett's work.

14. I take it that Muddiman's (2–3) insistence on determining the author of Ephesians stems from the fact that he counts this as essential for determining motives. Because he fails to distinguish motives from intentions, he ends up giving too much weight to the question.

our understanding of the linguistic, material, social, and historical factors that would have shaped the ways in which Christians in the latter half of the first century understood Ephesians as it was spoken or read to them might lead us to claim that despite this person's motives, they were unsuccessful. Moreover, as will become clearer below, one could only make such a case about Ephesians after, and relying upon, making a case about the communicative intention of the author. These and other obstacles work to ensure that biblical commentators (myself included) are generally interested in an author's communicative intention even when they do not use such terminology in describing their work.

To render an account of an author's communicative intention, one need not attend to an author's motives. Rather, such an account requires attention to, among other things, matters of semantics, the linguistic conventions operative at the time, and matters of implication and inference. In the case of dealing with the biblical writers, attention to these matters is inescapably historical. Indeed, in many respects the practices required to discern an author's communicative intention will be familiar to biblical critics even if they do not characterize their work as offering an account of an author's communicative intention. This historical work does not usually depend on a precise identification of an author.

Indeed, scholars on both sides of the authorship question in Ephesians engage in all of these historical exercises. This is because the notion of an author's communicative intention does not depend on having a textually mediated access to an autonomous, fully aware, authorial self. Rather, in the case of Paul—or the author of Ephesians, if they are not the same person—it depends on a knowledge of Greek and the linguistic conventions operative in the first century; on an ability to detect and explicate allusions, indirect references, implications, inferences, textually indicated rhetorical aims; and on a measure of familiarity with the general set of social conventions of which letter writing is a part. No doubt other elements might come into play as well. Further, the exact ways in which to mix and match all of these considerations will always be open to argument and debate. For example, there is no set formula or method that will tell one when to rely more heavily on semantics rather than social conventions or possible OT allusions. In fact, the great majority of interpretive arguments among professional biblical scholars could be cast as arguments about whether or not something should even count as a relevant piece of evidence and what sort of weight to give each piece of evidence. In adjudicating these arguments, a whole range of factors might be considered, but one element that is not obviously relevant is a concern with what is going on in that biblical author's consciousness at the particular moment he wrote something—assuming we could even know this.

It is clearly much easier to talk about an author's communicative intention in regard to epistolary discourse as opposed to narratives such as the Gospels. Since communicative intention is not dependent upon an author's motives or consciousness, then it would not be important precisely to identify the author whose motives one is not considering if one can confidently place a text within a relatively confined historical period. It is my judgment that regardless of whether Paul or a disciple of Paul's wrote Ephesians, both options fit within such a relatively confined historical period.

Pauline Theology and Biography

So far I have surveyed a number of interpretive interests and concerns that one might bring to Ephesians. I have tried to show that in order to pursue any of these interests, determining the authorship of Ephesians is not particularly important. The question of authorship, however, is crucial to at least two particular scholarly activities. These two activities are scholarly reconstructions of Paul's biography and the construction of Pauline theologies. These are both historical tasks, and for both of these projects it is essential to know as precisely as one can which texts are truly from Paul.

The way issues of authorship affect each of these projects, however, is different for each enterprise. If Paul did not write Ephesians, then the text is not at all relevant to the production of a biography of Paul except to the extent that a biography of Paul is concerned with the aftereffects of Paul's life on his immediate followers. Nevertheless, there seems to be little doubt that Paul went to Ephesus and participated in the founding of the Christian community in that city. Whether things happened precisely in the manner related in Acts 19 is a question that is largely independent of the Letter to the Ephesians. Ephesians makes little mention of Paul's personal circumstances other than a general account of Paul's ministry to Gentiles (3:1–13), an indication that Paul was in jail (3:1; 4:1; 6:20), and his intention to send Tychicus to Ephesus (6:21). The account of Paul's ministry is quite general and fits, but does not really add to, accounts in Galatians and Acts. It certainly could not be used to adjudicate differences between these texts. Paul was in jail numerous times, and the references in Ephesians do not add anything to what is already known about this.[15] The reference to Tychicus does not really tell us much about Paul. Moreover, the text does not provide us with a detailed account of the Christian community in Ephesus or elsewhere if the letter was not directed to Christians in Ephesus. Thus, regardless of whether Ephesians is Pauline, it is probably not a significant piece of evidence for constructing a biography of Paul. If the letter is by Paul, then the writing of Ephesians, however, would need to be placed within such a biographical account.

---

15. Cassidy (87–89), however, notes that if Ephesians is pseudepigraphic it is extraordinary that this Pauline follower would have identified himself with the imprisoned Paul. Such identification may indicate how central Paul's chains were to his identity for later Christians.

At the same time, this lack of specificity about life in the Ephesian church is taken by some to be evidence that Paul did not write the letter. This is particularly the case if one assumes that silence about particularities of church life in Ephesus is an indication that the author did not really know much about the church in Ephesus. Given the fact that all of Paul's Letters are occasional, it becomes difficult to use this as an argument for or against Pauline authorship. One would have to grant that specific situations can generate general comments just as readily as they can call forth highly specific comments.

Perhaps one place where the authorship of Ephesians might affect a Pauline biography has to do with the so-called household codes in Eph 5:21–6:9. If Ephesians is Pauline, this text, along with the similar text in Col 3:18–4:1, would count as significant evidence for the historical Paul's views about household relationships in Christ. Yet one must recognize that even if Paul did not write Ephesians, one might still take Colossians as Pauline and thus retain roughly the same evidence for Paul's views about familial relations. Moreover, as I will argue in the body of the commentary, there is little, if anything, in the household codes of either Ephesians or Colossians that does not come up somewhere else in the undisputed Letters. Further, as the account of these verses in the body of the commentary indicates, they should not be taken as evidence that Paul considers the patriarchal household to be God's particular preference for social relations.

The issue of authorship may be more significant for Pauline theology. To the extent that Pauline theologies aim to reconstruct and synthesize the historical Paul's views about God, the world, and the relationships between them, then Pauline theology is basically a form of intellectual biography; the same issues noted above would apply. To the extent that Pauline theologies aim to say something more broadly theological, they are a subspecies of biblical theology with all of its attendant problems and promise. If one is eager to demarcate the boundaries of this sort of biblical theology, then the authorship of Ephesians is a relevant question. It is not clear, however, why one would want to do this. As observed above, the theological significance of Ephesians is really independent of the question of authorship. The authorship of Ephesians might be relevant to where one situates the epistle within a larger biblical theology, but regardless of who wrote the epistle, one really could not exclude it from a biblical theology.

The Historical Question of Authorship

I have tried to indicate that questions about the authorship of Ephesians play little role in the theological interpretation of the epistle or discerning the communicative intention of the epistle. In addition, questions of authorship have clear but limited roles relative to constructions of Pauline biography or theology. In those few passages when a decision about authorship might influence the way a text is interpreted, I will, in the body of this commentary, try to lay out both options as best I can. These passages are relatively limited, however, and the interpretive differences are not all that significant.

Nevertheless, it is still a legitimate historical question of limited interpretive value to ask, "Did Paul write Ephesians?" Indeed, in my experience this is the first question clergy ask when they learn that I am writing a commentary on Ephesians. I will leave aside speculation on what this indicates about ministerial training in our time and focus on the historical question.

Questions over Pauline authorship of Ephesians may go back as far as Origen. However, serious scholarly dispute about the issue does not seem to have been a live question until the end the eighteenth century (discussed in Hoehner 6–20). Since then, the question seems to have divided scholars who have written on this subject more or less equally. In any straw poll of NT scholars today, I suspect that a majority would hold the view that Paul did not write Ephesians.

If one is interested in answering the historical question of the authorship of Ephesians, even though recognizing the limited interpretive and theological benefits derived from answering it, those on both sides of this issue tend to look at external and internal factors. Factors external to Ephesians include ancient attestation and the relationship of Ephesians to Colossians. Then there are criteria internal to Ephesians: vocabulary, style, and theme (including the use of the OT).

Those arguing against Pauline authorship tend to claim that despite its early attestation as Pauline, Ephesians is probably literarily dependent on Colossians. Being demonstrably later than Colossians, whose Pauline authorship is also in doubt, puts Ephesians into the postpauline period. Moreover, with regard to vocabulary, style, and theme, those opposed to Pauline authorship argue that the differences between Ephesians and the undisputed Pauline Epistles are so significant that it is unlikely that Paul wrote Ephesians.

Those favoring Pauline authorship look at the same criteria and argue that the connections between Ephesians and Colossians are too complex to argue for any straightforward account of literary dependence. Further, all of the Pauline Letters are specific to particular occasions and differ from one another in significant ways. Those supporting Pauline authorship argue that the differences between Ephesians and the other Letters are not sufficient to sustain the claim that Ephesians is not Pauline.

Before looking at these arguments in greater detail, it should already be clear that they are based on finely balanced judgments about probability. Hence there is no clear way of demonstrating with absolute certainty one way or another whether Paul wrote Ephesians. Rather, contemporary scholars tend to qualify their judgments with claims like "On balance it is unlikely that Paul wrote Ephesians," or "On balance it is probable that Paul wrote Ephesians." Because of this, no scholar should hold too tightly to views about the Pauline authorship of Ephesians. Strength of conviction should be in direct proportion to level of probability.

Attestation

No scholar doubts that a wide range of church fathers from Clement of Rome in the late first century through second-century writers such as Polycarp, Irenaeus, and Clement of Alexandria all treat Ephesians as Pauline (see Hoehner 2–4). Gnostic texts from Nag Hammadi such as *The Hypostasis of the Archons* and *The Exegesis of the Soul* treat Ephesians as Pauline.[16] Moreover, it is clear that at least some Christians from the second into the third centuries understood that some texts bearing the names of apostles were not written by those apostles.[17] For example, both Tertullian and the Muratorian Fragment in the late second or third century seem to indicate that although there were letters that claimed to be from Paul and were not taken to be Pauline, Ephesians was from Paul (Tertullian, *Praescr.* 36). Thus, in terms of early attestation, there is little doubt that Ephesians was reckoned as Pauline.

Ephesians and Colossians

Ephesians and Colossians are closer to each other in terms of shared themes and vocabulary than any other Pauline or deuteropauline Epistles. For example, only Ephesians (5:21–6:9) and Colossians (3:18–4:1) contain the household codes (though 1 Peter has similar material); they both mention and commend Tychicus (Eph 6:21–22; Col 4:7–8); they each speak of Paul's gospel as a mystery revealed to him (Eph 3:1–13; Col 1:24–29), though they each develop this idea differently. The question, of course, is what one should make of this.

If one argues that Paul wrote both epistles, then one can account for these similarities by observing that Paul and/or his secretary used similar phrasing and addressed some common themes in writing to two different churches that were geographically close to each other. Alternatively, one might argue that Paul or his secretary simply reworked the text so as to address a nearby congregation.

If one argues against Pauline authorship of Ephesians, then that case might be strengthened by showing that Ephesians is literarily dependent upon Colossians, that the author of Ephesians had access to the text of Colossians and reworked it to address a different congregation at a later date. If one can show both such literary dependence on Colossians and thus Colossians' temporal

---

16. Both *Hypostasis of the Archons* II.86.20–25 and *Exegesis of the Soul* II.6.131 quote Eph 6:12 and link the text to Paul.

17. In addition to the text from Tertullian noted here, see Eusebius, *Hist. eccl.* 6.12, quoting Serapion; and the Muratorian Fragment.

priority to Ephesians, then one can argue that it is at least probable that, no matter who wrote Colossians, Paul did not write Ephesians. Determining that Ephesians is dependent upon Colossians is one element in an overall argument against Pauline authorship of Ephesians. In reality, however, such judgments are more complex. For example, after arguing vigorously for the dependence of Ephesians on Colossians, Lincoln (*Ephesians* lv) concludes, "What has emerged from this overview is the dependence of Ephesians on a prior Colossians in terms of its overall structure and sequence, its themes and its wording. Yet what is also absolutely clear is that this is a free and creative dependence, not a slavish imitation or copying." This level of qualification may be significant. In the absence of other data, it seems that the connections between Colossians and Ephesians need to be sufficiently strong and of a nature that they serve as evidence that Colossians is clearly prior to Ephesians. It is not clear that "free and creative dependence" really provide evidence that the relationship between Colossians and Ephesians moved in only one direction. As a result, it is then unclear what data, other than scholarly custom, would lead one to presume that these connections argue for the temporal priority of Colossians over Ephesians.

To my mind, Best's 1997 article "Who Used Whom? The Relationship of Ephesians and Colossians" offers a very measured and persuasive argument that despite the obvious similarities between Colossians and Ephesians, there is insufficient evidence to argue that one is "dependent" upon the other. For example, the so-called vice lists in Col 3:5 and Eph 5:3–5 are significantly different from each other (Ephesians only repeats three of the five vices listed in Colossians) and substantially similar to material in 1 Cor 5:10–11; 6:9–10 and elsewhere. The greetings of Ephesians and Colossians are similar, but they use the standard Pauline formula. In addition, other supposed parallels appear rather to rely on material that either is similar to material found in other Pauline Letters or material that is considered traditional and part of a more-or-less common stock of Christian ideas and language. Thus these cannot be used to demonstrate the priority of one epistle to the other.

In addition, Best notes that if there is borrowing from Colossians, the author of Ephesians does so in a very haphazard way: "The random nature of the way A/Eph [the author of Ephesians] is supposed to have drawn on references from Colossians suggests that if he did depend on it, he did not have a copy of it in front of him as he wrote but had its words in his mind, and the same would be true of the way A/Col [the author of Colossians] would have used Ephesians" ("Who Used Whom?" 76).[18]

The mention of Tychicus in Eph 6:21–22 and Col 4:7–8 is the one parallel where it seems there is actual literary dependence between Ephesians and

---

18. Best contrasts this with the way Josephus's *Antiquities* uses the *Letter of Aristeas* or the way the writers of the Synoptics use each other.

Colossians. For various reasons, most modern scholars treat this as evidence that the writer of Ephesians had access to the text of Colossians. Best, however, decisively shows that there is no good reason to suppose the priority of Colossians to Ephesians in this matter. Indeed, the grammatical and stylistic problems of Eph 6:21–22 make it as likely that the author of Colossians revised and clarified Ephesians as that Ephesians copied Colossians and then made it obscure.

Although in this article Best is not primarily interested in solving questions of authorship, his argument leads to a very limited set of possibilities. One possibility is that both Ephesians and Colossians were written by followers of Paul who were in contact with each other as part of a "Pauline school." "In sum they would have developed Paul's thought differently in response to different situations and out of their different personalities" ("Who Used Whom?" 94). Best prefers this option. The other possibility is that a single author wrote both letters. Such a person could have been, but need not have been, Paul. Based on the evidence of Eph 6:21–22//Col 4:7–8, Best thinks it is more likely that, if there was a single author, Ephesians was written first, and in writing Colossians the author cleaned up Eph 6:21 and added further praise of Tychicus (95).

The upshot of all of this for the question of authorship is that the clear connections between Ephesians and Colossians sharpen and limit the possibilities regarding the authorship of each epistle but do not really help determine the authorship of either. In terms of the primary tasks of a commentary, it is crucial for a commentary on Ephesians to treat Colossians judiciously as a resource for understanding passages in Ephesians. In certain cases, similar phrases in Colossians can help illumine obscure passages in Ephesians. At the same time, one must be careful not to reduce Ephesians to Colossians by assuming similarities when there may actually be significant differences.

Vocabulary

With regard to vocabulary in relation to the authorship of Ephesians, some try to determine whether there are such substantial differences between the vocabulary of Ephesians and the vocabulary of the undisputed Letters as to make it unlikely that Paul is the author of Ephesians. The data here are as follows: Ephesians has 2,429 words, with a total vocabulary of 530 words.[19] Of these, 41 occur nowhere else in the NT; 84 words are not found elsewhere in the Pauline corpus but do appear in the rest of the NT. Galatians, for example, has 2,200 words, with a total vocabulary of 526 words. This makes it about 10 percent shorter than Ephesians. Of these words, 35 (not counting proper nouns) are unique to the NT, and 80 (not counting proper nouns) do not appear elsewhere in Paul but do appear in the NT. The point here is that the number of unusual words

---

19. See Hoehner 24, citing the statistics of Morgenthaler.

is about the same in Galatians and Ephesians even though Galatians is slightly shorter. Thus, on its own, this data cannot really tell against Pauline authorship.

Lincoln (*Ephesians* lxv) notes that Ephesians has a number of unique phrases such as "in the heavenlies" (1:3, 20; 2:6; 3:10; 6:12). In addition, Christ is called "the beloved one" (1:6). Further, Ephesians has phrases such as "the word of truth" (1:13) and "the Father of glory" (1:17) that do not appear in the undisputed Pauline Letters. Again, however, Galatians has roughly the same number of unique expressions. Schnackenburg (22 n. 19; followed by Lincoln, *Ephesians* lxv) argues that many of the unique words in Ephesians have a "greater affinity" with postapostolic literature. It is not exactly clear what "greater affinity" really means or what it might indicate if true. Given that there is early postapostolic attestation that Ephesians is canonical and that it touches on a variety of issues of interest to postapostolic theologians, it seems likely that they would make use of Ephesians and its vocabulary. This is not in itself evidence for a postpauline date for Ephesians.

Style

Ephesians has a number of very long sentences, often containing several subordinate clauses. The letter also tends to use two words when one would suffice. Although one can find similar stylistic patterns in the undisputed Pauline Letters, they do not occur with the frequency that one finds in Ephesians. Nobody argues that the stylistic differences are so extreme that it is absolutely impossible that Paul could have written Ephesians or that the differences are so slight that they raise no questions about Pauline authorship. The issues here concern how one weighs the relative difference in style between Ephesians and the other Pauline Letters and how one might account for this. In this matter, the temperament and taste of the scholar making the judgment plays a very significant role. If, for other reasons, one rejects Pauline authorship of Ephesians, then the argument about style will help cement that judgment. If one is committed to Pauline authorship on other grounds, the stylistic differences will not seem significant enough to threaten that judgment.

Themes

One of the pieces of evidence one might use for adjudicating the question of the authorship of Ephesians concerns the treatment of themes that appear in Ephesians relative to the ways similar themes are handled in the undisputed Letters. As with vocabulary and style, when comparing themes one is trying to discern how to weigh and account for the differences and similarities between texts. If one discerns that the differences between Ephesians and the undisputed Letters relative to any theme are so significant that they become differences of kind rather than differences of degree, then that would count against Pauline authorship. If one judges the differences to be differences of degree, then it may become more likely that Paul is the author of Ephesians. Of course, some differences might appear to be so severe that we should question whether we are really comparing like with like. In this light, it is worth examining two themes of note: eschatology and the use of the OT.

Eschatology

It is quite common for contemporary scholars to speak of Paul's view of time as apocalyptic. This can mean a variety of things. How one understands this term will have an impact on how one understands the continuities and discontinuities between Ephesians and the undisputed Pauline Letters. In the middle of the twentieth century, scholars tended to tie Paul's apocalyptic view to an ardent expectation that Christ would very soon return and establish the kingdom of God in its fullness. As Ernst Käsemann writes, "It is characteristic of the letters that the entire mission of Paul is determined by the expectation of the imminent end of the world."[20] Driven by this understanding of apocalyptic, most scholars understood the earliest churches as Spirit-inspired, dynamic places of fervent evangelistic activity. On this view, authority in these communities was derived from one's ability to command and display spiritual power.[21] Scholars assumed that these communities paid little attention to formal ecclesial structures because they only expected to be present for a relatively short time.

As time went on, so the argument goes, it became clear that the world might not end as quickly as the first generation of the followers of Jesus hoped. The next generation gradually became more interested in establishing formal ecclesial structures, regulating charismatic power, and domesticating the wild and disturbing power of the gospel.[22]

In the light of this understanding of Paul, Ephesians, and its interests in ecclesial life, its passages that have believers already seated in the heavenlies with Christ, among other characteristics, look like they come from someone living in this period of "early Catholicism" rather than from the apocalyptic Paul.

One will also have to say, however, that neither Galatians (sometimes thought to be the earliest of Paul's Letters) nor Philippians really displays the apocalyptic vision of an imminent Parousia that someone like Käsemann attributes to Paul. At the same time, they also do not bear the marks of "early Catholicism."

---

20. Käsemann, "Early Catholicism," 241; see also his definition of apocalyptic as the "expectation of an imminent Parousia," in "Primitive Christian Apocalyptic," 109 n. 1.

21. Käsemann uses the phrase "post-Easter enthusiasm," as in "Primitive Christian Apocalyptic," 109 n. 1.

22. In "Early Catholicism," Käsemann uses the term "early Catholicism," or "Frühkatholizmus."

In this light, scholars such as J. Louis Martyn have proposed revisions to our understanding of Paul's apocalyptic vision. Rather than imposing a preformed apocalyptic schema on Paul, Martyn (113) asks, "Could Galatians perhaps be allowed to play its own role in showing us precisely what the nature of Paul's apocalyptic was?"

If one extends Martyn's questions to the undisputed Pauline corpus as a whole, then Paul's apocalyptic view primarily emphasizes that in the life, death, and resurrection of Jesus, God has intervened in or even invaded our world in an unprecedented way, which has transformed everything. In the light of this revelation, Paul comes to understand that the life, death, and resurrection of Jesus divides all time into two ages. The age before Christ is characterized by Sin's rule over the cosmos and all of the attendant evils that come with this. Christ's resurrection inaugurates the new messianic age, which will reach its culmination when all things are put into their proper order under Christ's rule, and Christ hands over the kingdom to God the Father (1 Cor 15:20–28). Although the resurrection inaugurates the messianic age, it is clear that both Paul and we stand in the time when the two ages overlap. The ultimate victory of God is assured, but the present age still persists in its resistance to God's desires. The messianic age is both a present, and a yet-to-be-completed reality. In Paul's Letters one sees in various ways and to various degrees aspects of this tension that mark this present time. Moreover, it is also clear that Paul felt free to vary his use of eschatological themes and perspectives depending on his own purposes and the needs of the congregations he addressed.[23]

Paul's perspective is thoroughly apocalyptic in the sense that he recognizes that the manner, scope, timing, and implications of Christ's invasion of the cosmos are unprecedented and surprising, something that had to be revealed rather than something one could reason one's way to. It has disrupted everything, and much of Paul's writing is devoted to figuring out how to reconstitute his understanding of God and God's drama of salvation from this new perspective. One of the sharpest examples of this is Paul's reflection on his own life in Phil 3:4–14. In this text Paul recounts his significant achievements within Judaism, asserting both that his persecution of the church was a virtuous mark of his zeal and that according to the righteousness found in the law, he was blameless. In the light of being grabbed by Christ, he has thoroughly reevaluated his past so that now he sees those achievements as rubbish. Instead Paul now is devoted to knowing "Christ and the power of his resurrection and the sharing of his sufferings by becoming like him in his death" so that he might attain the resurrection of the dead (Phil 3:10–11). Paul goes on to admit that he has not yet achieved this, but he presses on toward this end. In addition, in 3:15–17 Paul encourages the Philippians to press on toward the same end also.

---

23. For a clear articulation of this issue, see Gorman 57–64.

This text in particular demonstrates that being thoroughly apocalyptic does not imply that Paul was convinced that the age in which he lived was only going to last for a very short period of time. Paul recognizes that the present age *may* end very soon, so one should be prepared for that. At the same time he also recognizes that such timing is fully in God's hands. Thus his churches need to be formed in ways that will enable them to be faithful over a possibly long period of time.[24]

On this view of Paul, there is no easy or clear way to mark a transition from charismatic to institutional Christianity. Interestingly, it is in Phil 1 that one finds the first mention of offices such as bishop and deacon. Further, the occasional nature of all of Paul's writings make it clear that we are not in a good position to chart clear patterns of development within Christianity in the middle decades of the first century.[25] More particularly, it also becomes difficult to situate Ephesians relative to this issue.

Ephesians also speaks in apocalyptic terms of God's drama of salvation. In particular the revelation that in Christ, Jews and Gentiles are united into one new body is a mystery hidden from prior generations and revealed to Paul and others (1:9; 3:1–10; 6:19). Ephesians also recognizes that the current time is not the age to come in its fullness. Thus Eph 1:21 speaks explicitly about the "age to come." In addition, Paul's own imprisonment and sufferings indicate that the messianic age has yet to be fulfilled. Alternatively, Eph 1:3 states that God has already blessed the Ephesians with spiritual blessings in the heavenly realms. Nevertheless, even in "the heavenly realms" there are powers that have yet to become subject to Christ. Although the imprisoned Paul understands that the principalities and powers still exercise some level of control in the world, in 1:22 he speaks of all things having been put under Christ's feet. Ephesians does seem to speak of the age to come as realized in some significant respects. Nevertheless verses such as 1:14; 2:7; 4:30; 5:5; 6:8, 13 all speak of future aspects of the age to come, recognizing that things are not yet what they will be.

In conclusion, as long as one understands the theme of eschatology as really a subtheme of Paul's apocalyptic view, it is more difficult to argue that any differences between Ephesians and the undisputed Letters are so significant as to be differences of kind. For example, 2 Cor 5 (and to a lesser degree Gal 3:27)

24. Some passages indicating this are Phil 1:27–2:18, where Paul urges the Philippians to order their common life in a manner worthy of the gospel (an ongoing activity) so that they will remain as a faithful witness in Philippi: their fidelity over the long term will indicate that Paul's work was not in vain. In addition, the moral injunctions in Gal 5–6, especially the fruit of the Spirit, seem directed to a community that may need to remain faithful over an extended period of time.

25. At a more general level, Michel Foucault's studies of such matters as the rise of hospitals and prisons shows that institutions rarely follow regularized and discernible patterns of development. See his works *The Birth of the Clinic*, trans. Alan Sheridan (New York: Vintage Books, 1975); and *Discipline and Punish*, trans. Alan Sheridan (New York: Vintage Books, 1979).

exhibits the same type of assertions about realized yet not completed eschatology as Ephesians does. If one were already convinced that Paul is unlikely to be the author of Ephesians, the epistle's eschatology would probably not persuade such a person otherwise. Likewise, someone disposed toward Pauline authorship will not have that conviction disturbed by the epistle's eschatology.

Use of the Old Testament in Ephesians

Readers of the undisputed Pauline Letters know that the apostle often quotes from and alludes to the OT. Paul mostly relies on the Psalms, Isaiah, and the Pentateuch (in their LXX form). Moreover, he often employs exegetical techniques that were common among Jewish interpreters of his day. Likewise, Ephesians both quotes from and alludes to the OT. Yet there appear to be several significant differences between the way the OT was handled in the undisputed Pauline Letters and the way Ephesians treats the OT, which might shift the scale of probability away from Pauline authorship.

Andrew Lincoln makes the most extensive case for this view in an article ("Use of OT") from 1982. He recognizes the similarities between Paul and Ephesians in both the range of texts used and the methods used to interpret them. Despite these formal similarities, there are some significant differences as well. First, the writer of Ephesians introduces an OT quote with some sort of formula only once in five cases (cf. 4:8–10, quoting Ps 68:18). In the undisputed Pauline Letters as a whole, introductory formulas occur with a much higher frequency, though this varies from letter to letter.[26]

Lincoln also examines the one OT text that appears both in Ephesians and in an undisputed letter. In Eph 5:31–32 Paul quotes Gen 2:24, "For this reason a man will leave his father and mother and be joined to his wife, and the two will become one flesh." Paul uses this text in Ephesians not only to indicate the unity that God intends between husband and wife, but also to assert that this unity characterizes the relationship between Christ and the church. This movement between human marital relations and the relationship of Christ to the church and back again is consistent throughout 5:21–33.

In 1 Cor 6:16 Paul quotes the latter part of Gen 2:24 as part of an argument to show the Corinthians that although "all things are lawful" (6:12), there is a deep theological incompatibility between life in Christ and continuing to frequent prostitutes. Genesis 2:24 serves to underwrite the claim that a liaison with a prostitute reflects a deeper union than the Corinthians seem willing to grant. One actually becomes one body with the prostitute. Paul then goes on to claim that in contrast, "Anyone united to the Lord becomes one spirit with him" (6:17).

---

26. One might make the case that the phrase "For this reason" in Eph 5:31 serves to introduce the quote from Gen 2:24 as well as actually being part of the quotation.

Lincoln sees significant differences here between Ephesians and 1 Corinthians ("Use of OT" 36). Ephesians uses Gen 2:24 to speak of the unity of Christ and the church. In 1 Cor 6 the union is between Christ and individual believers. Moreover, in 1 Cor 6 Paul does not explicitly support this claim with Gen 2:24. Rather, he says, "Anyone united to the Lord becomes one spirit with him." One might argue that the implication from the argument based on Gen 2:24 applies equally well to union with prostitutes and union with Christ. Paul does not, as Lincoln sees it, argue this way. Instead he counts becoming one flesh with a prostitute as a contrast with being united with the Lord and becoming "one spirit."

Yet these differences may be less pronounced than one might first imagine. In 1 Cor 6:15 Paul declares that the bodies of believers are members of Christ. In 6:19 he further states that the bodies of believers are the temple of the Holy Spirit. Thus, both before and after the quote from Gen 2:24, Paul has asserted that believers are bodily and spiritually united with Christ. Some Corinthians clearly understood the nature of their union with Christ to also be compatible with frequenting prostitutes. Being joined to the Lord and being "one spirit" may be exactly how they understood themselves. The use of Gen 2:24 in the context of 6:15–19 is part of Paul's argument against this understanding. In 1 Cor 6 Paul could have used Gen 2:24 to argue both against union with prostitutes and for the already-established bodily union with Christ that he asserts in 6:15 and repeats in 6:19. Nevertheless, in the context of this whole passage it appears that Paul's understanding of Gen 2:24 is compatible with the use of the same passage in Eph 5:31.

For Lincoln, the more pervasive difference between the use of the OT in Ephesians and in the undisputed Letters has to do with the absence of a promise-and-fulfillment pattern in Ephesians. For Lincoln the key text here is Eph 3:5, which notes that the "mystery of Christ," particularly Christ's reconciliation of Jew and Gentile, "was not made known to previous generations," but has only now been revealed to the "holy apostles and prophets" (AT). According to Lincoln, the writer is not talking about something that can with great difficulty be found in the OT. Instead, "The OT writers, therefore, were ignorant of the sort of blessing that was to come to the Gentiles" ("Use of OT" 47). There was no promise, no matter how dimly perceived. Hence, there could be no fulfillment.

Evaluating this claim really depends on one's understanding of the "mystery of Christ." The following verses in Eph 3 indicate that this mystery entails the following claims: That the Gentiles have become "fellow heirs, members of the same body, and sharers in the promise in Christ," with those Jews who believe. Moreover, these two groups, joined together into one church in Christ, are also to bear witness to God's wisdom and grace to the rulers and authorities in the heavenlies. Presumably this act of witness is tied to God's plan to bring all things to their proper end in Christ (1:10). Of course, the more precision and subtlety one adds to this account of the mystery of Christ in Ephesians, the more likely it becomes that the entirety of the plan really was unknown to prior generations.

On one level, this does sound quite different from Romans, where Paul thinks that the OT, understood rightly, indicates that God has always saved people by faith and that this continuity reveals God's righteousness. In addition, there is the explicit claim in Gal 3:8 that the gospel was "prepreached" to Abraham. At the same time, however, Gal 3:19–29 tells a story of Sin's work of obscuring the true end of the Law and using it instead to blind and enslave humanity. Moreover, in 2 Cor 3:12–18 Paul speaks of those Jews who are outside of Christ as being blind to the Law's true meaning in Christ.

Particularly in Romans and Galatians, in the light of Christ, Paul emphasizes the continuity of God's saving purposes over time. In addition, Paul pays attention to the foreshadowings and promises offered in the OT that are now seen to be fulfilled in Christ. Nevertheless, Paul does not think that before Christ these things were clearly understood. Indeed, prior to his own encounter with Christ, Paul himself was blinded and could never have read the OT in the ways that he later came to do.

Is this disposition compatible with the claim in Eph 3:5 that the "mystery of Christ" was unknown to earlier generations? To hold these two views together, one must emphasize the level of detail in the Ephesian understanding of the "mystery of Christ." That is, the more detailed account one can give of the mystery mentioned in Eph 3:5, the greater the possibility that one could say that this mystery in all its detail was unknown in previous generations. At the same time, one could also still affirm that Paul's gospel, which saw the promise to Abraham regarding the blessing of the nations as fulfilled in Christ, was both "prepreached" to Abraham *and* obscured by the work of Sin. In this light, Galatians represents a more general promise that is fulfilled in Christ. Ephesians refers to the utterly surprising nature of its specific fulfillment in the church and stresses the church's unanticipated role in witnessing to the powers. From a theological perspective one can hold these two views together. From the perspective of the narrower historical question of authorship, one can say that the same person could have written both Galatians and Ephesians, but it certainly does not require it to have been the same person.

Conclusions and Suggestions on Authorship

This rather long discussion of authorship has allowed for some important questioning of scholarly assumptions, some reflection on interpretive practice, and the separable nature of diverse interpretive and historical aims and concerns. I think this is its main value. At the same time, a reader might well wish to know where I stand on the historical question. I genuinely do not know whether Paul wrote Ephesians. As a matter of historical interest, I find the arguments so finely balanced that my decisions about this could vary from day to day. I understand when others find that the evidence speaks more clearly one way or another; I am less certain. As an interpreter of this text, however, I am not disturbed by this situation. I think the historical evidence leads one to conclude that either Paul wrote Ephesians or someone close to him wrote Ephesians within a decade or two after his death. Theologically and interpretively, it does not make much difference whether Paul or this close follower wrote the text. Further, despite one's views on authorship, one is left to struggle with the interpretive problems, subtleties, and inferences along with the insights of Ephesians as one engages the text as we currently have it. For the sake of avoiding alternative and often clumsy formulations, I will refer to the author of the Ephesians as Paul. This is the name the author chose for himself, and he certainly means to imply that he is the apostle.

Recipients and Occasion of Ephesians

When most scholars discuss the recipients of Ephesians, they are talking about the original audience of the letter. Identifying this audience is rendered more complex by the text-critical issues in 1:1. At the same time, from the perspective of interpreting the text of Ephesians, the identity of a single original recipient is rendered somewhat less critical by the fact that the epistle does not appear to address challenges or false teachings specific to a particular congregation. Although the vast majority of ancient MSS and the majority of the early Christian discussion of this text all take the letter to be addressed to the church in Ephesus, there are three very old MSS that omit "in Ephesus" ($\mathfrak{P}^{46}$, ℵ, B). Even these, however, contain superscriptions identifying the letter as "to the Ephesians."

On purely text-critical considerations, the MSS that omit "in Ephesus" present the more difficult reading. It is not easy, however, to account for either the insertion or deletion of "in Ephesus" without speculating well beyond the bounds of any evidence we have. Origen (*Cels.* 3.20) appears to know only texts of Ephesians that omit the phrase. At the same time, he lists Ephesians at the head of a list of Paul's Epistles. In addition, Clement (*Strom.* 4.60), Origen's predecessor in Alexandria, as well as Tertullian (*Marc.* 4.5; 5.11) both explicitly identify this epistle as that to the Ephesians. Irenaeus quotes Eph 2:13 as being from Paul's Letter to the Ephesians. Hence there is fairly wide patristic attestation from a time at least contemporary with $\mathfrak{P}^{46}$ identifying this letter as Paul's Letter to the Ephesians.

Most important, it is not clear that one gains any firmer interpretive foothold on the text if one argues that the original audience for the text was the church in Laodicea (e.g., Marcion,[27] initially) or Hierapolis (e.g., Kreitzer, most

---

27. Tertullian, *Marc.* 5.11–12, makes this claim about Marcion.

recently). Thus I will use terms like "Ephesus" and "Ephesians" to refer to the initial audience of the text without denying that there are grounds for disputing that this text was originally addressed to the Ephesians.[28]

This sort of agnosticism about the audience (as well as about the authorship) of this epistle is made much easier to accept by the fact that the letter does not reveal a great deal about the occasion of its writing. Paul (see the discussion on authorship above) writes from prison. Unlike Philippians, however, he makes no strong connections between his imprisonment and any hostility the Ephesians are facing. He does not expound on the challenges surrounding suffering for the gospel. He has not received a financial gift from the Ephesians that requires recognition.

In Ephesians, Paul speaks about the relationship between Jews and Gentiles in Christ. Unlike Galatians, however, there does not seem be any strong pressure on members of the congregation to supplement their faith in Christ by also taking on torah observance. Unlike Romans, Paul does not go to great lengths in Ephesians to justify God's righteousness relative to the calling of Israel and the salvation of the Gentiles. There does not appear to be any tension between Jewish and Gentile believers regarding their status before God. Indeed, although Paul deals with the issue of Jew and Gentile in Christ, the believers in Ephesus seem to be overwhelmingly Gentile. Moreover, they do not seem to have much to do with Jews or Jewish Christians.

Paul speaks of his apostolic mission in Eph 3 at some length. Unlike Galatians or the Corinthian Letters, however, Paul's status as an apostle does not appear to be in doubt. We have no reason to suspect that the Ephesians were inclined to reject his teaching or his advice.

Paul offers a variety of moral admonitions and exhortations in Ephesians. While these reveal something about the common life Paul desires for them, the Ephesians do not appear to have adopted any aberrant practices that require a swift rebuke. We do not gain the impression that the Ephesians were resisting any calls to walk in a manner worthy of their calling.

In this light it is easy to see why some would treat Ephesians as a compendium of Paul's writings rather than a letter in the strict sense of the term. The strongest argument one can make against treating Ephesians as a compendium is by showing that the various parts of the letter do fit together as a more or less unified argument, albeit a position at a more general level than in most other Pauline Letters. This is an argument that is ultimately only persuasive in the light of the whole of this commentary. In anticipation of offering just such a set of comments, I argue that Ephesians is, like all of Paul's Letters, an occasional letter. Whatever the occasion was, however, it was such that it evoked an

---

28. After surveying various options, Westcott (20) concludes, "Ephesus must have had a better right than any other single city to account itself the recipient of the Epistle."

argument and reflected a set of concerns that are relatively general in their scope and focus. Thus it does seem possible that, as with the Letter to the Colossians and the lost Letter to the Laodiceans, Paul intended this letter to be read widely in the various congregations in and around Ephesus (cf. Col 4:16).

Despite our desire to know more, we have little to go on when it comes to understanding what specific occasion might have led Paul to write Ephesians. At the same time, one can imagine that, in a world deeply interested in spiritual things and in a religiously pluralistic environment, Christians might have been tempted to supplement their faith in Christ in ways that would lead someone such as Paul to assert that God's plan is to bring all things to their proper end in Christ, who is both source and locus of all spiritual fullness. In a context where the church has become overwhelmingly Gentile, one can imagine a Christian community needing to be reminded of the priority of Israel, of their status as Gentiles, and of the astonishing work of reconciliation that God has willed to accomplish in the life, death, and resurrection of Christ. In a world that is often either ignorant of or indifferent to the claims of Christianity and the life of the church, it is easy to imagine a set of admonitions insisting that Christians live together in a manner worthy of their calling so that they might bear witness to the world at large. The striking thing is that one can easily and with historical accuracy imagine such a context *both* in Asia Minor between the years 60 and 80 *and* in Baltimore (where I write) in the first decades of the twenty-first century. I take this to be the source both of the historically frustrating nature of Ephesians and of its great theological promise.

COMMENTARY

Ephesians 1:1–2
Greeting

The epistle begins by identifying the sender and the recipients. This is the common way that Hellenistic letters begin. The use of grace and peace in the greeting is common among NT Letters (cf. 1 Cor 1:3; 2 Cor 1:2; Gal 1:3; Phil 1:2; Col 1:2; 1 Thess 1:1; 2 Thess 1:2; Phlm 3). The greeting here is identical to Philippians and the same as Colossians except for the addition of "and the Lord Jesus Christ." As with most beginnings, the terms, allusions, and ideas first appearing here will help shape how one might read the whole text.

1:1 Paul, an apostle of Christ Jesus by the will of God, to the holy ones[a] who are in Ephesus[b] and are faithful in Christ Jesus. 2 Grace to you and peace from God our Father and the Lord Jesus Christ.

a. The Greek word *hagioi* is translated as "holy ones." This term is sometimes rendered in the commentary as "saints." There is little if any difference in the meaning of the two terms. Here at the outset I have used "holy ones" to short-circuit the importation of contemporary connotations to the term "saints" that would not have been evident to Paul. Moreover, the term "saints" may obscure the allusion to Exod 19:6 and the connection between God's desires for the church and for Israel. Alternatively, the phrase "holy ones" may lead some to assume that the Ephesians have already achieved holiness in all its fullness. This is not the case. Thus I will use both "saints" and "holy ones" interchangeably throughout the commentary.

b. There is a significant textual issue in this verse. This concerns the phrase "in Ephesus." Three very early and significant manuscripts omit the phrase ($\mathfrak{P}^{46}$, ℵ*, and B*).[1] This, combined with the fact that the epistle does not seem to reflect a very specific church situation, has led some scholars to argue that Ephesians was originally an encyclical letter to Christians in general, and whoever read the epistle would insert the

---

1. In addition to these, MSS 6, 1739, 424^c also omit "in Ephesus." For a thorough breakdown of the MSS according to text types, see Hoehner *Ephesians*, 144–48, "Excursus 1."

name of the relevant city.[2] Yet no manuscript simply has a blank space or simply the preposition "in." Moreover, even the three manuscripts that omit "in Ephesus" contain the superscription "To the Ephesians." Thus in virtually all of the manuscripts we have, this epistle is identified with the church in Ephesus.[3] In addition, we do not have any manuscript of this letter that lists an alternative city as the destination.[4] When faced with Marcion's claim that this epistle was written to the Laodiceans, Tertullian responded, "Of what consequence are the titles, since in writing to a certain church the apostle did in fact write to all?" (*Marc.* 5.17). For believers, this is the appropriate disposition. Believers need not deny matters of historical specificity in any particular text, but they must also retain the expectation that a scriptural text is, in some sense, written to them. This is simply easier to do when the text speaks in general terms, as Ephesians often does.

[1–2] Paul begins by identifying himself as an apostle of Christ Jesus. Paul identifies himself this way at the beginning of Romans, 1 and 2 Corinthians, Galatians, Colossians, 1 and 2 Timothy, and Titus. To designate oneself as an apostle indicates that one is on a mission. An apostle is one who has been sent. The phrase "apostle of Christ" declares that Paul is sent by Christ and on Christ's behalf to pursue a mission given him by Christ (Heil, *Ephesians* 47). This becomes much clearer in 3:1–13. In addition, Paul uses this designation to indicate his office and authority—authority that is sometimes questioned (as in 1–2 Corinthians). Yet calling himself an apostle of Christ "by the will of God" locates Paul's authority outside himself. Paul's mission is not one he would have chosen for himself. Although being an apostle puts Paul in a position of power, this position is not one that Paul seeks. Rather, it is "the will of God" that makes Paul an apostle. This is part of a pattern found elsewhere in Paul's writings, where he both claims and exercises great authority, while also displacing himself as the source of that authority. Paul is able to do this in Ephesians and elsewhere because he understands himself to be a character within a larger drama driven by the will of God. This will become clearer in Eph 3.

Paul's use of the term "apostle" in 2:20; 3:5; and 4:11 also provides a fuller account of what being an apostle might mean. In 2:20 the "apostles and prophets" are the foundation upon which the church, "the household of God," is

---

2. See Percy 461–64.

3. For a more thorough examination of the text-critical issues, see Hoehner.

4. Here are some of the alternative destinations proposed for this letter: According to Tertullian, Marcion treated Ephesians as the letter that was presumably sent to Laodicea and then on to Colossae as mentioned in Col 4:16 (*Marc.* 5.17). Roon (72–85), followed by Lincoln (*Ephesians* 3–4), has argued in favor of Laodicea and Hierapolis as the destinations for the letter. Kreitzer (9–11) has argued for Hierapolis on its own. Yet each of these modern suggestions has no manuscript evidence for it. They are conjectures based on very limited evidence. As Muddiman (61–62) notes, if these conjectures are connected to support of Pauline authorship, they provide possible alternative destinations for the letter. If such conjectures are posited along with the argument that Ephesians is pseudepigraphic, then they are not very satisfying. For example, why not mention Epaphras as author, who according to Col 4:12–13 has labored on behalf of the churches in Laodicea and Hierapolis?

built, with Christ as the cornerstone. In 3:5 we again find "apostles and proph-ets" paired. These are the ones to whom the Spirit has revealed God's plan for including the Gentiles with the Jews into one body in Christ. In 4:11 "the apostles" are mentioned as the first gift given by the resurrected and ascended Christ for the building up of the church. Thus, by identifying himself as an apostle at the beginning of Ephesians, Paul situates himself within the group that serves as the locus for God's work of founding, directing, and maintaining the one body of Christ.

The recipients are located in Ephesus and identified as "holy" and "faithful in Christ Jesus." This designation "saints" or "holy ones" occurs also in the greeting of Romans, 1–2 Corinthians, Philippians, and Colossians as a way of identifying those to whom these Epistles are addressed.[5] What does this way of identifying Christian congregations indicate?

It is clear from Paul's unhesitating application of this word to the Corinthi-ans that "holy ones" is not primarily a reference to their moral achievements. Rather, Paul has taken over a word used to describe Israel in the LXX and applied it to these congregations. The allusions here go back to Exod 19:6 and 23:22 LXX, where the Lord speaks of setting Israel apart as a "kingdom of priests and a holy nation" (not in 23:22 MT). Further, in Leviticus the Lord repeatedly calls Israel to a divine holiness (11:44–45; 19:2; 20:7, 26). In part, this call is based on God's gracious activity of setting the people of Israel apart and delivering them up out of Egypt (Lev 11:45). Deuteronomy 7:6–8 again designates Israel as a holy people chosen and redeemed by God (see also 14:2, 21). Moreover, the LXX of Pss 15:3 [15:2 Eng.]; 33:10 [34:9]; 73:3 [74:3]; and 1 Macc 10:39 also uses "holy ones" to designate all or a part of the people of God in much the same way Paul seems to use the term.

Thus we can say that for the LXX and for Paul, the term "holy ones" appears to designate a body of people chosen by God. The term bespeaks God's forma-tion of a particular body of people and God's desires for them to be holy. By applying this language to the Ephesians, Paul seeks to connect them to God's activity of forming, redeeming, and sanctifying a people (cf. Eph 1:4; 2:19). "To us, the early Christian self-designation as 'the saints' is almost embarrass-ing. . . . But the word once expressed much of what was meant by 'contrast soci-ety.' The church understood itself to be the sacred people of God's possession, a people with a pattern of life which differed from that of the world" (Lohfink 131). In designating the congregations he addresses as "saints" or "holy ones," Paul is indicating that they are a people set apart, not because of their moral perfection, but by the work of God. At the same time, this phrase indicates the end for which God sets people apart: holiness.

---

5. The use of "saints" as a form of Christian self-designation is prominent until the Montanist crisis in the late second century.

In addition to being called holy ones, the Ephesians are "faithful in Christ Jesus." Grammatically, this clause is unusual. The absence of a definite article before "faithful" seems to indicate that "the saints" or "the holy ones" and "faithful" are to be taken together as a common designation of a single group, as in the very similar usage in Col 1:2.[6]

It is important to remember, however, that the Ephesians' status as "holy" and "faithful" is tied to being "in Christ Jesus" (cf. 2:19–22). On numerous occasions Paul uses "in Christ" to speak of a distinct group or community composed of believers.[7] In addition, recall that the use of "holy" is tied to the formation of a particular people. This indicates that identifying the Ephesians as "holy" and "faithful in Christ Jesus" defines both the parameters of a community and the character of that community. Being in Christ locates one within the community founded by Christ and thereby within the realm governed by Christ. It is easy to forget, however, that when Paul uses such language, he is speaking in political terms—not of partisan politics but of a community whose character and polity is defined by the lordship of Christ.

Paul's language here presumes a viewpoint that contemporary Christians must work hard to remember. If Christ's lordship is to have any material reality in the present, then there must also be a community of people whose faith and practice, whose hopes and desires, whose very life and death—all are shaped by their allegiance to their Lord. Apart from this, language about being in Christ and attempts to call Christ "Lord" begin to lose their coherence. As Gerhard Lohfink (127) states, "*Being in Christ* means living within the realm of Christ's rule—and that realm is the church." Clearly Christians are divided over questions about exactly how the church should be ordered and what all of its constitutive practices are. This very divisiveness is a profound wound in the body of Christ. Nevertheless, to follow Paul and speak of the church as the body of Christ demands the real material presence of a community of Christians, not simply individual Christians enjoying discrete inner transactions with God. The central Christian confession "Jesus Christ is Lord" calls forth and requires that community known as the church.[8]

In the next section Paul begins to articulate in greater detail what God has done for this community in and through Christ.

6. This is opposed to Kirby (170) and others who see two groups addressed here, "the saints" and "the faithful ones in Christ."

7. Outside of Ephesians, Paul uses "in Christ" in this way in at least these passages: Rom 6:11; 12:5; 1 Cor 1:2; 1:30; 15:22; 2 Cor 5:17; Gal 1:22; 3:28; 5:6; Phil 1:1; 1 Thess 1:1; Col 1:2. This is only a portion of the numerous times Paul uses the phrase "in Christ." A large amount of secondary literature treating this Pauline formulation is introduced by Allan; Wedderburn.

8. Although the context is quite different, this partly is what Cyprian understood when he indicated that "outside of the Church there is no salvation" (*Ep.* 73.21).

Ephesians 1:3–14
Introductory Blessing

This section calls on believers to bless God for the saving work God has accomplished and is accomplishing in the world. One can find similar passages in 2 Cor 1:3–4; 1 Pet 1:3–12; and Luke 1:68–76. This text formally resembles the blessings found in Tob 13:1–17; 1 Kgs 8:15, 56, where the phrase "Blessed be the LORD, the God of Israel" introduces a narrative of God's saving acts (cf. also LXX of Pss 65:20 [66:20 Eng.]; 67:36 [68:35]).

Although many scholars have proposed that this passage, as a whole or in part, replicates an early Christian hymn or liturgical formula, these suggestions are highly speculative.[1] Moreover, the present context of the epistle has to be determinative for interpreting these verses, not some reconstructed context for which we have limited, if any, evidence.

This passage begins with an expression of praise to God in v. 3. Verses 4–6 locate the reason for praising God in God's gracious choice of believers. The next verses go on to locate believers' redemption in Christ. In vv. 9–10 Paul speaks specifically about the results of redemption. Finally, vv. 11–14 refocus the dimensions of God's drama of salvation in Christ from the cosmos onto the lives of believers in Ephesus.

1:3 Blessed[a] is the God and Father of our Lord Jesus Christ, who has blessed us with every spiritual blessing in the heavenly realms[b] in Christ, **4** just as he chose us in him before the foundation of the world that we might be holy and blameless before him in love, **5** having predestined us for adoption as sons and daughters through Christ Jesus for himself according to the good pleasure of his will, **6** for[c] the praise of the glory of his grace,[d] which he has graciously bestowed on us in the Beloved. **7** In him we have redemption through his blood, the forgiveness of sins according to the riches of his grace, **8** which[e] he has lavished on us in all wisdom and prudence. **9** He has made known to us the mystery of his will according to his[f] good pleasure that he purposed in Christ **10** for

---

1. For surveys of NT hymns, see Sanders; Deichgräber. For an account explaining why these identifications largely fail, see Fowl, *Story of Christ*, ch. 2.

the administration of the fullness of times, to bring together all things in Christ, things both in heaven and on earth. 11 In Christ we have an allotment,ᵍ having been destined for this according to the purpose of the one who causes all things to work according to the counsel of his will 12 so that we who have already hoped in Christ might live to the praise of his glory. 13 You also are in him, having heard the word of truth, the gospel of your salvation. In him also you have been sealed by the promised Holy Spirit, 14 who is the down paymentʰ on our allotment, standing also as the promise of God's redemption of his own possession for his praise and glory.

a. Verses 3–14 are a single sentence in Greek. In fact, this is the longest sentence in the NT. Because of the numerous subordinate clauses here, it is not always clear how particular phrases are connected to each other. Moreover, decisions about how to connect certain phrases will play a significant role in the overall interpretation of the passage. To render these words into readable English, one needs to apply a number of interpretive glosses. Any translator would hope to keep these to a minimum. The translation above renders the single Greek sentence as six English sentences. Even so, some of these sentences are quite long and complex. Inserting such breaks represents interpretive decisions, albeit small ones. Given this situation, students would be well advised to read this passage in a number of different translations.

b. The Greek phrase *en tois epouraniois* is translated here as "in the heavenly realms." The phrase also occurs in 1:20; 2:6; 3:10; 6:12. In each of these cases it is used to describe a place or a location (Lincoln, *Ephesians* 20). In each of these cases the context indicates something about this location without ever presuming to offer a full description.

c. The Greek preposition *eis* can be translated here as "to." The translation above uses "for" to indicate that praise is one of the ends toward which God's predestining in directed.

d. The phrase "for the praise of his glory" (*eis epainon doxēs autou*) appears in 1:6, 12, 14. It is almost formulaic. Here in v. 6 we get the added phrase "of his grace" (i.e., "for the praise of the glory of his grace"). This series of genitive constructions is somewhat difficult to untangle and render into elegant English. Hoehner (202) is on the right track when he explicates the phrase as referring to "the praise of God's glory for his grace." This both retains the strong formulaic connections between 1:6, 12, 14 and indicates that here in v. 6 there is a more particular emphasis on God's grace.

e. I am following most commentators here in taking "grace" as the antecedent of the genitive relative pronoun in v. 8. Although this "grace" is the direct object of the aorist verb (*eperisseusen*) "to lavish," the relative pronoun is genitive by attraction to the genitive *charitos* (of [his] grace) in v. 7.

f. Although it is not clear in English, the Greek relative pronoun makes it clear that it is God's good pleasure that was purposed or resolved in Christ.

g. The Greek word *eklērōthēmen* is translated here as "allotment." This is the only time in the NT that the word appears. Elsewhere it is used to refer to choosing something by lots (1 Kgdms [1 Sam] 14:41). Colossians 1:12 uses the nominal form of this term, *klēros*, along with the noun *meris* to speak about believers' being allotted a portion with the holy ones. Such language is also used in passages like Num 26:55–56 to refer to the division of the promised land (also determined by lot). This lies behind attempts to translate this term as "inheritance" [NRSV]. The translation of "allotment" is preferable in that it does not invoke the image of passing on property through death. See the comments below for further refinement of this notion.

h. The Greek word translated as "down payment" (*arrabōn*) is a loanword from Hebrew (cf. Gen 38:17–20). In the OT it refers to an initial installment toward the purchase of something or as a loan repayment.

[3] There are formal affinities between this verse and numerous OT verses that bless or praise God by using some form of the Hebrew word (*bārak*). Nevertheless, the language here is decidedly Christian in its praise of the God and Father of our Lord Jesus Christ. The point here is not to identify two gods, but to identify the one God and God's particular relationship as Father of the Son (Thomas Aq. [Aquinas] 45).

The following clause explains why believers are to bless or praise God: God has blessed us. One should avoid thinking of this as a straightforward exchange of blessing between equals where we bless God in exchange for God's blessing us. God does not need human praise; we humans desperately need God's blessing. This verse concludes with three phrases each introduced by the Greek preposition (*en*). Each of those phrases serves to elucidate the nature of God's blessing.

Some interpreters take the first phrase "every spiritual blessing" to refer to spiritual as opposed to material blessings. Rather, "spiritual" here refers to the fact that God's blessing is related to and sustained by the work of the Spirit. This is made explicit in 1:13–14. It is also the way the adjective "spiritual" is used in 5:19.

These spiritual blessings are located "in the heavenly realms."[2] The Hebrew term for "heaven" is also a plural noun, and that usage seems to be reflected here. Hence Paul is probably not referring to a multilayered heaven such as one sees later in, for example, Irenaeus's account of Valentinian Gnosticism.[3] It is very clear from the five times the phrase "in the heavenly realms" occurs in Ephesians that this is a way of talking about a location (cf. 1:20; 2:6; 3:10; 6:12). "The heavenly realms" refers both to a place where Christ is seated at the right hand of God (1:20) and a place where hostile principalities and powers seek

2. The Greek phrase *en tois ouranois* appears in Paul (2 Cor 5:1; Eph 1:10; 3:15; 6:9; Phil 3:20; Col 1:5, 16, 20). The term *epouranios* occurs in various forms 5 times in 1 Cor 15:40–49. The phrase *en tois epouraniois* only occurs in Ephesians. This is often taken as a mark against Pauline authorship.

3. Schnackenburg (51) comments that although this refers to a place, it does not provide a topography of heaven.

to exercise authority (3:10; 6:12). It is also a place where believers have been raised with Christ and seated with him. It would appear, then, that the heavenly realms is a place that has been decisively marked by Christ's redemptive work, a foreshadowing of the final end of believers (Thomas Aq. 46). It is also a place whose final transformation into a place fully under Christ's rule has yet to be accomplished (Lincoln, *Ephesians* 21; Carr 94–96).

What does it mean, however, to say that God has blessed us with every spiritual blessing in the heavenly realms? What does the juxtaposition of divine blessing with this location convey? Although "the heavenly realms" have yet to be fully subjected to Christ's rule, it appears that this is "the place" where matters of the utmost significance happen. The one in control of the heavenly places is the one who ultimately exercises dominion over the earth (cf. Dan 7:1–14; Job 1:6–12). By declaring that God has blessed the Ephesians in the heavenly realms, Paul may be making a point about either the immutability of these blessings or their ultimate significance.

This is not to say that locating these blessings in the heavenly places means that God's blessings are not also material. Nevertheless, just as Paul indicates in Phil 4:10–13, such blessings are not tied to the material goods that may or may not come one's way. At the same time, in Eph 2:6 Paul asserts that believers have been raised with Christ and seated with him in the heavenly realms. Thus, in some sense, believers are already located in that place where God has blessed them. In some real though unspecified way, they are united with Christ in that place where God's blessings have been bestowed and where the most important things are. In addition, though, 3:10 and 6:12 make it clear that in some significant sense the heavenly realms are not yet fully under Christ's rule. As the heavenly realms are not yet under Christ's full control, so believers are clearly not yet fully resident there. The fact that Paul himself is in prison when he writes to the Ephesians makes this clear.

This line of thinking is not all that different from Paul's discussion in 2 Cor 5. There he uses the image of believers' having an eternal dwelling from God. The beginning of the chapter reminds the Corinthians, however, that there is a very real sense in which they have yet to inhabit this dwelling: they still remain clothed in mortality. Nevertheless, as in Eph 1:13–14, the presence of the Spirit in the lives of believers is God's guarantee that they will not be found naked but will come to their true home (2 Cor 5:4–5). Even as he recognizes that believers are not yet in their heavenly dwelling, Paul boldly asserts a few verses later that having abandoned an earthly point of view, one can see that in Christ the new creation is a reality: "everything has become new!" (2 Cor 5:16–17).[4]

Finally, in Eph 1:3 Paul says that these spiritual blessings, in the heavenly places, are also "in Christ." They are in, through, and by Christ, the one who

4. Galatians 3:27 also stresses what might be called a "realized eschatology."

sits at God's right hand in the heavenly places (1:20) and who will ultimately have all things subjected to him. "All that God resolved and performed for our salvation took place 'in Christ' and every blessing which comes upon us is bestowed 'in Christ.'"[5] In addition to asserting Christ's agency in making God's blessing available to the world, the phrase "in Christ" also includes the fact that believers' incorporation into Christ's body in baptism joins them to God's blessing (so Lincoln, *Ephesians* 22; MacDonald, *Ephesians* 191).

[4–6] It seems best to take the conjunction "just as" (*kathōs*) to indicate the cause of believers' praise of God for God's blessings.[6] This causal interpretation fits the formal structure where a blessing is offered or called for followed by the reasons for that blessing. as in Pss 67; 103; 113; or in the more familiar passage Luke 1:68–79.

The primary reason that God is blessed and believers are called to bless God is because God chose us in Christ to be holy and blameless before God (in love). The language here is redolent of Deut 7:6–8:

> For you are a people holy to the LORD your God; the LORD your God has chosen you out of all the peoples on earth to be his people, his treasured possession. It was not because you were more numerous than any other people that the LORD set his heart on you and chose you—for you were the fewest of all peoples. It was because the LORD loved you and kept the oath that he swore to your ancestors . . .

In the light of this text, it appears that Paul is telling or reminding the Ephesians that through Christ they have become participants in God's election of Israel, when God chose Abraham from among all people and graciously made a covenant with him. One of the reasons for God's call of Abraham and the establishment of an everlasting covenant with him is to bring a blessing to the nations (cf. Gen 12:1–3). Because of what God does with Israel, all the nations are to be drawn to God. As Isaiah, among others, declares, this will happen when Israel is redeemed (Isa 2:1–4; Amos 9:11–12). In Acts 15:15–17 James reads Amos as announcing the incorporation of Gentiles into the people of God.

Further, in Gal 3:6–18 Paul takes great pains to point out that Christ fulfills this promise to Abraham, as Gentiles are drawn to the renewed and redeemed people of God. In Eph 1:4 Paul simply indicates that God's election is in Christ. It will become clear in Eph 3, however, that this is part of the great "mystery," which has been revealed in the life, death, and resurrection of Christ.

Further, just as God's election of Israel is a call to holiness (Deut 7:6; also Exod 19:6; Lev 11:44; 19:2; 20:26), so also all those brought into this elect

---

5. Schnackenburg 51. Far too much scholarly energy has been expended in trying to limit the focus of the phrase "in Christ."

6. Hoehner (175); MacDonald, *Ephesians* (191). Barth's (2:79) claim that *kathōs* refers to statements made previously by another ignores the clear causal use of the conjunction in 5:3 as well as Rom 1:28; 1 Cor 1:6; 5:7; and Phil 1:7 without reference to any prior statement by another.

group through the life, death, and resurrection of Jesus are called to be "holy and blameless." As Thomas Aquinas (46) states, "He chose us, I say, not because we were holy—we had not yet come into existence—but that we should be holy in virtues and unspotted by vices." In addition, although it is important to strive for personal holiness, the use of these same terms, "holy and blameless," in 5:27 to describe the end of the church indicates that holiness is the communal end toward which God calls the church as a body.

More will be said about Israel's election and the inclusion of the Gentiles in Eph 2:11–22. Yet here we observe two things about Paul's understanding of the election of Israel and how the Gentiles have been incorporated into the people of God in Christ. First, Paul's claims about the incorporation of the Gentiles into the people of God do not assume the abrogation of the covenant. If God's everlasting covenant with Israel is either broken or superseded by some new covenant with Gentiles in Christ, then the character, fidelity, and righteousness of God would be called into question. A God who freely makes an everlasting covenant with Abraham and his heirs and then abandons that covenant in favor of a new one with Gentiles—such a God can hardly be called righteous, much less trustworthy.

Second, although Paul as a Jew is offering an account of how God fulfills the promise to Abraham by drawing Jews and Gentiles into one body in Christ, one should not assume that Paul's account was immediately acceptable to his Jewish contemporaries or to subsequent Jews. Nevertheless, as Eph 1:13–14 asserts, the presence of the Spirit in the lives of both Jewish and Gentile believers in the church confirms that they have been accepted by God as full members of the covenant people.

It is also important for readers, both ancient and modern, to understand some of the ways in which God's choosing is not like human choice. Paul does not offer such reflection himself. Presumably, however, when presented with such considerations, Paul would agree with them. These considerations reflect basic components of a Christian doctrine of God. This doctrine is the result of sustained and ordered reflection on Scripture, particularly the OT. Moreover, Christians (presumably including Paul) recognize that although our language about God can become ever more disciplined, clear, and beautiful, it can never fully comprehend God. Thus to claim that God chose us is not to say that God, having considered all the options and possibilities, selected us from among a variety of lesser options. God's choice is gracious and not the result of our superior properties. Further, in choosing us, God is not filling up some lack that God has or feels. God's choice is neither provoked nor coerced by any insufficiency in God. God does not need to elect anyone. Moreover, by claiming that this choosing took place before the foundation of the world, Paul declares that this election is not like our contingent choices, forced on us by opportunity or circumstance.

Moreover, we Americans are often so deeply shaped by our own notions of equality that we are offended by God's selectivity in choosing Abraham and his people. For us, it may be valuable to remember that the calling of Abraham and the formation of a chosen people, Israel, is part of God's plan to bring a blessing to all the families of the earth (Gen 12:3). God chooses Israel with the aim that the relationship between God and the people of Israel is to be so beautiful, fascinating, and compelling that it will draw all of the nations to God.

This verse ends with the phrase "in love." Grammatically, the phrase can either serve to complete v. 4 ("to be holy and blameless before him in love") or as the beginning of v. 5 ("In love he destined us for adoption as sons and daughters").[7] I am not sure there is any gain in limiting the ambiguity of the placement of this clause. One might take the phrase both as closing v. 4 *and* opening v. 5. As a closing to v. 4, one can read "in love" in the light of Phil 1:9 and 1 Thess 3:12–13, where a superabundance of *agapē* in the lives of believers provides the wisdom and grace they will need to be holy and blameless before Christ. As the beginning of v. 5, "in love" reminds readers that as mysterious as God's choosing and predestining is, the underlying motivation behind it is God's unsurpassed love for us.

Verses 4–5 really belong together since they express a single complex assertion: Out of God's love, God has predestined us through Christ to become sons and daughters of God. As with the notion of election, predestination presumes love (Thomas Aq. 48). This still raises the question of the relationship between the praise of God's election in v. 4 and God's predestining in v. 5. Grammatically, an aorist participle such as "he predestined" (*proorisas*) following a main verb such as "he chose" (*exelexato*) usually refers to contemporaneous actions (Porter 383–84). Moreover, in terms of God's will, there can be no temporal distinction. Humans, due to our finitude, first make plans and then try to execute them. God is outside of time and not subject to such finitude. Although our thinking (including our thinking about God) is temporally constrained, God is not.

Rather than focus on a temporal distinction between election and predestination, it is probably better to think of the discussion of God's predestining believers in v. 5 as a way of further explicating the nature of God's choosing believers so that they might be holy and blameless. That is, predestining believers to be adopted through Christ is the way in which God brings about believers' sanctity. There may be other ways to have done this, but this is how God acted.

Paul elaborates being adopted as children of the Father through Jesus Christ and uses that image to speak of the object or aim of God's predestining. There are several points to note here. First, the word translated above as "adoption" (*huiothesia*) had been in use for a couple of centuries before the NT. Paul,

---

7. Schnackenburg (47–48) argues that "in love" should begin v. 5. Lincoln (*Ephesians* 17, 24–55), Hoehner (183–84), and MacDonald (*Ephesians* 198) see it as going with v. 4.

however, is the only NT writer to use this word. Although the LXX does not use the word, there are a variety of occasions in the OT where someone might be thought of as adopting someone (levirate marriage in Deut 25:5–10; Abraham's provisional ceding of his goods to Eliezer in Gen 15:2; Jacob's adoption by Laban in Gen 29:14–30; and Moses' adoption by Pharaoh's daughter in Exod 2:5–10). Throughout the OT, relatives and others are expected to care and seek justice for orphans, yet the OT does not preserve clear evidence of a legal process for adopting a child (Walters 43).[8]

Roman law allowed adoption. There were two aspects to this process: Initially, the son's ties to his biological father were severed, and all of the father's considerable control was relinquished. This then allowed the son to come under the full control of the adoptive father (Lyall 86–99; Walters 52–55; Hoehner 196). This Roman pattern fits well with points Paul will make later in Ephesians. In Eph 2:1–5, Paul speaks of the Ephesians as formerly "sons and daughters of disobedience" and children of wrath (by nature)—as part of a more comprehensive description of their alienation from God, a situation rectified and altered in Christ.

In the light of this description, it appears that Paul uses the image of adoption through Christ here with its Roman overtones of breaking all former bonds to a natural father and coming under the domain of a new father. In this respect, adoption is not simply God's gracious act: it bespeaks the comprehensive and total transfer of one's passions, love, and allegiance from the world to God. Finally, we only obtain our share in this adoption through the true son, Christ. Paul spells this out more clearly in Gal 4:4–5 where "God sent his Son, born of a woman, . . . that we might receive adoption as sons and daughters" (AT).

The subsequent clause, "according to the good pleasure of his will" (Eph 1:5), reflects Hebrew phraseology (Lincoln, *Ephesians* 26, citing CD 3.15). The phrase reiterates the point that God's election of believers is not something wrested from the hand of an unwilling giver, but fully accords with God's most heartfelt desires (Barth 81, making a similar point).

Verse 6 begins by noting that the upshot of God's adoption of believers in Christ is praise. Praise is one of the ends toward which God's predestining is directed. Thus God is both the free initiator of believers' adoption, and praise of God is the end toward which such adoption is directed. The adoption of believers is God's gracious act, which leads not simply to praise of God, but to praise of God for this specific act of grace. The rest of v. 6, "which he has graciously bestowed on us in the Beloved," elaborates on this grace.

There are two ways of understanding this gracious gift that God has bestowed on believers in Christ. The first way is to recall that the aim of God's adoption of sons and daughters in Christ is that these believers might be holy and

---

8. Contra Scott, who thinks that Paul relies on a Jewish background for his concept of adoption.

blameless before him. In this light, believers can think of God's bestowing grace on them as part of the process of their sanctification. Thus grace enables believers' transformation from children of wrath (2:3) to holy and blameless sons and daughters of God through Christ. The second way of taking this passage is to read it in the light of the similar use of the verb "to bestow grace" (*charitoō*) in Gabriel's pronouncement to Mary in Luke 1:28. Here the emphasis is on the graciousness of God's choosing. It is an unmerited gift. The latter emphasizes the character of the giver; the former emphasizes the effects of the gift on believers. It is, however, the same grace. "Being highly favored with grace means, for the believing community, participation in that divine love with which the Father favored the Son, though the community's participation in this relationship is through adoption" (Lincoln, *Ephesians* 27).

This grace is bestowed on believers in the "Beloved one." This term is used of Israel in the LXX of Deut 32:15; 33:5, 26; and Isa 44:2. As Lincoln (*Ephesians* 21) notes, however, there is no evidence that the term was used with messianic overtones prior to Jesus (contra Schlier 56). In both Jesus' baptism and his transfiguration the voice of God uses the term "beloved" in authenticating Jesus' identity as the Son (Mark 1:11 par.; 9:7 par.). Moreover, Col 1:13 speaks of believers being "transferred into the kingdom of the Son of his love" (AT).

[7–8] These verses go on to explicate how God brings about the Ephesians' adoption in the Beloved. First, they are told that in the Beloved, they have redemption. Redemption occurs in Christ, in the realm or sphere defined by Christ's lordship. Paul uses the present tense of "have," indicating that redemption is more like an ongoing state rather than a onetime achievement.

The word translated here as "redemption" (*apolytrōsis*) is not very common in the NT. Three of its ten occurrences are in Ephesians. In all of its NT uses, the word refers to God's acting to release or deliver people from slavery (e.g., slavery to sin), danger (e.g., the danger of falling under God's just judgment), or distress. In the case of v. 7, redemption is specifically spoken of as "the forgiveness of sins." This shows that here God's redemption is directly tied to God's delivering believers from their slavery to sin. This slavery is further specified in Eph 2:1–10. It appears that, as in Rom 5–6, sin becomes a way of speaking both of the transgressions that individuals commit and of a power that captivates the world, bringing with it slavery and death. Redemption involves not only liberating believers from their slavery within the sphere ruled by Sin; it also includes transferring them into a new kingdom under the rule of the "son of his love" (cf. Col 1:13).

On this much, commentators largely agree. Modern commentators are divided, however, about whether the term always connotes the payment of some sort of ransom. Certainly this would be the case in more general Greek usage, where the term is often used to speak of the manumission of slaves (BDAG 117). In the NT the notion of some form of payment is clear in Rom

3:24 and Heb 9:15.[9] In passages such as Luke 21:28 and Rom 8:23, which speak of some future redemption, it is not clear whether redemption presumes some form of prior payment. In Eph 1:14, however, the term is used to speak of future redemption in a context where financial images of exchange abound. Moreover, the vast majority of patristic authors are all relatively comfortable in recognizing the notion of payment entailed in speaking of redemption here.[10]

In Eph 1:7 the reference to Christ's blood makes it clear that the death of Christ is the means through which God brings about redemption (see also Rom 3:24; Heb 9:15). We should be wary, however, of simply transferring images from the realm of commercial exchange directly into the life of God as if Christ's blood was a form of currency. Here are simply a few of the problems that would need careful attention: First, if we are slaves to Sin, then any ransom offered for our release must be paid to Sin or Satan.[11] Christians should be clear here: God has defeated Satan; God owes Satan nothing. Second, if we think of Christ's death as offering restitution to God for the damages incurred by our sin, we need to avoid two obvious corollary judgments one might also make. That is, we would need to avoid thinking that God is somehow damaged by our sin. Our sin damages us and our relationship with God. The incarnation, death, and resurrection of Christ is both a sign of God's continued desire for fellowship with us and an offering to God on our behalf to restore that relationship. Of course, the offering does not come from us; it is God's self-offering on our behalf. In this light, we should also avoid the notion that the Father wills the death of the Son as opposed to the Father willing the Son's perfect obedience. The Son's death may be the consequence of being obedient in a world marked by sin, but obedience rather than death would be the Father's desire.

Further, we should also be wary of thinking that somehow Jesus' death on the cross releases God's love for us. God loves us unconditionally, fully, and without reserve. The cross displays that love to the world. The cross manifests humanity's utter inability to abide the perfectly loving and obedient Son. Paradoxically, the cross also declares our forgiveness. It does not unleash God's love; the cross, rather, enables the sanctification for which we are created and for which this entire passage praises God. In this sense, if one thinks of restitution being made, it would be in the sense in which making restitution helps to transform the offender rather than to mollify the offended party.

9. Even in Heb 11:35 the image of release seems to imply payment in the form of renouncing one's faith. It is not a cash exchange, but a valuable exchange nevertheless.

10. The interesting question for these patristic interpreters concerns the one to whom payment is made.

11. Some modern commentators such as Muddiman (71) dismiss this line of interpretation, yet it attends much closer to the logic of the verse than any other alternative. This is why patristic authors often read the text this way, while at the same time acknowledging that God could not be in debt to Satan. See the list of patristic views in Lyonnet and Sabourin 207–10.

The mention of our redemption at the beginning of v. 7 quite naturally leads to mention of redemption's origin in the "riches of his grace." Paul explicates this grace further in the relative clause in v. 8, "which he has lavished on us in all wisdom and prudence." There is some ambiguity about whether "in all wisdom and prudence" refers to God's wisdom or whether wisdom and understanding are some of the manifestations of the grace that God has lavished on us. The wider context of v. 9, which stresses believers' apprehension of the mystery of God's will, along with v. 17, where Paul prays that the Ephesians may have a spirit of wisdom and so forth, indicates that here in v. 8 believers are the recipients of wisdom and prudence from God. The word "prudence" here may sound old-fashioned to contemporary readers. Both the RSV and NRSV translate the Greek word *phronēsis* with "insight." I think there are a couple of reasons to prefer "prudence." The Greek word *phronēsis* was used widely in classical moral philosophy to refer to practical wisdom, the ability to know how to apply general moral rules to specific situations in the right ways.[12] This requires both insight and a variety of habits that are born of practice. Paul clearly uses *phronēsis* in just this way throughout Philippians, where the vast majority of his uses of this term occur. Hence *phronēsis* means insight but also includes practice in life. When Christian theologians writing in Latin encounter *phronēsis*, they translate the term with *prudentia*. Thus prudence, while old-fashioned, may give readers pause to recall that Paul is not simply speaking of disembodied insight, but also of a way of life.

Paul's combination of "wisdom" and "prudence" here connects wisdom, which involves knowing God, including one's proper relation to God (e.g., Prov 1:2–7; Job 28:28; Ps 111:10; Isa 33:6), a wisdom that may stand in contrast to the wisdom of unbelievers (e.g., 1 Cor 1:21–25; 2:6–7; 3:19)—with prudence, which employs that right understanding of God and one's relationship to God in order to live faithfully in concrete situations.

Recall that the prepositional phrase "in love" at the end of v. 4 can refer back to the discussion of our election *and* modify the participle "he predestined" in v. 5. Similarly here the prepositional phrase "in all wisdom and prudence" both reflects back to the grace that God has caused to abound in believers *and* points forward to the participle at the beginning of v. 9, referring to the means by which God has enabled us to comprehend the "mystery of his will."

[9–10] When God lavishes wisdom and prudence on believers, one of the results is that they are able to apprehend the "mystery" of God's will, which he

---

12. The two terms wisdom (*sophia*) and prudence (*phronēsis*) are used in the classical world to refer to two different types of knowledge. Aristotle uses s*ophia* to speak of theoretical knowledge or something like speculative wisdom. "Prudence" is used to refer to understanding of practical matters. In a similar vein, both Philo (*Praem.* 14.81) and Thomas Aq. (58) independently distinguish between "wisdom" (*Sophia,* or *sapientia* in Latin), which concerns knowledge of God, and "prudence" (*phronēsis,* or *prudentia* in Latin), which concerns temporal affairs.

has made known to them. Paul uses the term "mystery" numerous times and with some variety (Rom 11:25; 16:25; 1 Cor 2:1, 7; 4:1; 13:2; 15:51; 2 Thess 2:7; also 1 Tim 3:9, 16). Moreover, the word appears relatively widely in both Greco-Roman and Jewish religious contexts (Caragounis 119–35). In Ephesians, Paul repeatedly speaks of the mystery that has been made known to him and that he proclaims as his gospel (3:3, 4, 9; 5:32; 6:19). From these references we can see that the "mystery" here is a shorthand for a much larger account of God's story of the redemption of the world (Caragounis 118). In Ephesians, Paul emphasizes two particular aspects of this larger story. First, redemption is accomplished in Christ. Second, redemption calls forth a unified body of Jews and Gentiles, which is Christ's body, the church.[13] What makes this a mystery, or a hidden truth requiring revelation, is that apart from the life, death, and resurrection of Jesus, and the presence of the Spirit in the church, no one could have reasoned their way to such an account. Of course, once Christ has been revealed and believers have received "all wisdom and prudence," this mystery becomes both evident and compelling. Moreover, it is a mystery that can be openly proclaimed. It is not a secret to be kept.

In v. 9 one finds a compilation of ways of asserting God's absolute control over this mystery. It is the mystery of God's "will," made known "according to his good pleasure," which God "purposed" or "resolved" in Christ. Although Paul is clear that this mystery has been hidden from humans, it has not been hidden from God. Rather, it is generated, executed, and sustained by God's will.

Verse 10 begins to explicate the nature of the mystery of God's will and good pleasure, which God has purposed in Christ. The focus of this mystery is on the "the administration of the fullness of times." The nature of this focus is that all things will be summed up in Christ. The phrase "fullness of times" is similar to Paul's usage in Gal 4:4 where in "the fullness of time . . . [Christ is] born of a woman." The difference is that in Galatians the birth of Christ signals the climactic moment in the world's history. In Ephesians the plural "of times" indicates the end point, or telos, of God's will, that toward which everything is ultimately moving.[14]

In its first-century context the Greek word *oikonomia* was used to refer either to an administrator or to the act of administration. In later patristic writings when the word is linked with God, it refers to God's economy or plan of salvation (Lampe 940–44). Although "administration" is the best way of taking this

13. This conforms to the use of "mystery" in Col 1:26–27; 2:2; 4:3.

14. This corresponds with the usage of the plural "times" (*kairoi*) in such texts as 1 Thess 5:1; Dan 2:21; 4:37 LXX; Tob 14:5; *4 Ezra* (= 2 Esd) 4.37. One sees here an image of history as a collection of "times." The fullness of times, then, would refer to some point of consummation. See also Lincoln, *Ephesians* 32. This image of history as a succession of times may also account for 1 Cor 10:11, where Paul speaks of the "ends of the ages."

word in Eph 1:10 (Reumann 156–57, 164), it also seems that for early Christian writers the word functions as a shorthand for Paul's larger assertion in Ephesians that God has willed that the fullness of times will be marked by Christ's rule over and ordering of all things. That is, the patristic usage of *oikonomia* seems to take all of this verse into account.

Paul continues the image of history being a succession of "times" by indicating that all things are to be summed up in Christ. The verb used here (*anakephalaiōsasthai*) is often used to indicate the drawing together of discrete points into a summative argument. Romans 13:9 uses the same term to sum up the law. Irenaeus (*Haer.* 1.10.1) uses the term to speak of that time when all things are brought together and subjected to the lordship of Christ, as in Phil 2:10–11, and thereby restored to their proper relationship to God and each other.[15] Tertullian, Jerome, and Thomas Aquinas, among others, all use this term to speak of the renewal of all things.[16] John Chrysostom says "the meaning of 'to sum up' is 'to knit together.'" He also uses several images to explain this term, including repairing and improving a decayed house, and establishing a union under one ruler.[17] What all of these early interpreters seem to be doing is explicating a term that normally applies to rhetoric — summing up the points of an argument — in the light of Paul's use of that term to describe Christ's role in all of history.

These patristic images point out that in this context the administration of the fullness of times is when God brings all things in heaven and earth to their proper end through and in relation to Christ. The array of various images for describing this point in time should remind Christians that this truly is a mystery. Nobody knows when this will happen, how it will happen, or exactly what it will look like. The result, however, will be in accord with God's will, and the result will represent the fulfillment of God's best intentions for creation. Thus it must require the renewal of all things rather than their destruction. Moreover, at this point humans will be brought into a new and ever-deepening union with God. All Christian discussion of these ends will need to operate at least within these parameters. Obviously, these parameters can comprehend a variety of other images; they also, however, exclude images suggesting that God's intentions can ultimately be thwarted or that Christ's lordship will be constrained in any way.

Although it is not spoken of in these verses, the summing up of all things in Christ presumes an account of prior brokenness and disorder. Based on the

---

15. See McHugh (302–9) for a fuller account of Irenaeus's understanding of this term.

16. Tertullian, *Mon.* 5; Jerome, in Heine 99; Thomas Aq. 59, quoting Amos 9:11//Acts 15:16.

17. John Chrysostom, *Hom. Eph.* 1, noting the parallels to Col 1:20.

whole of Eph 1–2, it becomes clear that Paul presumes that the principalities and powers created by God for the good ordering of the world have been hijacked or taken over by satanic forces so that they no longer serve their providentially ordered purposes (cf. 1:20–22; 2:1–3). Further, the consequences for humans of this disorder are death (2:1) and alienation from God. Moreover, this alienation is specifically manifested in the alienation of Gentiles from the children of Israel (2:13). One need not speculate about whether there was one particular and formal account of the world's disorder and alienation from God behind Paul's assertions in Ephesians (contra Schnackenburg 60–61). He simply argues as if his audience recognizes this.

At the same time that Ephesians expresses the full confidence that all things will be brought to their proper end in Christ, the letter also speaks of those outside of Christ as under God's wrath (2:1–4). In this respect Ephesians on a small scale manifests a phenomenon found in Paul and the rest of the NT. On the one hand, there are passages—such as Matt 5:25; all of Matt 25; Mark 3:29–30//Luke 12:10; John 12:48; Rom 3:9; 1 Cor 11:32; and others—that speak of a coming judgment in which some will be condemned. On the other hand, passages such as John 12:32; Rom 5:12–21; 2 Cor 5:19; Eph 1:10; 1 Tim 2:4–5; 4:10; 2 Pet 3:9, and others speak in various ways of God's will for the salvation of all. The NT itself never synthesizes these two positions into one coherent whole. All subsequent attempts by theologians and other believers to offer such a synthesis risk the sin of presuming to know more than we actually do about these matters. As Swiss theologian Hans Urs von Balthasar observes, the deep problem with presuming to know whether or not all will be saved is not that one might be wrong about such an important matter. Rather, presuming to know God's mind on this will naturally frustrate Christian hope for the salvation of all. In the face of a variety of attempts to build the NT's witness into a systematic approach to this question, Balthasar (45) states, "Still, one ought to stay well away from so systematic a statement and limit oneself to that Christian hope that does not mask a concealed knowing but rests essentially content with the Church's prayer, as called for in 1 Timothy 2:4, that God wills that all men be saved." As Balthasar (72–78) goes on to argue, presuming that one knows about the ultimate salvation of all not only frustrates Christian hope but also makes it ever more difficult to love others in the way that Christ commands. This is because one cannot truly love any particular person as Christ commands if, for example, one is convinced that such a person is destined for hell. In this light I invite readers to extend such scripturally regulated hopeful agnosticism to their study of Ephesians.

[11–14] These verses refocus the dimensions of God's drama of salvation in Christ from the cosmic to the lives of particular believers. Verse 11 reiterates many of the ideas surrounding God's call of believers first articulated in

v. 5. In Christ we have been assigned a portion in God's salvation, preordained according to the purpose of the one who brings all things to pass according to his will.

The major interpretive question of this verse concerns the Greek term *eklērōthēmen*, "we have an allotment." This word appears only here in the NT. When it appears elsewhere in Greek (including 1 Kgdms [1 Sam] 14:41), it refers to being chosen or appointed by lots. Both Chrysostom (*Hom. Eph.* 2) and Thomas Aquinas (61) are eager to distance this verse from any super-stitious practice or random choosing on God's part. The context of the verse, however, clearly rules out the idea that God chooses on such a random basis. Colossians 1:12 uses the noun related to this verb, *klēros*, along with the noun *meris* to speak about believers' being allotted a portion with the holy ones. Similar language, which also has connections to choosing by lot (cf. Num 26:55–56), is often used in Deuteronomy to speak of God's choosing Israel as God's special possession (Deut 4:20; 9:26, 29; 32:9). If one uses this image to help explain Eph 1:11, then it appears that Paul employs images reflecting God's providential and preordained election of Israel to speak of believers in Christ.[18] Rather than being the result of some sort of a divine roll of the dice, believers are spoken of as being appointed as God's possession. As will be clear in Eph 2, Paul does not think that Israel's status has simply been transferred to a (nearly exclusively) Gentile church. Rather, through Christ, Gentiles have been brought within God's purposes for all creation as manifested through the calling of Israel.

Verse 12 continues this thought by specifying the purpose and goal of that appointment, that believers who hope in Christ might now live to the praise of God's glory. Here in 1:12 and also in 1:6, 14, Paul affirms that the purpose and goal of the people of God is to praise God's glory ("the glory of his grace" [1:6] or "glorious grace," as in NRSV). In their various ways, the Psalms (e.g., 95; 100; 145–50), the church's catechesis, and its liturgy all remind Christians that the vocation and proper end of all creatures is the praise of God.[19] For Paul,

18. There is some dispute among commentators concerning those referred to here by "we" and "you." Some take "we" here to refer to Paul and his companions specifically (and believers, more generally) and "you" to refer to the Ephesians. Others take "we" as a more specific refer-ence to Paul and other Jewish Christians and "you" to refer to Ephesian Gentile Christians. See Hoehner (230–33) for a concise account locating most major commentators on this issue. On the one hand, Yoder Neufeld (54–55) and others are correct in noting that the two options are not that far apart since the overwhelming majority of those who first hoped in Christ (among whom are Paul and his companions) were Jews. Furthermore, the Ephesian church was probably all or virtually all Gentile. Although this is the case here in 1:11, one should not allow this narrow distinction between "we" Jewish Christians and "you" Gentile Christians in Ephesus to persist throughout the entire epistle.

19. See also the powerful beginning of Augustine's *Confessions*.

the striking, surprising, and mysterious element is that God has providentially ordered things so that believers are brought to their proper end through the crucified and resurrected Christ.

Should the Ephesians have any doubt about this, vv. 13–14 remind them that the presence of the Spirit in their midst is God's confirmation and promise that, through Christ, they will be brought to their proper end. In these verses, Paul rehearses how the Ephesians came to be in Christ. They heard the word of truth, the gospel of their salvation. They believed and were sealed by the promised Holy Spirit.

"The gospel of your salvation" is "the word of truth" (cf. Jas 1:18). In the later chapters of Ephesians, Paul emphasizes the importance of truth (4:21, 24, 25; 5:9; 6:14). Indeed, in 4:21 Paul reminds the Ephesians that in their hearing about Jesus and learning of Jesus, they were taught that "truth is in Jesus." The Ephesians (as well as most other believers) lived in an environment where numerous religious and philosophical movements made claims to truthfulness and sought their attention. Paul reminds the Ephesians that the gospel of their salvation is true. Moreover, they can be sure of this. This assurance does not, however, come by amassing more true propositions than any other alternative. Rather, assurance is found in the confirming presence of the Holy Spirit, which results from hearing the word of truth and believing.[20]

At the end of v. 13 Paul identifies the Spirit as the "promised Holy Spirit." Both Joel 2:28–29 (particularly as interpreted in Acts 2:17–21) and Jesus (in Luke 24:49; John 14:16–17; 15:26) speak of God's promised outpouring of the Spirit.[21] The presence of the Spirit in the lives of the Ephesian believers is the confirmation that the gospel of their salvation in Christ is true. As v. 14 begins, Paul elaborates on this notion by claiming that sealing the Ephesians with the Holy Spirit is God's down payment on their allotment or heritage, first mentioned in v. 11. Such a "down payment" both promises full payment in the future and signifies the good faith of the purchaser/debtor. The only times Paul uses this term (*arrabōn*) outside Ephesians are 2 Cor 1:22 and 5:5. In each of these cases, as in Ephesians, Paul links this down payment to the pouring out of the Spirit in the lives of believers. It indicates God's commitment to bring to completion the redemption achieved by Christ's resurrection, which awaits completion at his second coming. For Christians living in that time between the accomplishment of our redemption in the cross and resurrection, and the consummation of that redemption at the day of Christ, the pouring out of the Spirit is God's promise to bring this work of redemption to completion. This idea is similar to Paul's confident claim in Phil 1:6 that the one who

---

20. As Perkins (43) notes, later Christian practice linked sealing with the Spirit to Christian baptism; yet such a link, though not ruled out, is probably not implied here.

21. Chrysostom makes similar links in *Hom. Eph.* 2.

began a good work in the Philippians will bring it to completion at the day of Christ.[22]

As it stands, however, this claim needs further elaboration. The image of the Spirit as God's down payment on some yet-to-be-completed purchase indicates several things. First, it confirms the truth of the gospel and the Ephesians' reception of the gospel in faith. Second, it implies God's fidelity to the promise both to send the Spirit and to bring believers to their ultimate end in Christ. Finally, however, the metaphor of God's sending the Spirit as down payment has the unfortunate and unacceptable implication of making God appear to be a debtor. Thus the image of down payment is supplemented by the claim that this down payment is really more a promise to redeem God's own possession. God is not buying something that God does not already own. Rather, God is redeeming a people who already belong to God yet have been alienated from God.[23]

Although the Greek word *peripoiēsis*, "possession," is not common in the LXX or NT, it is used very significantly in 1 Pet 2:9. There believers are spoken of as "a chosen people, a royal priesthood, a holy nation, God's own possession" (AT; cf. LXX: Hag 2:9; Mal 3:17). Allowing the usage in 1 Pet 2:9 to clarify this clause in Eph 1:14 makes it clear that sending the Spirit as a down payment of our redemption does not render God a debtor because believers are already God's possession. Moreover, speaking of believers as God's possession reintroduces language that ties the Ephesian believers to the people of Israel.

In Ephesians the pouring out of the Spirit confirms God's commitment to bring the Ephesians into the heritage that has been granted to them in Christ, their portion among the people of God. As we have seen in 1:6 and 1:12, the ultimate end of God's sealing and redeeming results in praise and glory for God.

Whatever one can say about the prehistory of this text (and we can say very little with confidence), in its current context this passage is in the form of praise to God (v. 3). In the light of the movement of the passage as a whole, however, it seems equally clear that this passage aims to reaffirm an account of the redemption of the world in Christ and the Ephesians' place in that yet-to-be-completed story. Moreover, this passage uses language often associated with God's calling of Israel to describe the calling of Ephesian Gentile Christians. For these Ephesian Christians, at the very least, this reminds or reaffirms their

---

22. Thomas Aq. (67) notes the following difference between a pledge and earnest money: "An earnest, however, does not differ from the object in place of which it is given, nor is it returned since it is a partial payment of the price itself, which is not to be withdrawn, but completed. God communicates charity to us as a pledge, through the Holy Spirit who is the Spirit of truth and love. Hence, this is nothing else than an individual and imperfect participation in the divine charity and love; it must not be withdrawn but brought to perfection."

23. "The Spirit is seen as the power of the age to come given ahead of time in history, but as still only the beginning and guarantee of the full salvation of that age which is yet to come" (Lincoln, *Ephesians* 41).

roots in God's redeeming Israel. The overall tone of praise, however, is never abandoned. This is because at various points throughout this passage we are reminded that the first and ultimate purpose of God's redemption of the world is that the world should fulfill its proper vocation of praising God.

In the next passage Paul connects this overview of the drama of redemption more concretely to the faith of the Ephesians. At the same time, he will also commend their attention to and love for the saints, both in Ephesus and elsewhere.

Ephesians 1:15–23
Paul's Prayer for the Ephesians

This is another very long sentence in Greek. As with 1:3–14, the translation breaks a single Greek sentence into several English sentences for ease of understanding. It is not very common for a Pauline letter to include two passages of blessing and/or thanksgiving in a single letter. In this respect, Phlm 4–5; 1 Thess 1:2–10; 2:13–17; 2 Thess 1:3–4; 2:13–15; as well as Col 1:3–4, 9–14 (cf. also Dan 2:20–23) provide the closest stylistic parallels to Ephesians.[1] In other thanksgiving passages and in other passages where Paul expresses his prayers for a community, one can often learn a good deal about how Paul views the situation of the community. That is less obvious in Ephesians. Paul's commendation of the Ephesians' faith in Christ and love for the saints, as well as his prayer for their growth in wisdom, could apply to almost any Christian community.

It should become evident that 1:15–23 expands upon and presumes both the praise of God and the articulation of the drama of salvation that Paul presents in 1:3–14. The focus of 1:3–14 is clearly God, God's redemptive activity in the world through Christ, and the Ephesians' incorporation into the people of God. The prayer embedded in 1:15–23 shifts the focus from God to Paul's desire to see the Ephesians grow in their wisdom and knowledge of God so that having been incorporated into the body of Christ, they can continue to move toward their ultimate end in Christ.

This passage begins with Paul's recounting his knowledge of and concern for the Ephesians in vv. 15–16. From this, he offers a prayer for them in vv. 17–19. This leads to a more general discussion of God's unsurpassed power as displayed in the resurrection of Jesus.

---

1. As with almost all of the stylistic quirks of Ephesians, this one has been used to argue both for and against Pauline authorship. Schubert (*Form and Function* 44) argues that including both types of introductory thanksgivings is a crude mimicking of Pauline style by a later author: "The fact that it is superfluous after the liturgical proömium (1.3–14) indicates that it is a highly conscious effort on the part of the author to omit nothing which he considered formally essential in Pauline epistolography." O'Brien in "Ephesians 1" counters Schubert by arguing that the very distinct and precise use of *eulogētos* and *eucharisteō* could only have been penned by Paul himself. Without determining the issue of authorship here, such discussion on this passage tends to flatten out the distinct focus and nuance of both 1:3–14 and 1:15–23.

1:15 Therefore I also, having heard of your faith in the Lord Jesus Christ and[a] the love that you have for all the saints, 16 have not ceased to give thanks for you, remembering you in my prayers. 17 I pray that the God of our Lord Jesus Christ, the Father of glory, may give you the Spirit of wisdom and revelation in knowledge of him 18 so that, the eyes of your heart having been enlightened,[b] you may come to know what is the hope of his calling; what are the riches of the glory of his inheritance among the saints; 19 and what is the limitless greatness of his power toward us who believe, according to the working of his mighty strength. 20 God[c] demonstrated this power in raising Christ from the dead and seating him at his right hand in the heavenly realms, 21 far above all rule, authority, power, dominion, and every name named in this age and in the age to come. 22 God[d] has put all things under his feet and gave Christ as head of all things to the church, 23 which[e] is his body, the fullness of him who is filled in every way.

a. Several MSS ($\mathfrak{P}^{46}$, ℵ, A, B, et al.) omit the phrase "and the love that you have." In these MSS, Paul mentions that he has heard of the Ephesians' faith "in the Lord Jesus Christ and in all the saints." According to this reading, it appears that Paul does not distinguish between the Ephesians' faith in Christ and their faith in other believers. This would be very unusual. Philemon 5 would be the only close parallel. It is mostly in Alexandrian texts that "and the love that you have" appears (e.g., ℵ², D², et al.). This also seems to fit the context better. Moreover, as Metzger (533) notes, one can account for the missing text as a scribal error due to the repetition of the Greek article *tēn*. Hence it has been included here in the translation.

b. The participial phrase translated above as "the eyes of your heart having been enlightened" is somewhat obscure in Greek. It is unclear why it is accusative and how it is connected to the indirect object ("you," in the dative case) of the verb "give" (in v. 17), I follow Hoehner (261) and Lincoln (*Ephesians*, 47), who treat this as a subsidiary part of Paul's prayer request for the Ephesians. The phrase then is taken as an accusative absolute. Yet Best (*Ephesians*, 164) is correct in stating that in this case the meaning is clear although the syntax is not.

c. In Greek the sentence continues with a relative clause whose antecedent is the word "power" (*energeia*) in 1:19. The main verb of this relative clause is *enērgēsen*, which plays upon *energeia*. The translation above starts with a new sentence and therefore needs to articulate the subject of the verb.

d. Although the translation starts a new sentence, the Greek continues as a single sentence. Because of this I have explicitly named God as the subject of the action and Christ as the one on whom God acts. The Greek simply uses pronouns.

e. This verse is grammatically obscure. There is no simple or definitive way to address its problems. There are three primary interpretive problems here: Should the Greek word *plērōma* (fullness) be understood actively or passively, and how is it related to the preceding phrases? Should the Greek participle *tou plēroumenou* be understood as a middle voice or passive voice (e.g., the one who fills or the one who is filled)?

Finally, should the phrase *ta panta en pasin* be understood as an adverbial or adjectival phrase (e.g., the fullness of him who fills *all things*, or the fullness of him who is filled *in every way*)? For a fuller accounting of the options and reasons for choosing various options, see the commentary below. For now I have followed Hoehner (294–300), Best (*Ephesians*, 183–86), and Dawes (241–50) in taking *plērōma* in a passive sense, *tou plēroumenou* as a passive voice, and *ta panta en pasin* as an adverbial phrase. The result of these decisions is reflected in the translation above.

[15–16] Paul begins to insert himself into the epistle here by reporting that he has heard of the Ephesians' faith in Christ and their "love for all the saints." According to some commentators, this way of writing reflects, at best, an indirect connection to the Ephesian community by a nonpauline author (see Best's arguments, *Ephesians* 158–59; Lincoln, *Ephesians* 54). Others (e.g., Hoehner 248) note that it may have been six or seven years since Paul was with the Ephesians. His knowledge of their faith and love could not have been anything other than secondhand. If Ephesians is Pauline, then Hoehner's explanation must be the best.

The authorship issue should not distract one from recognizing Paul's presumption that Christianity entails a relationship both to Christ and to other Christians. Faith in Christ apart from love for the saints is dead or incomplete; love for the saints apart from faith in Christ reduces the church to just another social service provider.[2]

Although Paul's current connection to the Ephesians comes only through hearing, he thanks God for them and prays for them. On the one hand, for a writer to give thanks to the gods for the health of the recipients is quite conventional in Hellenistic letters. On the other hand, the extent and detail of Paul's thanksgiving in Ephesians, and elsewhere, is not conventional. The language here goes well beyond conventional expressions of good wishes.[3]

As in Rom 1:8–10; Col 1:3; 1 Thess 1:3; and Phlm 4, here also in Eph 1:15–16 Paul's thanksgiving to God for a particular group of Christians is tied to praying for them. Paul's claim never to cease thanking God for the Ephesians must be hyperbolic. It expresses the view that Paul's concern for the Ephesians is not fleeting. Further, in these two verses Paul establishes the three-way

2. My allusions here to James complement Thomas Aquinas's reference (68) to John 13:34–35: "By this everyone will know that you are my disciples, if you have love for one another." Best does not think the reference to love is original in Eph 1:15 (*Ephesians* 160). He does think that it truncates Jesus' teaching of love for all. Alternatively, Chrysostom (*Hom. Eph.* 3) sees the same reference to the Ephesians' love "for all the saints" to be a sign of the catholicity of their love, reaching well beyond the bounds of those in Ephesus.

3. Several scholars note that this part of Ephesians seems closer to the praise hymns of the Dead Sea Scrolls (e.g., 1QH hymns 2, 3, 7, 8, 10, 12) than to a typical Hellenistic letter. See, e.g., Robinson; Lincoln, *Ephesians* 48–49. This seems to reflect Paul's use of conventional Jewish forms for expressing praise to God.

relationship between God, the Ephesians, and Paul that governs the rest of the epistle. As one will see in the subsequent verses, Paul offers a prayer to God that conveys Paul's longings for the Ephesians. At the same time, he also presents those longings to the Ephesians as a token of his affection.

[17–19] Having articulated a disposition to pray for the Ephesians, Paul begins here to describe the content of that prayer. In short, Paul prays that God will give the Ephesians the Spirit and the spiritual resources they need to grow in their knowledge of God. Thus Paul's prayer begins by explaining the spiritual resources the Ephesians will need if they are to grow in their knowledge of God. In doing this, Paul further identifies the God whom the Ephesians and all Christians seek to know and love.

Paul's request is that God will give the Ephesians "the Spirit of wisdom and revelation." The Greek word translated as "Spirit" here could refer either to the Holy Spirit or to a general human spirit of wisdom. Although there is no definite article, which would identify the Spirit as opposed to a spirit, the context here makes it fairly clear that Paul is referring to the Holy Spirit.[4] Nearby 1:13–14 has just mentioned the work of the Spirit in the lives of the Ephesians, sealing them and assuring them of their incorporation into the people of God. Moreover, while a "spirit of wisdom" might refer to a general human quality or disposition, the addition of "revelation" here could only be the work of God through the Spirit. Once this phrase is read as a reference to the Holy Spirit, the distinction between receiving the "Spirit of wisdom and revelation" and the formation within believers of a spirit of wisdom and revelation diminishes.

The combination of "wisdom and revelation" in 1:17 helps to explicate the notion of the "knowledge" of God, which Paul prays will be the result of the Spirit's work. The wisdom of the world (cf. 1 Cor 2:11–12) or human intellectual power cannot independently produce knowledge of the true God.[5] In many respects, 1:17 recapitulates ideas first broached in 1:7–8 (Macdonald, *Ephesians* 216). At the same time, Paul's prayer indicates that the work of the Spirit is not a onetime event. Rather, through the Spirit's work, the life of the believer is to be characterized by an ongoing desire for and growth in knowledge of God.[6]

The mention of a Spirit of wisdom, and of revelation and understanding, may allude to Isa 11:2, where the shoot that springs from the stump of Jesse will have the Spirit of the Lord resting on him. This Spirit is further identified

4. The Greek word for "spirit" (*pneuma*) is used without the article to refer to the Holy Spirit in other places as well (e.g., Matt 12:28; Mark 1:8; Luke 1:15, 35, 41, 67; Rom 1:4; 1 Pet 1:2). In each of these cases, as here, the context makes it clear that the Holy Spirit is in view.

5. Thomas Aq. (71) reads this verse in the light of Wis 9:17, "Who has learned your counsel, unless you have given wisdom and sent your holy spirit from above?"

6. Schnackenburg (71) also sees a link here to the work of the Spirit mentioned in 1:13.

as the "spirit of wisdom and understanding, the spirit of counsel and might, the spirit of knowledge and the fear of the LORD." In this case, Paul is praying that the same Spirit that fell upon Christ, as anticipated by Isaiah, may also fall upon believers in Ephesus.

Paul identifies this God who gives the Spirit of wisdom and revelation as "the God of our Lord Jesus Christ, the Father of glory." Several things can be said here. First, in using the term Lord with regard to Christ, Paul places Christ within the identity of the one God of Israel.[7] This God is also the one who gives the Spirit. On the one hand, it seems right to say that Paul does not presume a doctrine of the Trinity here. On the other hand, Paul's language here and elsewhere strikingly places Christ and the Spirit within the identity of the one God of Israel without any qualms and without any clear way of resolving the tension such language places on the singularity of Israel's God. Rather than think of later Trinitarian doctrine as the imposition of an alien and rigid Greek metaphysical system on the biblical text, Christians should understand that later Trinitarian doctrine can be seen as providing a scripturally regulated way of ordering and resolving the tensions that the language of Scripture generates but does not directly resolve.

Second, Paul identifies God as the "Father of glory." This is an unusual phrase. The phrases "God of glory" (Ps 29:3 [28:3 LXX]; Acts 7:2), "LORD of glory" (Num 24:11 LXX; 1 Cor 2:8), and "king of glory" (Pss 24:7, 8, 9, 10 [23:7, 8, 9, 10 LXX]) all occur in Scripture. In addition the phrase "glory of the LORD" occurs frequently. Moreover, God's "glory" appears three times in the previous passage (1:6, 12, 14) as the object of human praise. Although one could translate this phrase as "glorious Father," the phrase "Father of glory" allows several significant overtones to come through. The phrase correctly identifies the God and Father of Jesus Christ (1:3) as the source of glory. The OT certainly makes it abundantly clear that the glory of Israel's God is unsurpassed and not shared with any other (Isa 42:8). Glory is also a way of referring to manifestations of the invisible God. Throughout the LXX the visible manifestation of God is associated with God's glory (Exod 16:10; 24:16–17; 33:17–23; 40:34–38; 1 Kgs 8:11; Isa 6:3; Ezek 1:28; 43:2; 44:4; 1 Macc 15:9; 2 Macc 2:8; also *1 En.* 14.21; *T. Levi* 3.4; *Ascen. Isa.* 10.16). Often this glory is manifested in God's great works of power. Specifically in Eph 1:19–22, God's glory is linked to the resurrection and enthronement of Christ. Finally, and more distantly, the phrase recalls that surprising Christian logic within which the glory of the one true God is revealed in Christ's willed self-emptying and obedience to the point of death on the cross, an obedience that God vindicates in the resurrection (cf. Phil 2:6–11).

---

7. The importance and implications of such an identification are explicated by Bauckham; Hurtado.

In 1:18 Paul anticipates that the gift of the Spirit will enlighten the eyes of the Ephesians' heart. Such enlightenment comes from the gift of the Spirit and will enable the Ephesians to know the hope of God's call, the riches of God's inheritance among the saints, and the greatness of God's power as demonstrated in the resurrection. The work of the Spirit enlightens the eyes of the heart. It is not simply the eyes that are enlightened, nor simply the heart. Rather, the metaphors are combined.[8] The perfect participle in the phrase "having the eyes of your heart enlightened" invites commentators to try to find a distinct point in time when this enlightening occurred (e.g., conversion, baptism, etc.; cf. Lincoln, *Ephesians* 58; Macdonald, *Ephesians* 217).[9] If Colossians is one's guide in this matter, then Paul thinks that there is distinct movement from darkness into light when one becomes a believer (Col 1:12–13). In confirmation, Eph 2 speaks similarly, although without the specific images of movement from darkness to light. Moreover we remember that the object of this enlightenment is the knowledge of God. Although Paul looks forward to a time when he will know as fully as he has been known (1 Cor 13:12), there is also a strong element within the Christian tradition arguing that there can never really be a completion to this process of coming to know God.[10]

Through the end of v. 18 and into v. 19, Paul adds several layers of precision or focus to his prayer. First, Paul prays that the Spirit may enlighten the Ephesians as to the hope of God's calling. Presumably God's call is directly tied to God's choosing, first articulated in 1:4. On the one hand, then, God's call is "before the foundation of the world" (1:4). On the other hand, following 1:10–14, God's call to us to participate in the drama of redemption is a call that awaits its full realization in Christ. Hence believers are called to hope. Here hope is not primarily a reference to an evanescent emotion. Rather, it is a conviction founded on God's fidelity. The God who calls us in Christ to live in a world that is not yet fully redeemed will ultimately put all things in subjection to Christ.

The next aspect of Paul's prayer is that the Ephesians, enlightened by the Spirit, may come to know "the riches of the glory of his inheritance among the saints." The language here seems to draw quite heavily on 1:14. Lincoln (*Ephesians* 59), however, is right to note that 1:14 speaks of believers' inheritance while 1:18 is speaking of God's inheritance. These are not vastly different notions for they are each speaking about the salvation of the people of God. Nevertheless, v. 18 approaches this from a different angle than does v. 14. In the OT the people of Israel are often spoken of as God's inheritance (cf. Deut

8. See Jeal 99; the composite metaphor also appears *1 Clem.* 36.2; 59.3.

9. In Justin Martyr, *1 Apol.* 61.12; 65.1; *Dial.* 39.2; 122.1, 2, 6; and *Odes Sol.* 15, "enlightenment" does become a technical term for baptism.

10. One of the early proponents of this is Gregory of Nyssa (in *Life of Moses* §§219–55), who argues this point against Origen.

4:20; 9:26, 29; 2 Sam 21:3; 1 Kgs 8:51, 53; 2 Kgs 21:14; Pss 28:9; 33:12; 68:9; 78:62, 71; 94:14; 106:5, 40; Isa 19:25; 47:6; 63:17; Jer 10:16; 51:19). In the vast majority of these cases the notion of the people of God as God's inheritance indicates that there has been or is about to be some sort of separation between God and the people. Sometimes this refers to the separation caused by slavery in Egypt (e.g., Deut 4:20; 9:26, 29; 1 Kgs 8:51). Other times it is the separation related to Israel's sin and subsequent exile (e.g., Ps 78:62; Isa 47:6). Whatever the cause, the image of the inheritance of God seems to convey the idea that God's true possession has become alienated from God and awaits restoration. In Ephesians, Paul takes this image, which in the OT applies to the people of Israel, and now uses it to describe redeemed Israel, the body of Christ composed of Jews and Gentiles. As already noted in regard to 1:7–14, this redemption is both rich beyond our imagination, and the manifestation in the world of redeemed Israel redounds to God's glory.

There is some interpretive dispute about whether "among the saints" here (1:18) refers to believers or to angels. Those preferring angels notice the use of the word translated here as "saints" (lit., "holy ones," *hagioi*) to refer to angels in such texts as the LXX of Job 15:15; Ps 88:6, 8 [89:5, 7 Eng.]; Isa 57:15; Amos 4:2; and Dan 8:13. Moreover, they argue, Paul seems to use the word to refer to angels in Col 1:12.[11] The majority of commentators, however, take this reference to holy ones as meaning believers, saints (cf. 1:15).

Although 1:19 is hard to translate into elegant English, it is not hard to understand. Paul piles a combination of words together to speak of God's power. It is probably a mistake to try to read various nuances into these terms. They all work together to convey the sense of God's unparalleled and unsurpassed power. The important thing for the Ephesians to understand, the eyes of their heart having been enlightened, is that this power has been deployed on their behalf and on behalf of all who believe. Paul prepares for the emphasis on Christ's relationship to the created powers and principalities in v. 21 by asserting that God's power is unsurpassed and cannot be challenged by created forces. Thus, although the powers and principalities are not yet fully subjected to Christ (1 Cor 15:24–28), they cannot ultimately resist his power.

[20–23] After offering an account of God's unsurpassed power in 1:19, Paul offers the paradigmatic example of God's power in his discussion of Christ's resurrection and ascension in 1:20–23. In some ways Paul's prayer for the Ephesians in this passage corresponds to Paul's own desire for himself in Phil 3:10. Paul's prayer for the Ephesians is that they would grow in their knowledge of God and in particular their knowledge of God's power as displayed in the resurrection. Although Paul often reflects on the cross and resurrection as

11. Those holding this view include Schnackenburg 75; Best, *Ephesians* 168. Lincoln (*Paradise* 144) held this view but changed his mind in *Ephesians* 60.

a demonstration of God's vindication of Christ's self-emptying obedience and weakness, there are other passages that speak of the resurrection primarily in terms of God's power (cf. Rom 1:4; 1 Cor 6:14; Phil 3:10; Col 2:12). In Eph 2:5–6 Paul will claim that this same resurrecting power will work in the lives of believers in Christ.[12] Here in 1:20–23 the focus is on God's power demonstrated in Christ's resurrection.

God's power both raised Christ from the dead and also works to seat him at God's right hand in the heavenly realms. Although this is not a precise quotation from Ps 110:1 [109:1 LXX], Eph 1:20–23 certainly seems to reflect the very early use of this psalm to describe Christ's exalted status at the right hand of God (cf. Rom 8:34; 1 Cor 15:24–25; Col 3:1; Matt 22:44).[13] Clearly in Ps 110 to be seated at God's right hand is to have a place of favor and to participate in God's power, which will subdue all the enemies of God (cf. also Exod 15:6; Ps 89:13; Isa 41:10). Further, Christ is not only seated at God's right hand but is also "in the heavenly realms." From 1:3 we have already learned that the blessings with which God has blessed the Ephesians are "in the heavenly realms." It would appear that this is the place where matters of the utmost significance are decided, where God's rule is ultimately and fully exercised. It seems to be the most fitting place to locate the God who has unsurpassed power. The imagery here is all spatial, "at his right hand," "in the heavenly realms," "above all . . ." One of the aims of this spatial language seems to be to set up relationships of comparative power and status, which are articulated more fully in 1:21–23.

Verse 21 initiates this comparison by declaring that Christ's location at the right hand of God in the heavenly realms situates him far above all powers, authorities, and so forth. Although the Greek word *hyperanō* usually signifies a location, it is also used metaphorically to speak of authority, power, or status relative to others (cf. Deut 28:1; Philo, *Conf.* 137; *T. Levi* 3.4). In the case of 1:21, locating Christ above all of these powers signifies his superiority to them.

Paul then lists a series of terms used to refer to a variety of spiritual forces (*archē* [rule], *exousia* [authority], *dynamis* [power], *kyriotēs* [dominion]). Similar lists appear in Eph 3:10; 6:12; Col 1:16; Rom 8:38; 1 Pet 3:22. As with this passage in Ephesians, these passages all assert Christ's comprehensive superiority and power over all alternatives. These terms appear widely in Jewish texts (such as Dan 7:24; 10:10–21; *1 En.* 61.10; *2 En.* 20–22; 2 Macc 3:22–28; *T. Levi* 3.8; Philo, *Spec.* 2.45; *Plant.* 14).[14] These texts indicate that

12. Lest one draw too sharp a distinction between 1:20 and 2:5–6, however, see Thomas Aquinas's (74) comment on this verse: "The divine activity in Christ is the form and exemplar of the divine activity in us." Although he does not say so as succinctly, Calvin (136) holds the same view.

13. See the work of Hay. Yet Hay's (98–99) treatment of Ephesians tends to overstress the extent to which Paul sees Christ's rule as realized.

14. As Arnold (53–69) reports, these terms also appear in Hellenistic magical texts (esp. those influenced by Judaism).

within Judaism at this time, there are certain speculative views arguing that the nations, in particular, are overseen by angelic powers. These powers are in part responsible for the idolatrous practices of the nations. Moreover, these powers have an impact on all aspects of life (cf. Deut 32:8; Dan 10:10–21; *Jub.* 2.2).[15] Such angelic forces would stand behind those practices, dispositions, and structures that alienate people from the God of Israel.

If Arnold is right about the context of Ephesians, then this language also fits within the context of first-century Ephesus, where both magical practices and the cult of Artemis were widely observed (Arnold 13–40; cf. Acts 19). Thus, in addressing converts from this milieu, Paul reminds them both of the superiority and sufficiency of God's power in Christ and of their need to make a clean break from their past spiritual attachments (Arnold, esp. chs. 4–6).

One cannot decisively answer the question of the precise background to these terms regarding the powers. There is, however, a current consensus among scholars that Paul does not "demythologize" the powers by reducing them to concrete social and political forces, thereby eliminating or reducing the notion that these powers are spiritual, angelic, or demonic forces.[16] Nevertheless, one should also recognize that in the ancient world there was no hard-and-fast boundary between spiritual forces and social and material forces. The NT recognizes that spiritual forces manifest themselves in a variety of concrete structures and events (cf. Rom 13; Rev 13), and in pagan worship (1 Cor 10:20). In these cases, the point of power, spiritual or political, was to influence or control people and events (Best, *Ephesians* 176).

Further, scholars now generally agree that in Ephesians, as well as in the NT more generally, the powers are either hostile to or alienated from God and God's purposes in Christ.[17] From a theological standpoint, however, this does not say enough. Christ's superiority to all possible powers must in part depend on the fact that these powers, unlike the Son, are created (cf. Col 1:15–16). As such, they must have initially been part of God's good creation, a claim a Jew, such as Paul, would probably accept.[18] Moreover, it is certainly consistent with Eph 1:7–10 and 2:1–10 that these created powers had become hostile to or

---

15. An analogous view is represented in Rev 1–3, where each of the seven churches has an angel.

16. See the earlier discussion in O'Brien, "Principalities" 111–128; and Arnold 41–51.

17. This claim is largely directed against Carr's (98–99) argument that the powers in Paul represent pure angelic hosts surrounding the throne of God. Carr is able to hold this position because he argues that the primary text against his view, Eph 6:12, is a later interpolation (104–8).

18. For an alternative Jewish position that there were chaotic spiritual forces present prior to creation, see Levenson. Levering (*Scripture and Metaphysics*, ch. 3) shows how Levenson's view is but one way of construing the scriptural account. Moreover, taking Scripture in that way would render a God who was neither capable of bringing about the salvation of the world nor worthy of human worship.

alienated from God. They will, ultimately, with all other things, be reconciled and brought to their proper end in Christ (cf. 1:10). Thus Ephesians indicates that Christ is both comprehensively superior to these powers and the means by which they will be restored to their proper place in God.

We should not think that this list of powers is comprehensive. Moreover, in case Paul's list leaves any out, he concludes 1:21 by asserting that Christ is far above any and all names that might be named.[19] The mention of two ages here, this one and the age to come, points to the fact that although Christ's rule over all things is already determined and established, it has yet to be consummated.

As stated above, 1:20 includes an allusion to a christological interpretation of Ps 110:1. Here in 1:22 there is a quotation from Ps 8:6 [8:7 LXX] that is also applied to Christ (cf. 1 Cor 15:24–28; Heb 2:5–9, 14; and Heb 1:13 citing Ps 110:1). God has set all things under Christ's feet. In Ps 8 the image of setting something under the feet of another is used to convey humans' mastery over the rest of creation. Here Paul uses the image to invoke Christ's comprehensive superiority to the powers and all other things. Thus Christ is not simply superior to them in rank, but all things are subjected to him and all things will recognize Christ's superiority (Best, *Ephesians* 180).

The next clause of 1:22 runs into v. 23. God gave Christ to the church as head over all things. This leads to a further comment, identifying the church as the body of Christ. One might be tempted to treat these verses in the light of conventional Hellenistic use of the metaphor: the head's relationship to the body as a relationship of authority; yet there are some reasons to be cautious about doing so.[20] This verse does not directly identify Christ as the head of the church, his body, as in 5:23 or in Col 1:18. Rather, Christ, the head of all things, is given to the church, his body. Of course, being "head of all things" would certainly include the church. Nevertheless, the image of rule and authority, which comes from being "head of all things," is not sufficient to account for the relationship between Christ as the head and the church as his body here in 1:22–23. Instead, one should view the relationship in the light of 4:15–16, where the head provides both the rationale (and telos) for the growth of the body and the unifying principle that holds together the various parts of the body.[21] Thus the image of Christ as head in 1:22–23 seems to perform a dual function. First, it is an image of superiority and rule: Christ is head over all things. Second, Christ is head of his body, the church. This conveys the image

19. The term translated here as "name" (*onoma*) is widespread in the magical papyri. Reciting or calling upon the name of a deity or power was crucial to the practice of magic (Arnold 54–55). In Phil 2:9, similarly, Christ is given the name above all names.

20. For a list of references for the conventional metaphor, see Best, *Ephesians* 195–96.

21. In Philo (*QE* 2.117), for example, the *Logos* is seen as the head or ruling principle of the cosmos, which is referred to as a body. This notion of the head-body relationship does not, however, seem as rich as the notion expressed in Colossians or Ephesians.

of rule yet also of the integral and almost organic connection between Christ and the church (Benoit 73–75).

The use of the verb "give" enhances this image further. Christ has been given to the church.[22] Thinking of Christ as a gift from God to the church reinforces the image that Christ's role as head of the church is as the church's graciously given end, or telos, and as the church's unifying force.

Commentators are united in thinking that the final phrase of 1:23 is the most obscure in the epistle and one of the most obscure in the entire NT. There are no firmly fixed points on which to build an interpretation of the whole. Thus any interpretation must be somewhat provisional. Here is a list of some of the interpretive questions and ambiguities in this phrase: To whom or what does the phrase refer? Should the word *plērōma* (fullness) be understood passively (that which is filled) or actively (that which fills)? Does the participle *tou plēroumenou* have a passive voice (the one who is filled) or a middle voice with an active sense (the one who fills)? To whom or what does it refer? What is the sense of the words *ta panta en pasin*? Moreover, because of the interconnections between these terms, decisions about any one of these questions shape and limit the possibilities for the others.

In my judgment, one of the best and clearest discussions is offered by Gregory Dawes in an appendix to his book *The Body in Question*. He suggests that the participle be read as passive given that in the rest of the NT, LXX, Philo, and papyri the verb is never used in the middle voice (241).[23] Thus the participle refers to the one who is filled.

This move pushes one to interpret the phrase *ta panta en pasin* adverbially to mean "in every way."[24] The referent of this participial phrase is Christ, the one who is filled in every way. The subject of this phrase, the one who fills Christ in every way, would be God. Alternatively, if it is the church that fills or completes the one who is filled in every way, then the whole phrase simply becomes redundant, repeating the force of *plērōma*. God is the one who puts all things under Christ; God gives Christ to the church as head over all things; God is the one whose power is decisively displayed in raising Christ. It therefore seems reasonable to take God as the one who fills Christ in every way. The primary objection to this interpretation comes from the fact that the present tense of the participle usually indicates that the action involved is ongoing, or yet to be completed (Lincoln, *Ephesians* 76; Hoehner 300). Dawes (244) notes, however, that 1 Thess 1:10; 2:12; 5:24 all use present participles to describe actions that appear to be onetime or completed actions.

---

22. With MacDonald (*Ephesians* 220) and against Barth (57–58), who reads the Greek verb with the sense of "appoint."

23. Here Dawes is following La Potterie, who is also followed by Benoit; and Hoehner (298–99).

24. Moule (160) links it to the classical word *pantapasi*. Hoehner (296) offers further defense for this reading.

If one accepts these interpretive moves, then one is drawn to read *plērōma* in a passive sense, that which is filled or "the fullness," and as a reference to the church. The alternative would be to read *plērōma* as that which fills. This would be problematic since the idea that the church is that which fills Christ seems incompatible with the idea that all things are subject to Christ.

All of these moves yield the following sets of assertions: God has given Christ as head over all things to the church. The church is the body of Christ, "the fullness of the one who is filled in every way" by God. This is not the only plausible reading of this verse. Nevertheless, it has a sufficient level of plausibility to be taken as an acceptable reading; as such, it leads to several conclusions.

First, God's gift of Christ to the church is the greatest possible gift. Christ is filled in every way by God, and that fullness is manifested in his body, the church. If believers in Ephesus or elsewhere were tempted to supplement their faith in Christ through taking on the law (as in Galatians), through ascetic practices designed to lead to visions (as in Colossians), through manifestations of certain spiritual gifts (1 Corinthians), in submission to or veneration of the powers, or through any other means—they are reminded here in 1:23 that the fullness found by becoming a member of Christ's body is complete, absolute, and lacking in nothing. Indeed, to gloss Cyprian, there is no real fullness outside the church. At the same time, Eph 4:13 indicates that this fullness is yet to be consummated.

Second, this verse is an implicit claim about God's character. The God who has blessed believers with every spiritual blessing in the heavenly realms (1:3) has given the church the greatest possible gift, the One whom God fills in every way. Christ is God's ultimate gift to the church, a gift that reflects the goodness and grace of the Giver.

This section begins with Paul's thankful remembrance of the Ephesians and his prayerful desires for them. These desires focus on God's granting the Ephesians (through the Spirit's work) a deeper knowledge of God's comprehensive power, Christ's full participation in that power, and the Ephesians' own connection to that power through their membership in the body of Christ. As chapter 2 begins, Paul will turn to reflect on a larger and more explicit account of how the Ephesians came to be in Christ.

Excursus 1: An Alternative Reading of 1:23

Although I think there are good reasons to interpret 1:23 in the manner laid out above, the obscurity of the verse allows for at least one other plausible reading. This reading begins by taking the participial phrase as a middle with an active sense, yielding the translation "God has given Christ as head to the church, which is his body, the fullness of the one who fills all things" (vv. 22b–23). Such a reading is adopted by NRSV, NIV, and most other major English translations. As with the interpretation above, this way of taking the verse locates the fullness of Christ distinctively with his body, the church. This way of taking the verse does not focus so much on the character of God, who gives Christ to the church. Instead, it emphasizes Christ's role in filling all things or bringing all things to their proper end or completion, and it emphasizes that the church is the unique locus of that filling.[25] The first reading hearkens back to 1:3 and the God who blesses believers; this second interpretation seems to reflect the ideas of 1:9–10, that in Christ all things are brought to their proper end.

From a grammatical standpoint, there is no clear way to assert one of these readings over the other. Each has difficulties. Moreover, within the context of Ephesians each reading is consistent with themes found elsewhere in the epistle. And from a theological standpoint, there is no need to choose one over the other: each interpretation edifies. Although their emphases are different, each speaks truthfully about God, Christ, and the church: neither transgresses any theological dogma. From a Christian standpoint, there is simply a fruitful ambiguity in the verse.

Paul's prayer for the Ephesians concludes with 1:23. As chapter 2 begins, Paul continues to reflect on the great and powerful works of God. In particular, he focuses on how the Ephesians have been caught up in this drama of God's salvation of the world.

25. This is similar to the view of Lincoln, *Ephesians* 77–78; and Schnackenburg 80–84.

Ephesians 2:1–10
Once Dead, Now Alive in Christ

Over the next several verses starting Eph 2, the thanksgiving and prayer that starts in 1:15 shifts into an exposition of God's great power, particularly as it is manifested in Christ's superiority over all things. Without the prayer formally ending (as happens in varying degrees in 1 Cor 1:9; Phil 1:11; 1 Thess 1:10, this exposition continues into chapter 2. Stylistically, this continuation is signaled by the use of the conjunction *kai* (and) in both 2:1 and 2:5.

These verses focus on how Christ's superiority over all things enables him to free the Ephesians from their bondage to sin. The first part of this exposition establishes the Ephesians' comprehensive alienation from God. They lived and acted within the realm dominated by oppressive powers opposed to God. They were dead. Although the Ephesians were captivated by their attachments to sin, through God's gracious activity they have been raised together with Christ and seated with Christ in the heavenly realms. Although this passage assumes a cosmic conflict in which God defeats all antidivine powers and brings all things to their proper end in Christ (cf. 1:10, 20–23), this passage is not really part of a narrative of divine cosmic conflict (contra Gombis, "Ephesians 2"). Rather, it is more like a commentary on the aftermath of such a conflict and its implications and possibilities for the Ephesian Christians.

Structurally, the passage begins (2:1–3) with a description of the Ephesians' state prior to Christ. Then Paul in some detail proceeds to describe God's work in making the Ephesians alive in Christ in three basic moves: The transition from death to life (v. 4) and then two descriptions of salvation in Christ (vv. 5–7, 8–10).

> **2:1** And you were[a] dead because[b] of your transgressions and sins **2** in which you once walked, according to the age of this cosmos, according to the ruler of the realm[c] of the air, of the spirit[d] that is now at work among the children[e] of disobedience; **3** among whom[f] we all also once lived in the desires of our flesh, performing the wishes[g] of our flesh and of our thoughts. We were by nature children of wrath, just like the rest. **4** But God, being rich in mercy, because of his great love, with which he loved us, **5** made us alive together with Christ even though we were dead

in our transgressions—by grace you have been saved— 6 and he raised you together with Christ and seated you in the heavenly realms together in Christ Jesus, 7 so that in the ages to come God might demonstrate the unlimited riches of his grace in kindness toward us in Christ Jesus. 8 For you have been saved by grace through faith, and this does not come from you. Rather, it is God's gift. 9 It does not come from works, so that nobody may boast. 10 For we are God's work, created in Christ Jesus to walk in good works, which God has prepared beforehand for us.

a. The main verb is a present participle of the verb "to be." The translation above renders this in the past tense in English. This is because the context clearly refers to the Ephesians' state before their conversion, a state they are no longer in.

b. I take the dative here to indicate cause.

c. The Greek word translated here as "realm" is the same word translated as "authority" in 1:21. To translate this term here as "authority" would introduce a redundancy with the word "ruler." Moreover, in Col 1:13 the same word, *exousia*, is used to refer to the dominion or realm of darkness (see Lincoln, *Ephesians* 95; Hoehner 311–12).

d. Following Lincoln (*Ephesians* 95–96) and Hoehner (315), I take the genitive *tou pneumatos* (of the spirit) to be a parallel construction with *tēs exousias* (of the realm), thus describing another aspect of Satan's rule. This makes the best sense of the genitive construction without forcing the phrase into grammatically or semantically difficult appositional relations to either "air" or "ruler."

e. Further, "the children of disobedience" are more literally "the sons of disobedience." The phrase "children of wrath" in 2:3, however, is literally "children."

f. With Lincoln (*Ephesians* 96), Best (*Ephesians* 207), and Hoehner (317), I take the relative pronoun to refer back to "children of disobedience" rather than "transgressions."

g. The term translated here as "wishes" is the same Greek word translated as "will" in reference to the will of God in 1:1, 5, 9, 11. This term may well be used here in 2:3 to contrast God's will with the results of lives lived outside of that will (MacDonald, *Ephesians* 230).

[1–3] Paul here is addressing the Ephesian believers as a group. Among others, Barth (211–12) argues that the second-person plural pronoun is used to refer to "you" Gentile Christians as opposed to "we" Jewish Christians. Although it is true that Paul takes the audience to be predominantly if not exclusively Gentile, it is not possible to determine this by means of the pronouns. Neither is it possible to maintain such a distinction in pronoun use throughout the epistle (Lincoln, *Ephesians* 88).

The Ephesians were dead in their trespasses and sins. Paul assumes that, from the perspective of being in Christ, the description Paul offers of the Ephesians' past will be relatively clear and straightforward. What modern readers of Ephesians may forget is that prior to being in Christ, the Ephesians would in all likelihood not have recognized Paul's characterization of them as dead in their trespasses and sins. Thinking of oneself as dead outside of Christ already presumes that one knows something about being alive in Christ. Thus Paul is offering an account of their past, but one that really only becomes intelligible from the perspective of being in Christ.[1]

The Ephesians' transgressions and sins have led to their death. It seems most likely that the terms "transgressions and sins" are used synonymously here rather than as a reference to two distinct types of act.[2] Paul is referring to things done or things left undone that rupture or damage one's relationship with God. This conforms to the use of the same Greek word translated here as "transgressions," which also appears in 1:7. In 1:7 the redemption accomplished by Christ's blood is further specified as the forgiveness of sins.

In Rom 5:12–21 Paul declares that Adam's disobedience leads to death. He also goes on to speak of Sin as a distinct power that seeks to rule the earth and uses death as one of its instruments of oppression. Although Paul does not contrast Adam with Christ in Ephesians, nor does he use "Sin" in the singular as a way of speaking about a power, the line of thinking here is very similar to Romans.[3] Death is both a way of speaking of the Ephesians' alienation from God and the characteristic result of Sin's reign. Further, although Paul is here clearly speaking of spiritual death and alienation from God, Christians should not forget that physical death in the way that we know it is also the result of our sins and trespasses. Death is not part of God's purposes in creation; as Paul declares in 1 Cor 15, death is our enemy.

These trespasses and sins are not only the cause of the Ephesians' death; they also constitute the realm in which the Ephesians used to "walk."[4] On numerous occasions Paul uses the metaphor of walking to refer to one's conduct or moral life (cf. Eph 2:10; 4:1, 17; 5:2, 8, 15; also Rom 6:4; 1 Cor 3:3; Gal 5:16; et al.). It can refer to either positive or negative conduct. The force of the metaphor depends on the ways in which it is qualified. Here in 2:1 the Ephesians formerly walked "in" their transgressions and sins. The use of the preposition "in" (*en*) seems to indicate that "transgressions and sins" constitute a realm in which one might live. In Rom 6:1–11, Paul clearly sees Sin as the ruler of a realm within which believers used to live. Within this way of thinking, Sin, or in this case "transgressions and sins," stand for that political space ruled and dominated by powers hostile to or alienated from God. The Ephesians were formerly citizens (or slaves) of this realm and have now been transferred or liberated from that realm into a new realm under Christ's rule (cf. Col 1:13–14).

---

1. Paul offers a similar account from the perspective of being in Christ in Rom 7 and Phil 3:1–10.

2. Thomas Aq. (85) sees "transgressions" as sins of omission.

3. Depending on one's perspective, it is precisely this partial similarity to Romans that indicates either Pauline authorship (because the similarity is so close) or argues against Pauline authorship (because the similarity is close, yet also different enough to be ascribed to a Pauline imitator).

4. The relative pronoun in Greek takes its gender (feminine) from its nearness to "sins."

The next several clauses further explicate the character of that realm within which the Ephesians formerly walked.[5] The rest of v. 2 is composed of three descriptions of this realm. The first of these is "the age of this cosmos." The Greek term *aiōn* can be used to refer to a specific deity.[6] In the Bible the term usually refers to a period of time (long or short). This is the way the term is also used in Eph 1:21 and 2:7. It appears that it should also be read this way here (with Lincoln, *Ephesians* 95; Arnold 133; Hoehner 310). What would it mean to walk according to the "age of this cosmos"? In all likelihood it is a reference to living in accord with the standards of this current world, a world that has yet to become subject to Christ, a world that could not abide the presence of the obedient Son of God and nailed him to a cross.

The second clause refers to "the ruler of the realm of the air." If the notion of the "age of this cosmos" speaks of a type of mind-set or standard of life, this clause personalizes the forces operating on the Ephesians in their pre-Christian state. Thus, instead of speaking of an "age," Paul now speaks of a "ruler." There is little doubt that the text is a reference to Satan.[7] Although Paul uses the phrase "the devil" (*ho diabolos*) in 4:27 and 6:11, he does not use the term Satan in Ephesians. One reason may be that the designations used here would resonate more clearly with a Gentile audience.[8] Ruling the "air" is not to exercise dominion over a morally neutral space. Rather, there are numerous Hellenistic and Jewish texts which treat the "air" as a realm within which forces hostile to humans dwell, and from which they make their assaults on humanity (e.g., *T. Levi* 3.1–3; *T. Benj.* 3.4; *Ascen. Isa.* 7.9–12; Plutarch, *Mor.* 274B).

The ruler of the realm of the air is further identified as "the ruler over the spirit that is now at work among the children of disobedience." The phrase "children of disobedience" also occurs in 5:6. Although the use of "child" can refer to a biological relationship, within the NT to call someone a child of something can often play upon the biological relationship in order to speak about a dominant characteristic or affiliation of that person (e.g., Matt 23:15, "child of hell"; Luke 16:8, "children of this age"; Acts 4:36, Barnabas is the "son of encouragement"). Thus, when Paul identifies the Ephesians as formerly walking according to the ruler of the spirit at work among the children

---

5. See the similar use of the metaphor of walking with the Greek preposition *kata* in Rom 8:4; 2 Cor 10:2.

6. See Irenaeus, *Haer.* 1.1.1; 30.2.11; Hippolytus, *Haer.* 6.14.6. Origen (in Heine 121) suggests that some consider the "Aeon of this world" to be a separate being from the "Ruler of the realm of the air," and some see the both terms as referring to the devil. Jerome (in Heine 121) follows this latter view.

7. Clement of Alexandria (*Protr.* 1.8.1) and Jerome (in Heine 121) are all early witnesses to the use of this description and the following one to identify Satan.

8. Best (*Ephesians* 204) suggests this. Alternatively, some point to this as evidence against Pauline authorship (cf. Lincoln, *Ephesians* 95).

of disobedience, he speaks of their fundamental disposition. This is not simply a failure to keep God's commandments. Rather, their lives reflect active and comprehensive turning away from God. As it turns out, "children of disobedience" are quite obedient. They simply are not obedient to God (Yoder Neufeld, *Ephesians* 91). It is unclear whether the spirit spoken of here causes the disobedience, or whether a person with a disobedient disposition places oneself under the dominion of such a spirit. After analysis, it does not directly matter. The picture painted in 2:2 is of people who are in the thrall of forces opposed to God. Satan has captivated them; they are under Satan's dominion.

As 2:3 makes clear, this situation is not unique to Ephesus. Paul indicates that "we all" once lived among the children of disobedience. In saying this, Paul declares that, outside of being in Christ, all people stand with the children of disobedience. The Greek word translated above as "live" is, like the verb "to walk," often used to refer to a pattern of conduct or way of life (cf. 4:22; LXX: Prov 20:7 and Ezek 22:30; 2 Cor 1:12; 1 Tim 3:15; Heb 13:18; 1 Pet 1:17; 2 Pet 2:18).

Paul goes on to characterize further this former way of life. His first description notes that we all lived "in the desires of our flesh."[9] This description echoes language found in Gal 5:16–24, where the "desires of the flesh" are contrasted with the "fruit of the Spirit." In Ephesians these desires are not enumerated as the works are in Gal 5. It is not the case that desire in and of itself draws humans away from God. Rather, in this context the desires of "our flesh" locates these desires within the same realm dominated by the powers identified in v. 2. Thus, without indicating the precise nature or focus of these desires, Paul locates them in the realm opposed to the dominion of Christ. They cannot help but serve to alienate people from God.[10] Moreover, if we read this phrase in the light of Rom 1:18–32, it appears that one form of God's judgment on the children of disobedience is handing them over to the desires of their heart. Thus "living in the desires of our flesh" would be a sign both of alienation from God and of God's judgment for such disobedience.

This clause is further amplified by the odd formulation "performing the wishes of our flesh and of our thoughts." The use of the plural "thoughts" is a bit unusual. It appears in the LXX of Num 15:39; 32:7; Josh 5:1; 1 Esd 4:26; Dan 11:14. In these cases it appears that rather than referring to episodic thoughts,

9. In the light of passages such as Phil 3:2–10 or Rom 2, it is clear that Paul does not see this to be a uniquely Gentile situation. Rather, Gentiles and Jews are both captive to ungodly desires (cf. Rom 3). They manifest this captivity differently, but nonetheless they are both captive.

10. Best (*Ephesians* 209) quite insightfully notes the difference between phrases like "the desires of the flesh" in Gal 5:16 (and other places in Paul) and "the desires of our flesh" here in Ephesians. He asserts that with a personal pronoun the term "flesh" becomes simply equivalent to the personal pronoun (e.g., "our flesh" = us). Even if this is the case, living according to our desires cannot be a good sign when the context clearly talks about lives completely in the thrall of sin.

the word refers to a general pattern of thinking or mind-set. Some commentators take the phrase "performing the wishes of the flesh and the thoughts" to introduce an unpauline distinction between "flesh" and "mind-set," between the sensual and the mental (Best, *Ephesians* 209; Lincoln, *Ephesians* 98). The context here is primarily designed to point out the comprehensive difference between being in Christ and being "dead because of your transgressions and sins."[11] Rather than making fine anthropological distinctions, this language reinforces the comprehensive picture of alienation from God outside of Christ.[12]

Finally, Paul claims that "we were by nature children of wrath, just like the rest." Being a child of wrath is not a way of speaking about someone's ill temper. Rather, a child of wrath is someone subject to wrath, presumably God's wrath in this case. For example, in *Apoc. Mos. (L.A.E. Apoc.)* 3.2, Cain is called a son of wrath. Although there is clearly the idea that God's wrath is tied to an eschatological judgment, Paul is also capable of talking about the wrath of God revealed in the present as humans are given over to the desires of their own hearts (cf. Rom 1:18–32). It may well be the case that here in 2:2–3 Paul also understands God's wrath to be revealed in giving humans over to their own desires (contra Schnackenburg 93).

Paul indicates that we are children of wrath "by nature." The Greek term *physis*, like the English word "nature," has a wide range of meanings. Paul uses it in Gal 2:15 to speak about being a Jew "by nature." In this sense it is a reference to origin or birth. In Rom 11:21, 24 the term is used to refer to what is normally the case in the natural world. In 1 Cor 11:14 (the case of men's having long hair) and perhaps also in Rom 1:26 (natural sexual relations), the term seems to reflect the violation of a well-established convention. Hoehner (322–23) and Lincoln (*Ephesians* 98–99) are probably correct to allow the other times Paul uses the dative form, *physei* (as found in Rom 2:14; Gal 2:15; 4:8), to guide the interpretation of this same form in Eph 2:3. Even in these verses, however, the term is used with various shades of meaning. Thus Rom 2:14 refers to Gentiles' following the law instinctively; Gal 2:15 refers to birth or origin; in Gal 4:8 the term is used to talk about things that "in reality" are not gods. So even in the closest parallel contexts, Paul could be saying that the Ephesians are children of wrath according to their deepest instincts, by virtue of their birth as humans, or in reality (as opposed to appearance).

Further, each of these possibilities says something important about human sinfulness. That is, outside of Christ, humans' dispositions and inclinations are so captivated by Sin that we become subject to God's wrath (cf. Rom 7:14–25).

---

11. These same commentators do not see transgressions as one thing and sins as another similar yet different thing.

12. Given that distinction, it seems to be an open question whether the scope of Paul's "style" can comprehend such usage.

By birth as humans we become Adam's heirs, inhabitants of and participants in a world dominated by the power of Sin (cf. Rom 5:12–21). Finally, despite our presumptions otherwise, in reality humans are captivated by Sin and thereby subject to God's wrath (cf. John 8:31–47). I can see no clear way to determine which of these interpretations is correct if it means ruling out the others. Each is consistent with the context, and each is consistent with larger Christian convictions about human sinfulness. There is no reason to limit one's options here.

The concluding phrase "just like the rest" is a reference to the rest of humanity. Having spoken of the Ephesians' pre-Christian state as simply one example of the state of all people outside of Christ, in vv. 4–7 Paul is going to speak about the transition from being dead in sin to being alive in Christ.

[4] To make this transition, Paul begins in v. 4 with God. Verses 1–2 offer a discussion of the Ephesians' prior condition, death. Verse 3 explains that the Ephesians' state is simply one example of the condition "we all" find ourselves in. Verse 4 begins with the decisive conjunction "but God."[13] "We all" were once alienated from God, living in the thrall of forces hostile to God, handed over to pursue our own desires, "children of wrath." But God is rich in mercy. Mercy is posited as the alternative or antidote to wrath. In this respect the use of "mercy" here is closer to Rom 11:30–32, where mercy is seen as the antidote to disobedience, than to Luke 10:37, where "mercy" describes the response of the Samaritan to the undeserved misfortune of the man traveling from Jerusalem to Jericho.[14] That person did not deserve to be mugged, and Jesus makes it clear that mercy is the response called forth by the law of loving one's neighbor as oneself. But in the Ephesians' case, God's wrath is not some undeserved misfortune that befalls us. Rather, it is precisely what one might expect when one has been captivated by sin. The great surprise here is that God is not rich in wrath. Instead, God is rich in mercy. Indeed, Christians are taught that God's "nature is always to have mercy."[15]

Verse 4 begins with the assertion that God simply is rich in mercy. We then learn of the motive that leads to the particular demonstration of mercy described in vv. 5–6. It is "because of his great love, with which he loved us." This phrase joyfully notes that God's great love is directed toward us (Hoehner 327). As an expansion on this assertion, Thomas Aquinas (90) lists four specific ways in which God's great love is directed toward humans: (1) It brought us into existence (cf. Wis 11:24, "You love all things which you have made"). (2) We are made in God's image and thus "capable of enjoying his own beatitude" (cf.

13. Yoder Neufeld (*Ephesians* 94) calls these the two most important words in the epistle.

14. Lincoln (*Ephesians* 100) sees similar connections to Rom 11:30–32.

15. This phrase comes from the prayer of humble access from the eucharistic liturgy of the Book of Common Prayer. This is the same respect in which God's "mercy" is reflected in God's steadfast love and loyalty to the covenant, or his *ḥesed*. The Greek word *eleos*, which appears here in Ephesians as "mercy," is the same word that often translates *ḥesed* in the LXX.

Deut 33:2–3 [Vulg.; NRSV mg.]). (3) God renewed humans corrupted by sin, citing Jer 31:3, "I have loved them with an everlasting love; therefore I have drawn you, taking pity on you." (4) God gave his own Son for our salvation (John 3:16). Thomas's expansion here reminds readers of several significant facts. Just as God's nature is always to have mercy, God's love is eternal. It is not something that God revived in rescuing the Ephesians and/or us from our captivity to sin. Rather, as Thomas's preference for OT citations shows, God's love is at work from before the foundation of the world, in the calling of Israel and in the redemption of the world in Christ.

[5–7] Verse 5 begins in a manner stylistically similar to 2:1. Instead of stating "You were dead," however, the verse begins "We were dead." Further, v. 5 presents God's answer to death right away. God "made us alive together with Christ even though we were dead in our transgressions." Being "made alive" is the obvious solution to being spiritually dead. Paul's assertion goes beyond this to claim that God has made believers alive together with Christ. The verb used here, *synezōopoiēsen* (made alive together), occurs in the NT only here and in the similar passage in Col 2:13.[16] Paul does not use the simpler verb *zōopoiēsen* (making alive) very often either. When he does, the context is almost always referring to resurrection (Rom 4:17; 8:11; 1 Cor 15:22, 36, 45). These are either direct references to Christ's bodily resurrection or analogous extensions of Christ's resurrection to talk about a future bodily resurrection for believers. In Ephesians it appears that Paul is speaking of something slightly different. Being made alive together with Christ must include some notion of future bodily resurrection. It must also speak of the quality of the new life and some of its present effects (see also Allen 106). Thus the new life of believers is the same as Christ's new life. Being made alive together with Christ means sharing in Christ's new life and not some derivative form of Christ's new life, similar yet inferior. It is important to recognize, on the one hand, that humans participate fully in this new life. There is nothing more they either need or can achieve in this regard. On the other hand, humans, even resurrected humans, will still be creatures and not God.

The new life that God gives is nothing less than union with Christ. Obviously, this union has yet to be consummated. Nevertheless, Paul speaks of believers' new life as something already present. Indeed, there is no talk here

---

16. The two passages are very close linguistically: Col 2:13 adds that the Colossians were dead in their transgressions and in the uncircumcision of their flesh and that being made alive together with Christ forgives all their transgressions. Moreover, the Colossian context is baptismal: being made alive together is predicated on having died with Christ in baptism. There are also some close parallels in phraseology with material from Qumran, particularly 1QH 11 (= *olim* 3).19–22; 19 (= 11).10–12. These have been noted by Mussner, who says, "The heavenly and the terrestrial communities already form a unity and a communion whose main purpose is 'the praise of his glory,' both according to Eph 1:6, 12, 14 and the Essenes (1QH [11 =] 3:23; [17 =] 9:14)."

of dying with Christ; Paul has already established that the Ephesians were formerly dead in their transgressions. In this light, being made alive together with Christ must be a way of speaking about the Ephesians' rescue from their captivity to sin and the powers mentioned in 2:3–4 (Yoder Neufeld, *Ephesians* 96).

This verse also emphasizes that it is God who makes believers alive together with Christ. This is not something one can do for oneself.[17] Moreover, the contrast between being made alive with Christ and being "dead" in one's trespasses indicates that there is nothing about the state of being dead that would render humans deserving of being made alive. Thus Paul interjects the phrase "by grace you have been saved." This phrase is repeated in 2:8. Its presence here is taken to be a joyful interjection.

The perfect passive participle *sesōsmenoi* (you have been saved) usually indicates a completed action with ongoing effects. Although it is more usual for Paul to speak of salvation as a future activity (cf. Rom 5:9, 10; 10:9, 13; 13:11; 1 Cor 5:5; Phil 3:20; et al.), he can also speak of salvation as a present state of affairs (1 Cor 1:18; 2 Cor 2:15; Phil 2:12). Paul speaks of salvation as having past, present, and future elements (Lincoln, *Ephesians* 104). Hence one should not make too much of this difference in shaping judgments about authorship. Nevertheless, it is striking to Lincoln that in the undisputed Pauline Letters, Paul does not use "by grace" or "by faith" with "salvation." Rather, he speaks of "justification" "by grace" or "by faith" (Lincoln, *Ephesians* 104).

Whether this phrase is characteristic of Pauline usage or not, it fits quite well within the context of Ephesians.[18] From 1:3 onward, Paul has been describing what God has already done for the Ephesians. There seems to be far less emphasis on what awaits believers in the future than one finds in the Corinthian Letters, for example. Paul never denies that there is a future and yet-to-be-completed element in the Ephesians' life with God (see esp. 2:7). His emphasis here, however, is twofold. First, he makes the bold assertion that God has rescued the Ephesians from death, from their captivity to sin. This is accomplished by means of Christ's defeat and subjugation of the powers opposed to God's claim on the world. This defeat allows the church to be established as a political space or realm that recognizes Christ's dominion.[19] Thus the Ephesians have been liberated from their captivity to sin by means of their inclusion in the church. According to this emphasis, salvation here seems to have more to do with ecclesiology than eschatology. The second emphasis is on the fact that the Ephesians' transfer from the realm of sin to the realm of

17. On this aspect Best (*Ephesians* 215) notes, "We can arrange neither to be born nor to be reborn."

18. Schnackenburg (95) also makes a similar point.

19. Allen (106) speaks of Christ as ruler of a new age. Phrasing the matter in this way allows Allen to pick up some of the temporal imagery of 2:7. Yet it does so at the expense of the moral and political force of the spatial imagery.

Christ is accomplished by God through God's overflowing mercy, great love, and grace. Hence this way of talking about salvation is fundamentally a way of speaking about God's character. That is, the uncompromising assertion that salvation is God's act is also implicitly a judgment about the character of the actor.

Excursus 2: The Death of Christ in Ephesians

The previous paragraphs observed that in 2:1–10 (or elsewhere in Ephesians) Paul does not speak about believers' dying with Christ. The Ephesians are made alive with Christ, but this is not preceded by being crucified with Christ. For many scholars, this is a significant deviation from Paul's views in the undisputed Letters and thus a reason to doubt Pauline authorship of Ephesians. As mentioned above, my stake in the question of authorship is relatively small. Regardless of the question of authorship, however, it is worth examining what Ephesians has to say about Christ's death and how that is related to what one finds in the undisputed Pauline Letters. One should note two points at the outset of this excursus, however. First, nothing said here is likely to be decisive for the historical question of the authorship of Ephesians. Second, the issue of Christ's death for Paul is an enormous and contested matter among Pauline scholars. Many of the issues addressed here are the subjects of monographs in their own right. This excursus can offer little more than an overview of the terrain.[20]

In Romans and Galatians, Paul repeatedly speaks of dying (and rising) with Christ; he also speaks of being crucified with Christ. Romans 5–6 and Galatians 2 are the primary, but not the only, places where Paul speaks about this. In Romans and Galatians, Paul is at pains to emphasize that both Gentiles and Jews are under Sin's captivity. Christ's death and resurrection breaks Sin's hold over the world and opens up a new space in which to live. This is the realm governed, shaped, and determined by Christ. Believers transfer their citizenship from the realm of Sin into the realm of Christ by participating in both Christ's death and Christ's resurrection.

In the Corinthian letters, especially 1 Cor 1–4, Paul emphasizes that Christ's death on the cross is the manifestation of God's wisdom. God's wisdom, the wisdom of the cross, runs counter to the wisdom of the world; God's wisdom undermines conventional notions of power and reconfigures notions of strength and status in a world where these matters are taken very seriously. Such reflection on the cross provides Paul with a basis from which he can address a community divided along status lines, where "the strong" are not attentive to "the weak," and where Paul's own apostolic suffering is often misconstrued.

In Philippians, Paul speaks of Christ's death as the supreme demonstration of Christ's self-emptying obedience to God on behalf of others (2:6–8). The resurrection is God's vindication of this self-emptying pattern of obedience on behalf of others (2:9–11). This way of looking at Christ's death and resurrection provides the Philippians with the pattern of thinking, feeling, and acting that they should display toward one another, even amid suffering. Paul does not speak of dying and rising with Christ in Philippians.

---

20. Those seeking a fuller introduction to this issue will benefit from reading Gorman, ch. 7.

Instead, Christ's self-emptying love, a love that leads to death on the cross, becomes the pattern to which Paul hopes his life (and the Philippians' lives) might conform (3:10–12).

In 1 Thessalonians, Paul says little about the death of Christ. There is a brief mention of imitating the Lord in the midst of hostility (1:6–7), which is a much less developed notion than one finds in Philippians. In 1:10 Paul speaks of the resurrected Christ rescuing the Thessalonians from the wrath that is coming, which is a much less developed notion than one finds in Eph 2:1–10.

In Eph 2:1–10 Paul speaks of being made alive in Christ, but there is no mention of dying with Christ. Before becoming believers, the Ephesians were already dead. Instead, in Ephesians the death of Christ destroys the hostility that alienated Jews and Gentiles from each other and from God. Christ's death brings "those who were far off" and "those who were near" into one body (2:11–18). Christ's death brings to a climax God's drama of salvation. One of the crucial episodes of that drama is the blessing of Abraham, a blessing through which all the nations are blessed. In the cross, God's surprising plan to draw Jews and Gentiles together into one body in Christ is decisively revealed to the world (Eph 3:7–13).

In Ephesians and in these other Letters, Paul unpacks the significance of the death of Christ in a variety of ways. Paul's decision to develop any one of these aspects rather than others would largely be shaped by the specific situation of each community, even if, as in Ephesians, the epistle reveals little of that situation. None of these ways of explicating the significance of Christ's death excludes the others.

I do, however, think that there is one thing that does unite these diverse and particular expositions of the death of Christ. Although the things Paul says about Christ's crucifixion are of immense significance for the lives of believers and for the world as a whole, the focus that unites Paul's various thoughts about the death of Christ is that all of these reflections say something about God. For Paul, first and foremost, the cross is the self-revelation of God's character. In whichever direction Paul expounds the significance of the cross, it always reveals something about the character of God.

Verse 6 goes on to explicate the idea of being made alive together with Christ. It means being raised together and seated together with Christ in the heavenly realms. The language here reflects Paul's claims about Christ in 1:20, where we learn that God raised Christ and seated Christ at his right hand in the heavenly realms. Now in 2:6 we learn that believers have been joined with Christ in just these two respects: Raised with Christ and seated with him. In the light of 1:20, the heavenly realms are now characterized as "in Christ." Christ's enthronement in 1:20 now establishes the heavenly realms as Christ's territory. Even so, however, there is no mention here of believers as either undergoing some form of death through baptism or as putting to death elements of their lives. In Colossians (e.g., 2:11–3:3) the emphasis seems to be on having believers make a clean break with their pagan past. In Ephesians, Paul stresses that the Ephesians' salvation is as full and complete as it could possibly be. They have been raised with Christ and seated with Christ. Nothing, in principle, stands between them and union with Christ. God has given them nothing less than what God gave Christ.

There are a variety of other places in Ephesians where it is clear that in several important respects, salvation has yet to be completed, that the end is not fully realized in the present. For example, in the very next verse, Paul will speak of the "ages to come." Further, powers hostile to God still hold sway in this age. The heavenly realms still contain powers that have yet to be subjected to Christ. There is still suffering. Paul in particular suffers and is imprisoned. Thus, rather than saying something about the relationships between the Ephesians and the eschaton, it may well be that one aim of vv. 5–6 is to say something about God and the quality of God's mercy and great love.[21]

One of the aims of God's exaltation of believers is to "demonstrate the unlimited riches of his grace in kindness toward us in Christ Jesus." The abundant riches of God's grace are demonstrated in the raising and exalting of believers together with Christ. The same word translated here as "unlimited" is used in 1:19 to speak of God's "limitless" power. It also appears in 3:19, where it is used to talk about Christ's love. As Lincoln explains, "It can be said that if the raising of Christ from death to sit in the heavenly realms was the supreme demonstration of God's surpassing power, then the raising of believers from spiritual death to sit with Christ in the heavenly realms is the supreme demonstration of God's surpassing grace" (*Ephesians* 110).

Paul goes on to elaborate that the abundance of God's grace is demonstrated to us in God's kindness to us in Christ. We understand this "kindness" in the light of the "mercy" that is basic to God's character (2:4). Thus God's kindness toward us in Christ is a manifestation of God's constant and abiding character. This kindness is displayed toward us "in Christ Jesus." The form and placement of this phrase allows it to make a dual point. First, God's kindness is decisively displayed in the life, death, and resurrection of Jesus Christ. Second, "in Christ Jesus" describes a particular place: God's kindness to us "in Christ Jesus" indicates that God's kindness is found and mediated to us in the body of Christ, the church.

The initial clause of this verse makes it clear that the demonstration of God's grace is something to be displayed both now and into the future. The phrase "in the ages to come" is somewhat unusual. It is more common to speak in the singular of the age to come (cf. 1:21; also Mark 10:30; Luke 18:30; Matt 12:32; Heb 6:5). This more common formulation is a relatively clear reference to the Parousia. It is probably best to read this phrase in v. 7 in the light of 1:10, where Paul speaks of the "fullness of times." The image there and here is of the future as a succession of ages or temporal periods, which reach their

---

21. Although he elaborates this in slightly different ways, Schnackenburg (96–97) also notes the theocentric and ecclesiological emphases of this passage.

conclusion in the Parousia or in the ultimate bringing together of all things under Christ's dominion. It points to a succession of ages leading to the end of time (Lincoln, *Ephesians* 110–11; Hoehner 337–38). Of course, one cannot know precisely where one is in this succession of ages until the Parousia. The phrase emphasizes that God has both acted decisively and that God will bring that work to its proper end at some point in the future (cf. Phil 1:6). It is more common for Paul to speak of the time between cross and resurrection on the one hand, and the Parousia on the other hand, as one undifferentiated age. Even here Paul will use a variety of images (e.g., "The present form of this world is passing away," 1 Cor 7:31; one long night that leads to day, Rom 13:11–13; "the fullness of time," Gal 4:4; an ongoing work of God, started and brought to completion, Phil 1:6). As long as one reads this passage in Eph 2:7 as dividing this in-between time into a series of ages and not a series of discrete moments of consummation, or repeated Parousias, then the thinking here, if not the wording, fits within a Pauline scheme.

[8–10] Verse 8 begins with a repetition of the declaration initially inserted into v. 5. In this case the claim that the Ephesians have been saved by grace serves further to illustrate the nature of God's abundant grace. The key addition here is the phrase "through faith."[22] Believers are saved through faith.

Although Pauline scholars debate whether Paul is primarily interested in Christ's faithfulness or believers' trust in Christ, here he is clearly speaking of the faith of believers. Paul is referring to the trust or reliance that believers put in God to bring about their salvation, a salvation that flows from God's superabundant love rather than from human desert.

In the following clause, "and this is not from yourselves; it is a gift from God," the crucial interpretive issue has to do with the antecedent of the pronoun "this." If "this" is a reference to "faith," then it further emphasizes the idea that humans do not generate their own response to God. Rather, faith is a gift.[23] Even though this is true, it is more likely that "this" refers to the entire process of salvation.[24] The gracious, gifted nature of salvation certainly says something about humans, a point that is picked up in v. 9. It also says something about God. Humans neither deserve salvation, nor does saving us fulfill some lack or need in God. It is pure gift. Moreover, it is a gift that believers can never hope

---

22. In Romans and Galatians, Paul tends to use the phrase *ek pisteōs* more or less interchangeably with *dia pisteōs* (Rom 3:30; Gal 2:16). The phrase *ek pisteōs* appears only in Romans and Galatians, while *dia pisteōs* appears in Romans, Galatians, 2 Corinthians, Philippians, Colossians, 2 Timothy, as well as here in Eph 2:8.

23. Chrysostom (*Hom. Eph.* 4) was one of the first to read the passage this way.

24. Lincoln, *Ephesians* 112; Best, *Ephesians* 226; Hoehner 343. The grammatical problem is that the neuter *touto*, "this," does not agree with the gender of any of the nouns in the previous clause, including "faith."

to reciprocate. Instead, believers are to respond by repeating God's gift-giving grace in their worship, words, and deeds. Christians do not do this as a way of repaying God, but because our lives are analogously to display the character of the God who gives us gifts (see v. 10 below).

Verse 9 reminds the Ephesians that they are not capable of saving themselves. When Paul says that the Ephesians' salvation is not brought about "by works," he does not here mean works of the law, as in Gal 2:16 or Rom 3:27. The text does not have the phrase "of the law." Neither does the context indicate that Paul intends such a specific reference. Rather, Paul is referring to human striving and performance in hopes of winning God's approval (cf. 2 Tim 1:9; Titus 3:5). Although it is tempting to think of salvation on the model of some transaction between God and believers, there is nothing humans can do to evoke God's salvation or to earn it. In the societies of late capitalism, where almost every encounter can be reduced to a set of transactions between autonomous agents, this is a hard notion to accept. This may be the case for contemporary believers; yet as the argument of Ephesians indicates, it does not appear that the Ephesians themselves were in any danger of thinking that their own striving would accomplish their salvation apart from grace. For example, the ascetic philosophy to which the Colossians seem to be tempted (cf. Col 2:16–23) does not appear to play a role in Ephesians (Lincoln, *Ephesians* 113).

The recognition that human salvation is "not from works" rules out "boasting." In our world, boasting is often seen as inappropriate; Paul is not unconditionally opposed to boasting. Rather, the key for Paul is boasting in the correct thing or person. In this, Paul follows Jer 9:24 and writes, "Let the one who boasts, boast in the Lord" (2 Cor 10:17; cf. Rom 5:11; 1 Cor 1:29–31; 15:31; Phil 1:26; 3:3; boasting in the cross of Christ, Gal 6:14). Boasting in the Lord reflects the appropriate recognition of one's status relative to God and the role of God's grace in one's life. Failure to recognize this would lead one perhaps to boast in one's own works or efforts. As Lincoln observes, "Boasting perverts human autonomy by making it the object of trust" (*Ephesians* 113). This is precisely the boasting ruled out in Eph 2:9.

Verse 10 continues to explicate the notion that salvation is not of human origin. This is because "we are God's work." The term used here for work is *poiēma*. Within the LXX the term is widely used to refer to the work of an artisan, to general types of human commerce and activity, and to God's own activity (cf. 1 Sam 8:8; Judg 13:12; 1 Chr 29:3; Eccl 2:4; 8:9, 14, 17; Isa 29:16; Ps 63:10 [64:9 Eng.]). The range of meaning here is particularly wide. In Ephesians this term points to a contrast between the futility of human works in 2:9 and the sufficiency of God's work in 2:10 (Hoehner 347; Lincoln, *Ephesians* 113). Given the next clause's clear emphasis on creation, it is probably best to see the emphasis here on salvation as God's action rather than human action.

As the verse goes on to elaborate, believers as God's work are "created in Christ Jesus." The verb translated here as "create" (*ktizō*) is only used in the NT to refer to God's creative activity (cf. Matt 19:4; Mark 13:19; Rom 1:25; Eph 3:9; Col 1:16; 3:10). This verse seems to reflect the same idea found in 2 Cor 5:17, "If anyone is in Christ, there is a new creation." The same idea is also found in Gal 6:15, "Neither circumcision nor uncircumcision ultimately matter. What matters is a new creation" (AT). Later in Ephesians, Paul will say, "Clothe yourselves with the new human, created according to the likeness of God" (4:24). In each of these cases, there is the sense that salvation in Christ inaugurates a new creation, or more properly, a renewal of the original creation. This creation is not simply the natural development of the created order. Neither is it the result of sustained human labor. Rather, this new creation is the dramatic and unanticipated renewal of all things in Christ, accomplished by God's grace through the death and resurrection of Christ. This clause picks up the notion that though believers were dead in their transgressions and sins, God has made them alive again. Resurrection and new creation complement each other as images of God's saving activity.

The purpose of God's new creation in Christ is so that the inhabitants of this new creation might "walk in good works, which God has prepared beforehand." The verb "to walk" is again used to speak of a manner of life, as in 2:2 (cf. also 4:1, 17; 5:2, 8, 15). The good works mentioned here contrast with the failed works mentioned in 2:9. Those failed works were designed to generate or bring about human salvation. Good works are not the means to salvation, but the result of having been graciously incorporated into God's new creation in Christ. These good works reflect the initial and formative work of God's grace on the lives of believers. God's gift generates further giving: good works. The good works do not provoke God's gift. These good works have been prepared by God beforehand for believers to walk in them. The grammar here makes it clear that it is the works, rather than the humans, which God prepared beforehand.[25] Nevertheless, this notion also seems to reflect the ideas of 1:4–5, 11–12, which speak of God's eternal choosing of believers.[26]

As with salvation generally, this verse points to the idea that even the good works that believers do are in some sense a gift from God. Expanding on this idea, Thomas Aquinas (97) reads this verse through Isa 28:12, "O Lord, you will ordain peace for us, for indeed, all that we have done, you have done for us." This, too, focuses the direction of our boasting away from ourselves and toward God.

---

25. The only other time the verb translated here as "prepare beforehand" is used in the NT is Rom 9:23, which also reflects on God's eternal choices.

26. Best (*Ephesians* 231) also posits that the plural "good works" corresponds to the plural "trespasses and sins," which characterized the Ephesians' "walk" prior to Christ.

Modern readers immediately want to know how this claim fits with notions of human freedom. If God eternally prepared these good works for believers to walk in them, how can believers be considered agents who "walk" rather than robots performing preprogrammed tasks? The problem here may lie more with particular notions of human freedom. For example, if human freedom is conceived of as acting without any prior shaping or constraint, then we cannot make sense of this notion of freedom. We are always acting under the influence, constraint, and encouragement of things, processes, circumstances, and people outside of ourselves. Sometimes we recognize these influences; often we are unaware of their effects on us. Even if we could attain such a state of freedom, it is not clear how we could know that we had. The notion of freedom as freedom from all constraint is simply unintelligible. Nevertheless, we generally think of ourselves as free enough to consider our actions to be our own, for which we are responsible.

Although Paul did not have the benefits of modern psychology or sociology, he understood that humans are often constrained by things and people beyond themselves. For Paul, humans are always under authorities outside of themselves. Indeed, in some respects he thinks of human life as always being a sort of slavery. Given this, the question is whether one is a slave to the oppressive power of Sin, or a slave of the one God who can truly make one free. In the light of 2:1–10 as a whole, it should be clear that Paul does not imagine that believers have gone from a state of freedom into a state where they have become automata when they become Christians. Rather, humans were (are) slaves to Sin outside of Christ. Being outside of Christ is servitude to oppressive and tyrannical masters. "The sons of disobedience serve their own wishes without hesitation, all the while following orders."[27] Participating in God's new creation in Christ opens the prospect of participating in the dramatic outworking of God's salvation. This too is a form of service to a master, a master in whose "service is perfect freedom."[28] As Paul sees it, those are the options available to humans. Of course, he would understand that humans both act and are responsible for their actions. The more important issue for Paul is where one's allegiance lies, who one's master is.

In 2:1–10 Paul presents a relatively brief account of the Ephesians' comprehensive attachment to sin. Their activity renders them "dead," pliant servants of forces opposed to God. Unlike Romans, however, there is little sense of despair here. The Ephesians seem to have been unaware and unbothered by their alienation from God. Perhaps this is the most profound sense in which we all are dead outside of Christ. Absent our own anxiety, and clearly apart from

---

27. This elegant way of putting the matter comes from Yoder Neufeld, *Ephesians* 91.

28. This phrase comes from the Collect for Peace in the service of Morning Prayer in the Book of Common Prayer.

any merit in us, God acts to save us, bringing us into union with Christ. Here there is little emphasis on the future aspect of salvation. Rather, the focus is on God's mercy and love. Salvation becomes an occasion for displaying some of the deepest elements of God's eternal character. Rather than focusing on the salvation of individuals or of the church, this passage displays a strongly theocentric focus. In the following section, 2:11–22, Paul's attention moves to discuss the ecclesiological significance and implications of God's saving activity.

Ephesians 2:11–22
Remember That You Were Gentiles

Several aspects of this passage reflect ideas first presented in 2:1–10. The most obvious is the contrast between what the Ephesians were and what they now are. Each passage also reflects on the salvation that God has brought about in the lives of the Ephesian believers. This reflection comes from two different perspectives, however. In 2:1–10 God graciously transforms the Ephesians' death—death through their sin and their captivity to powers hostile to God—into new life in Christ. This perspective on the Ephesians' salvation reflects the cosmic drama of salvation laid out in chapter 1. Here in 2:11–22 Paul reflects on the Ephesians' salvation in terms of their relationship to Israel. Although one does not find the same sort of explicit connection to the cosmic drama of salvation laid out in chapter 1 that one finds in 2:1–10, there are some connections. For example, the focus on God's choosing in 1:11 along with the language of promise and inheritance in 1:13–14 call to mind God's dealings with Israel in the OT. Further, the emphasis on holiness in 1:4 runs throughout 2:11–22.

In 2:11–22 Paul reflects on the relationships between Jews and Gentiles in Christ. In both Romans and Galatians, one finds a similar concern with the relationship between Jew and Gentile in Christ. In those two epistles one gathers the very clear impression that there is significant tension within each of these communities over how these issues are to be resolved. It does not, however, appear that the Christians in Ephesus are under any pressure to take on circumcision or the yoke of torah observance, or that Gentile Christians are treating their Jewish brothers and sisters as second-class citizens in God's kingdom. Indeed, it does not seem that the Ephesian Christians have much, if any, direct contact with Jewish Christians.[1] Thus we should expect that the discussion in 2:11–22 will be of a different sort from Romans or Galatians.

---

1. In Acts 19 Paul preaches regularly in the synagogue in Ephesus. There is widespread evidence of Jews in the city, but Acts indicates that Paul's preaching in the synagogue was not particularly successful. It would not be wise to suggest that there were absolutely no Jewish members of the Ephesian church. Nevertheless, if their presence raised any particular issues for the church, one could not determine this from anything said in the epistle.

In terms of its structure, this passage has three main parts. Ephesians 2:11–13 presents the contrast between the Ephesians' past and their present in Christ. As in 2:1–10, there is a contrast between what was "once" the case and what is "now" the case. The linchpin in the transition between once and now is the advent of Christ. Verses 14–18 spell out in detail the effects of Christ's work relative to the Ephesians' alienation from God and from the people of Israel. Finally, vv. 18–22 articulate the new relationship in Christ between the Ephesians and the people of Israel.

2:11 Therefore remember that once you were Gentiles in the flesh, called "uncircumcised"[a] by those who are called "the circumcision," a circumcision of the flesh by human hands; 12 recall also that at that time you were apart from Christ, excluded from the commonwealth of Israel, strangers to the covenants of promise, having no hope and without God in the world. 13 But now in Christ Jesus you, who were once far off, have been brought near by the blood of Christ. 14 For he is our peace; he has made both groups into one, breaking down the dividing wall,[b] nullifying in his flesh the hostility, 15 which was the law of commandments and decrees, in order that he might create in himself one new person in place of the two, thereby making peace. 16 He has reconciled the two groups to God in one body through the cross, putting to death the hostility in himself. So when he came he preached peace to you who were far off and peace to those who were near, 18 for through him we both have access to the Father in the one Spirit.

19 Hence you are no longer strangers and aliens, but you have become fellow citizens with the saints and members of the household of God, 20 built upon the foundation of the apostles and prophets, with Christ Jesus himself as the cornerstone.[c] 21 In him the whole building[d] is joined together and is growing into a holy temple in the Lord. 22 In him you also are built together in the Spirit into a dwelling place for God.

a. The use of the participle "called" here has led to the use of scare quotes around the terms "circumcision" and "uncircumcision." Another way to translate this might have been to take the participle as "so-called." In either case the point is to indicate that the application of these terms to particular groups may not be as clear as one might think.

b. The phrase "dividing wall" is a translation of the Greek *mesotoichon tou phragmou*. The term *mesotoichon* only occurs here in the NT. It refers to a dividing or partition wall. The appositional noun *tou phragmou* is used primarily in the LXX and NT to refer to a hedge or fence surrounding a vineyard (Num 22:24; Matt 21:33) or more generally as a wall to keep out intruders (cf. LXX: Pss 61:4 [62:3 Eng.]; 79:13 [80:12]; Prov 24:31).

It is not clear what this additional appositional description adds to the original, and it has been left untranslated.

c. The Greek here is a bit ambiguous. See the discussion below about whether Christ should be thought of as cornerstone or capstone.

d. There is a textual variant here in the phrase translated as "the whole building." In the preferred Greek text, there is no definite article. Some Greek manuscripts ($\aleph^1$, A, C, et al.) insert a definite article here. The weight of textual evidence favors omitting the article, which might render the translation "every building." Nevertheless, the translation "the whole building" is certainly possible without the article and makes the best sense of the context.

[11–13] The transitional admonition "Therefore remember" draws on the previous verses. Most precisely it relies on the notion that believers are participants in God's new creation and that such participation enjoins walking in good works (cf. 2:10).[2] Verse 11 would thus indicate that the immediate good work in view is the work of memory. The Ephesians are challenged here to remember their past. Indeed, the call here may be to remember their past in a new way. In this respect one can think of "remembering" as an example of being "transformed by the renewing of your minds," as advocated in Rom 12:2. Whatever else might be involved, the renewal of one's mind must include a repair or restoration of one's memory. Recall also that the call to renew one's mind in Rom 12 is contrasted with the admonition to avoid being conformed "this age." A renewed mind will not be conformed to this age. In Eph 2:2 Paul speaks of the Ephesians' deathly state outside of Christ as walking according to the "age of this cosmos." This present age is both a location of death and a cast of mind that one leaves behind in the light of being in Christ. Regardless of whether the connection to Rom 12:2 would have been evident to the first readers of this text or is my own edifying gloss, it helps to reinforce the point here in 2:11 that one of the primary good works that God has prepared beforehand for believers to walk in is the renewal, reconstruction, or repair of memory. This is so that both Ephesian and contemporary believers come to see their past (and their present and future) from the perspective of God's saving activity.

In 2:2–3 the Ephesians' state prior to Christ is simply described. Here in 2:11 the Ephesians are called to remember their identity as Gentiles. This is not as straightforward as it might seem. Romans, Greeks, and other non-Jews in Ephesus (or elsewhere) would never refer to themselves as Gentiles. That designation only had currency within Judaism or in relation to Judaism. From the perspective of being in Christ, and as part of their remembering, Roman or Greek

---

2. Chrysostom (*Hom. Eph.* 5) also sees the connection to 2:1–10, and to v. 10 in particular, but with an emphasis different from the one offered here.

or Scythian Ephesians need to learn that they are Gentiles.[3] They need to remember (or reconceive) of their past as a Gentile past. They need to learn both what being a Gentile meant when they were outside of Christ and what it means now that they are in Christ.

On the one hand, it seems most obvious that being a Gentile meant that one was uncircumcised. Nevertheless, Paul here seems to relativize the importance of circumcision for Gentile identity. He does not say that because "you were Gentiles, you were uncircumcised"—though this was true. Rather, he says that "you were called 'uncircumcised' by those called 'the circumcision.'" Paul then goes on to raise further doubts about the significance of this identification, suggesting that those who are called the circumcised simply have a circumcision of the flesh, done by human hands. The adjective "made by human hands" (*cheiropoiētou*) is used in the LXX to speak about idols (Lev 26:1, 30; Isa 2:18; Dan 5:4). In Acts 17:24 the term is used to describe pagan shrines. Elsewhere in the NT it refers to the Jerusalem temple (Mark 14:58; Acts 7:48; Heb 9:11, 24). In each instance it is meant to imply the transitory importance of the temple. When used of circumcision "in the flesh," as here in 2:11, it appears to invoke the distinction between the circumcision of the flesh as opposed to the circumcision of the heart (Deut 30:6; Jer 4:4; Ezek 44:7, 9; Rom 2:25–29). It is not so much that these instances undermine fleshly circumcision as stressing that someone does not benefit from fleshly circumcision apart from a circumcised heart.

Paul's point here is that those who refer to the Gentiles as "the uncircumcised" may not be the most reliable guides in this matter. This raises significant issues. Recall that one of the points of this section is to enable the Ephesians to remember their past as a Gentile past. Nevertheless, Paul's comments here in v. 11 undermine the reliability of what most would take to be one of the certain ways of identifying Gentiles. Paul seems to imply that the most visible way of identifying Gentiles might not be the most reliable or significant way. It thus appears that one implication of Paul's remarks here is that uncircumcision may not be a reliable way of identifying Gentiles because circumcision of the flesh may not be a sufficiently reliable way of identifying Jews.[4]

This indicates that coming to understand one's past outside of Christ as a Gentile past is a contested matter. At the very least it will involve learning to see Gentileness in a very particular way, which many Jews might not accept. In

3. Yee, ch. 3. In stressing the fact that this identification is offered by a Jew (he underplays the fact that the author is a Jewish Christian), Yee misses the point that the Ephesians would not normally have understood themselves as Gentiles and that the thrust of this passage is to try to get them to take on this identity.

4. Despite the many virtues of his study, Yee (76–83) is so intent on presenting a clear and distinct picture between insider (Jew) and outsider (Gentile) that he is inattentive to how Paul's Christianity leads him to reconceptualize his and all believers' Judaism in ways that blur the clear ethnic distinctions upon which Yee relies.

addition, Paul's account of citizenship in Israel and how it is obtained is going to be a contested matter. Thus it is not only important that the Ephesians learn to identify their past as Gentile and that they come to see their present as part of Israel, but that they must identify their Gentileness and their relation to Israel in a particular way, a way that other Jews may well contest.

Having indicated that uncircumcision is not the most significant thing in remembering one's Gentile past, Paul in v. 12 goes on to specify things he takes to be crucial to Gentile identity.[5] Interestingly, being a Gentile does not begin with understanding oneself in relation to Jews, but in relation to Christ, the Messiah of Israel (Lincoln, *Ephesians* 137). Being a Gentile is not primarily about uncircumcision, but about alienation from the Messiah. The use of the preposition translated here as "apart from" to speak of Gentiles' relation to Christ is somewhat unusual. Yet it does provide an appropriate contrast to the assertions of 2:6, which declare that believers have been raised together and seated together with Christ.

The next element of Gentile identity is their exclusion from the commonwealth of Israel.[6] The word translated here as "commonwealth" has a wide range of meanings.[7] For example, it is used in 2 Macc 8:17 and 4 Macc 8:7 to refer to a Jewish way of life. This is probably not in view here in 2:12 given the claims of 2:19. In 2 Macc 13:14 and 4 Macc 17:9[8] it refers to a political entity and could be translated as "nation" or "state" as long as one also recognized the sharp differences between ancient political orders and modern nation-states. In addition, we should remember that by Paul's time Israel has ceased to exist as an independent political unit. Given the way that the rest of this section runs, it appears that the "commonwealth of Israel" is a reference to the gathered people of God as a social and political entity, called and formed by God and endowed with God's promises and everlasting covenant (see Yee 95). Remembering one's Gentile past, then, entails understanding oneself as physically and spiritually excluded from this commonwealth.

Moreover, Gentiles were strangers to the "covenants of promise." In Rom 9:4 Paul speaks of the covenants and the promises as Jewish advantages. Here

---

5. Many commentators note parallels between this list and Rom 9:4, where Paul gives a list of the advantages of the Jew. There are some overlaps, but here the focus is on Gentile identity rather than Jewish advantage.

6. The verb translated here as "excluded" appears in the NT only here, in 4:18, and in Col 1:21. In each case it can be translated as "alienated" or "excluded." In each of these contexts, the verb is used to describe one's state before being reconciled with God.

7. See the variety of citations in Yee 91–93.

8. 4 Macc 17:9 is less obviously political than the other examples given. The NRSV translates *politeia* as "way of life," presumably in light of the term "religion" (*eusebeia*) in 17:7. I would argue that 17:9 sees *politeia* as the object of an attack by a "tyrant," and that in 17:10, it is the "nation" (*genos*) that is vindicated by the Maccabees' actions, and thus has political force.

the phrase is "covenants of promise." This probably refers to the covenants with Abraham in Gen 12:1–14; reiterated and expanded in 13:14–17; 15:18–21; 17:21; with Isaac in Gen 26:2–5; with Jacob in Gen 28:13–15; with David in 2 Sam 7 (cf. Lincoln, *Ephesians* 137; Schnackenburg 110). Given the negative comments in Eph 2:15 about the "law of commandments and decrees," Paul is probably not referring to the Mosaic covenant.[9] Aside from the negative example of 2:15, however, there is little in the text or its context that would specify which covenants are in question here. Further, such distinctions do not seem significant for Paul here. The advantage of those who are part of the "commonwealth of Israel" is that they, and not the Gentiles, are friends of the God who makes extravagant gracious promises on their behalf and for their benefit. The point here is not to determine the Gentiles' exclusion from some covenants rather than others. Instead, the point is to emphasize their alienation from the God who calls a people into being in order to bless them and make them a blessing to the nations.

Because being a Gentile means alienation from the "commonwealth of Israel" and "the covenants of promise," it also means that Gentiles are without "hope and without God in the world." This should not be taken to mean that outside of Christ, Ephesians or any other Gentiles were constantly in a state of despair. It is only from the perspective of being in Christ that the Ephesians are even called to remember their past as a Gentile past. From that perspective, however, they should recognize the truth about how hopeless their situation was.

This is the only time in the NT that the term *atheoi* (without God) is used. In Greek literature the term can refer to someone who does not believe in a god or gods either willfully or out of ignorance.[10] The term can also apply to the impious who believe in the gods but disdain them or to someone forsaken by God or the gods.[11] In this particular case, Paul probably means to indicate that Gentiles are alienated from God (Lincoln, *Ephesians* 139; Best, *Ephesians* 243).

As part of the good work prepared by God for the Ephesians, they are to remember their past from the perspective of being Gentiles. They are called upon to think about this past identity in a way that only seems possible for those who are in Christ. This act of remembering their past as a Gentile past has a dual function. First, by recalling their state as Gentiles before God, the Ephesians can come to see themselves in the very particular ways in which God saw them. They still remain Gentiles, but in recognizing their past as a Gentile past, they

9. See Hoehner 358–59. If this is the case, then Ephesians would be similar to Romans and Galatians in presuming that the temporal priority of the Abrahamic covenant allows it theologically to trump the Mosaic covenant.

10. The early Christians and Jews were often accused by the Romans of being "atheists" in just this sense of not believing in the god or gods of the empire (see *Mart. Pol.* 9.2; Justin *1 Apol.* 5–6).

11. See LSJ 31.

can come to appreciate the depths of their former alienation from God and to rejoice in what God has graciously done for them.

It is equally important, however, that by remembering their past as a Gentile past, a past that is thereby in relation (albeit a negative one) to Judaism, Paul can begin to describe more precisely the nature of the reconciliation accomplished in Christ. In fact, if Christians fail to grasp this, they may end up misperceiving what is involved in reconciliation today.

Verse 13 is a transitional verse. It points back to vv. 11–12, offering the alternative to Gentile alienation from Israel and from God in Christ. It also serves to introduce the more developed discussion of Christ's activity of reconciliation in vv. 14–18.

This verse establishes a contrast between what was "once" the case (vv. 11–12) and what is "now" the case. It may well be that this should also come under that same act of memory. Even as the verse refers to the present, "now," it is a present that has been decisively shaped by Christ's action in the past. Thus Paul calls upon the Ephesians to understand their present situation in the very particular light of Christ's reconciling work.

This verse reminds the Ephesians that they were "far off." In some ways this spatial designation summarizes the full scope of the alienation of their Gentile past as described in vv. 11–12.[12] Although the Ephesian Gentiles were "far off," now that they are in Christ, they have been brought near.[13] As vv. 11–12 illustrated, the Gentiles' alienation from God was also an alienation from Israel. On the one hand, vv. 15–22 indicate that by coming near, the Gentiles have not come to occupy exactly the same space as Israel. The people of Israel too are "near" (cf. Ps 148:14) and have not been supplanted by Gentile believers. Rather, in Christ both Jews and Gentiles have been brought near to God. On the other hand, coming near to God must involve also coming near to Israel (Best, *Ephesians* 245).

The passive voice of the phrase "you have been brought near" makes it clear that the Gentiles did not move themselves closer to God or to Israel. Rather, they were moved. In an abstract sense, they must have been moved by God. More precisely, the text speaks of being brought near "by the blood of Christ." Christ's death and resurrection are the agent that brings the Gentiles near, establishing and healing their memory so that they can truly understand who they were, where they were, where they now are, and how that relates to Israel. This

12. In the OT the term "far off" is sometimes used of Gentiles (Deut 28:49; 29:22; 1 Kgs 8:41; Isa 5:26; Jer 5:15). These are all literal references to distant Gentile lands. Thomas Aq. (155), however, finds the parallel with Ps 119 [118 LXX]:155: "Salvation is far from the wicked, for they do not seek your statutes."

13. In rabbinic and Qumran literature the verb "to come near" is used of proselytes (e.g., 1QS 6.13–22; 7.21; 8.18; 9.15; *b. Šabb.* 31a; *Num. Rab.* 8.4). See also J. Loader, "An Explanation of the Term *prosēlytos*," *NovT* 15 (1973): 270–77.

claim thus builds upon and elaborates on the assertion of 1:7 that believers have redemption "through his blood."

[14–18] Bringing the Gentiles near is simply one aspect of Christ's work of reconciliation. Verses 14–18 spell out this work in greater detail, beginning with the assertion that Christ is our peace.[14] As the following verses go on to show, this is a peace between Gentile and Jew and also their common peace with God. Given the description of Gentile alienation from God and Israel, it is fitting to talk of the work of Christ as a work of peacemaking. This fits with, but is not directly dependent upon, a christological reading of Isa 9:6, which identifies the expected Christ as the "Prince of Peace."[15] In this light, one might also recall Isa 2:1–4, which presents a vision of Israel's redemption that is so compelling that Gentiles are drawn to the mountain of the Lord. There they abandon war and live in peace. Finally, this peace could be contrasted with the so-called Pax Romana, the peace established by the empire.[16] This would have been peace in the much more limited sense of the cessation or suppression of outbreaks of violence. Paul is, rather, talking about *shalom*, the peace that results from the restoration of right relationships with God and others.

The verse then goes on to describe Jesus' peacemaking in terms of making "both into one." The reference here must be to the two groups mentioned in the previous verses, Gentiles and Jews. Thus the focus shifts from "you" Ephesians to us, meaning all Christians (Best, *Ephesians* 252). The making of two into one is described in ways that make it clear that the two are not dissolved into one. Peacemaking here is not homogenizing. Rather, as the passage indicates, it involves eliminating the hostility that divided Jew and Gentile.

Paul describes this peace as "breaking down the dividing wall." Best (*Ephesians*, 256–57) is probably right in asserting that this is simply a standard metaphorical use of wall to describe a fundamental division between Jew and Gentile. There are two further ways in which this phrase is sometimes taken. Some see this as a reference to the "wall" in the Jerusalem temple that separated the court of the Gentiles from the inner courts and sanctuary, where Jews could enter. This balustrade was about four feet high and was inscribed with warnings that Gentiles passing this point risked death (cf. Josephus, *Ant.* 15.11.5; *J.W.* 5.5.2; a pillar with such a warning was found in 1871). This quite literally was a wall dividing Gentile from Jew. It seems unlikely, however, that Ephesian Gentile Christians would have known of this wall, especially if the epistle is written after 70 C.E. Moreover, the inscription we have does not use the terms

14. Many commentators see elements of preformed traditional material here in 2:14–18. As I indicated earlier, the evidence for this is very thin, and the reasoning is not very strong. Best (*Ephesians* 250–51) also raises a set of points against seeing this as preformed material.

15. See Barth 261 n. 38; and Peter Stuhlmacher, *Reconciliation, Law, and Righteousness: Essays in Biblical Theology* (Philadelphia: Fortress, 1986), 182–200.

16. Yorke (118–22) emphasizes this connection.

for dividing wall used in Ephesians. Nevertheless, for those who do know of this wall, the allusion can be quite powerful.

The other option is to see the Jewish law as the dividing wall between Jew and Gentile. The law of commandments and decrees appears in the next clause as a bearer of hostility. Moreover, the *Letter of Aristeas* (139, 142) speaks of the law as a hedge or fence separating Jews from the idolatrous practices of the Gentiles surrounding them (also Philo, *Virt.* 186; *m.* ʾ*Abot* 3:18; *1 En.* 93.6). Again, the vocabulary used in Ephesians differs from these texts (see also Yee 146–47). Moreover, taking the dividing wall in this way could lead one to think that the law had been destroyed by Christ. This would directly contradict the Gospels, Romans, and Galatians. It could also feed a theology that has God making everlasting covenants with Israel only to break those promises in favor of promises to Christians. Nevertheless, there may well be certain circumstances under which some of these elements can usefully resonate behind the image of a "dividing wall." Modern readers, like those first readers in Ephesus, are probably best served by treating this as a straightforward image of separation.

What follows in the rest of v. 14 and into v. 15 is deeply contested in terms of syntax, vocabulary, and content. The syntactical concerns focus on how the words here are related to the two participles, "break down" and "nullify." Resolving those questions, however, still leaves issues about how to understand what is written.

The first question concerns the term "hostility." Should it be taken with "break down" or as the object of "nullify"? The Greek is capable of supporting either reading. Rather than take the term "hostility" with "break down," the translation above treats the term as the direct object of the verb "nullify."[17] The translations of the AV, RV, ASV, NASB, JB, and NJB read the matter this way. In addition, then, the phrase "in his flesh" becomes a reference to the manner in which this nullification of hostility occurred. Finally, in this light the phrase "the law of commandments and decrees" further clarifies the nature of the "hostility" between Jews and Gentiles.[18]

In terms of the vocabulary, it is crucial to note that the verb *katargeō* appears frequently enough in Paul, particularly in discussions about the law. In these cases Paul is at pains to argue that he does not wish to abolish or destroy the law (cf. Rom 3:3, 31; 4:14; 7:2, 6; Gal 3:17; also the repeated use of the term in 2 Cor 3:7–14). Thus it is probably not accurate to translate the same term

17. In Greek this is the participle *katargēsas* in v. 15.

18. With Bruce 54–55; Robinson 161; Dahl, "Christ, Creation" 437; Calvin 150–51. To my mind the strongest reason against the interpretation advocated above is that it requires the phrase "in his flesh" to be inserted between the "hostility" and the appositional phrase "law of commandments and decrees." See Hoehner 373. Although this is awkward, it is the least problematic of a problematic set of options in that it does not require a series of theologically dubious assertions about the law.

in Ephesians as "abolish" or "destroy" unless one has already decided to read Ephesians against Paul's views expressed in Romans and Galatians.[19] Instead, English verbs like nullify or void do better justice to the Greek. The phrase "the law of commandments and decrees" is unusual for Paul. The phrase does not refer to civil laws but to the torah in its totality.[20] Most commentators take the addition of "commandments and decrees" to be typical of the style of Ephesians (recall the repetitive combination of "dividing wall" and "fence" in 2:14). These decisions have led to the above translation identifying Christ as "nullifying in his flesh the hostility, which was the law of commandments and decrees."

Having looked at the various issues related to syntax and semantics in this verse, one should also recognize two basic strategies that one can take in interpreting this verse. One can read it against Paul's comments in Romans and Galatians. That is, one can take this verse in Ephesians as asserting that in Christ the law is abolished or nullified.[21] More precisely, if one takes the phrase "in his flesh" (v. 14) to be a reference to the passion of Christ (cf. 2:16), then it is Christ's death that abolishes the law. In whichever way one takes the various complex issues around Paul and the law in Romans and Galatians, Paul does not think the law is abolished. Death might void the law's claims over someone (cf. the use of *katargeō* in Rom 7:6), but that presumes that the law itself has not been abolished. Indeed it is precisely the charge that Paul has abolished the law (again *katargeō*) that Paul is at pains to refute in Rom 3:31–4:25.

If one takes Eph 2:14–15 to speak of the abolition of the law, one then has to account for this discontinuity with Romans and Galatians. There are a variety of ways of doing this. If Ephesians is not Pauline, the sting of discontinuity is lessened but not removed. How, for example, could a second-generation Paulinist have misunderstood Paul so badly on such a central matter? One explanation is that by this point in time, the tensions with Jewish Christians had diminished due to the fact that the church was overwhelmingly Gentile. The more subtle arguments that Paul uses in Romans and Galatians were not required even if they were understood. As a historical argument, this is no more than a possibility. It is based on claims about what was not required in a situation or what was not known or understood by an author. Further, it assumes that the arguments in Romans and Galatians about the enduring nature of the law are primarily about relations between Jewish and Gentile Christians rather than about the righteousness of God. Moreover, it becomes difficult to account for the fact that Eph 6:2 explicitly relies on a commandment of the law with the idea of its

19. Lincoln (*Ephesians* 143) and Barth (264) use "abolish."

20. There is a similar use of "decrees" in Col 2:14.

21. Hoehner's (374–76) insistence on translating the term "nullify" as "inoperative" does not really help. In Rom 3:31 Paul uses the same verb, *katargeō*, in a rhetorical question to deny that he is rendering the law "null" or "inoperative." The issue remains whether one reads Ephesians with or against the rest of the NT.

continuing validity. Theologically, this simply will not suffice. For Christians, it is crucial to try the second option, which is to read this claim in Ephesians in a way that is continuous with Paul's views in Romans and Galatians—regardless of whether Paul wrote Ephesians.

Traditionally, Christian theologians have treated this discussion in Eph 2 in the light of a distinction between moral and ceremonial laws. Both Thomas Aquinas and Calvin, for example, argue that in Eph 2:15 Paul is claiming that Christ abolishes the ceremonial laws as opposed to the moral laws. The ceremonial laws referred to such practices as circumcision, washings, and rules regarding sacrifices. These laws are particular to Israel (and thus mutable) in order to help the Israelites express their love for God. In contrast, the moral laws represent manifestations of the divine law that orders the universe and is designed to help all humans achieve ever deeper friendship with God.[22] It is precisely these ceremonial laws that divide Gentiles from Jews. Thus Christ's activity in breaking down the dividing wall directly refers to these laws that divided Jews from Gentiles. The historical points that the torah itself does not make such a distinction between moral and ceremonial laws and that such distinctions were not known in Paul's time are important to remember, but not directly relevant to the theological issues at hand.[23] The distinction between moral and ceremonial laws is best taken as a theological argument about how the NT's various claims about the law can be fitted into a larger scheme of divine lawgiving. Its successes or failures can really only be determined theologically.

From the perspective of a commentary on Ephesians, it seems incumbent upon the commentator also to offer some explanation of how the specific comments made in Ephesians can be held together with other very specific comments offered elsewhere in Paul's Letters in ways consonant with the logic of those letters. The key here seems to be to distinguish between the law as given by God on the one hand as holy, just, and good (Rom 7:12), and on the other hand as a source and agent of hostility. In both Romans and Galatians one finds the idea that the torah is a good gift from God. It holds the promise of life to Jews and promises the redemption of the Gentiles. For Paul and those who think like him, Christ is the end point, or telos, of the torah's redemptive and life-giving role for both Jews (first) and Gentiles (cf. Rom 10:4). This was manifestly not the way the vast majority of first-century Jews, and those few Gentiles who cared, understood the torah.

From the Jewish perspective, obedience to the law in the ways that Saul the Pharisee would have displayed was the key to living faithfully before the one

---

22. For a helpful discussion of this distinction in Thomas Aq., see Levering, *Christ's Fulfillment* 20–30.

23. Later Jews and Christians divide the torah into various categories, aiming to help people know and love God better.

God of Israel. All others were merely idolaters, and little could be expected from them (cf. *Jub.* 15.26; *Ps. Sol.* 17.24–25). Some Gentiles were attracted to the law and Judaism even if they were not willing to submit to circumcision. These so-called God-fearers found obedience to the law appealing (cf. Josephus, *Ant.* 3.217, 318–19; 2 Macc 3:35). For most other Gentiles who had views about the law, it was one of the main things that made Jews alien and hateful people (cf. 3 Macc 3:3–4).[24]

From Paul's perspective, the torah was not operating in the way that God intended. This situation reflected the work of Sin. Sin gained a foothold in God's good creation through Adam's transgression (Rom 5:12–19). It then began to distort all aspects of human life, including the torah (Rom 7:7–14; Gal 3:22). Instead of bringing life and redemption, instead of pointing clearly to Christ, the torah simply became one more of Sin's instruments of death and oppression. Under Sin's dominion, the law left the Jews misguided about their proper ends in God (cf. Rom 10:2, "They have zeal without knowledge" [AT]) and left the Gentiles alienated from both God and the promise of blessing made to Abraham.

Paul assumes that the torah, as given by God and properly understood, would lead to the unity of Jews and Gentiles in Christ, each being reconciled to God. Under Sin's influence the torah became both a source and an instrument of hostility. Ephesians asserts that in his passion (i.e., "in his flesh") Christ nullifies this hostility, fulfilling the law rather than abolishing it. In nullifying this hostility and thereby freeing the law to fulfill its proper role of pointing to Christ, Paul asserts that Jews and Gentiles have had the wall between them broken down. This enables their reconciliation with God and with each other.[25]

The aim of breaking down the dividing wall is the creation of a single new person in Christ out of two separate and alienated people. This claim here at the end of 2:15 recalls the image of a new creation in 2:10, which concluded the previous passage. It also provides a concrete description of the movement to bring all things together under Christ as articulated in 1:10 (Lincoln, *Ephesians* 145).

There is some scholarly discussion about whether this claim primarily involves individuals or groups (see Best, *Ephesians* 261–62). The question seems to be about whether this verse is talking about interpersonal or communal reconciliation. Such a question is probably misplaced. The image of two people separated by a dividing wall is already in place in v. 14. The upshot of vv. 14–15a is that the basis for their hostility and division has been removed. The next step, not necessarily entailed in the removal of the dividing wall, is the bringing together of these two into one. This is an image of reconciliation.

---

24. See Donaldson (50–78) for a fuller accounting of Jewish views on Gentiles.

25. Barth (290–91) presents a similar view. He does not, however, attend to the very Pauline notion that Sin has hijacked the law. Rather, he focuses on a variety of ways in which the law becomes divisive. Christ abolishes this power to divide.

It is unclear what is gained by limiting its scope to either corporate, communal entities or to individuals. Presumably the reconciliation imagined here permeates the entirety of life.

It is much more important to understand the nature of that reconciliation. The two, Jew and Gentile, are not simply left standing next to each other with the dividing wall removed. They are transformed into something new, "a new person." This new person is created "in him." That is, it is due to Christ's life, death, and resurrection; it is animated and sustained by the Spirit of Christ; it draws its identity and coherence from Christ's body. Reconciliation does not happen simply by removing the dividing wall. It happens in the creation of a new person in, through, and by Christ.

Further, it is important to reflect on the nature of this "new person." It is clear that participation in this new person does not require the Ephesians or any other Gentile to become Jews in the sense of needing to be circumcised and so forth. Nevertheless, vv. 11–13 demand that the Ephesians rethink their pre-Christian identity as a Gentile identity. Conceiving of their pre-Christian past as simply pagan is not enough. They must understand their alienation from God as Gentile alienation. That is, their alienation from God must also include an understanding of their alienation from Israel and God's particular dealings with Israel.

Though Ephesians does not devote much space to this matter, one should acknowledge that Jews, like Paul, needed to radically reconceive their perception of their Judaism. This reconception involved recognizing that proper torah obedience is best understood and practiced in Christ and that in the body of Christ the redemption of Israel was being accomplished, that the nations were flocking to the mountain of the Lord (Isa 2:1–4). There will be more to say about this reconciliation in the pages below. For now let it suffice to say that the new person created in Christ brings Jews and Gentiles together into one body without requiring them to submit to a homogenizing erasure of their identity as Jews and Gentiles. Nevertheless, participation in this new creation requires changes from both of them. Erstwhile pagans must come to understand themselves as Gentiles; Jews must come to understand their Judaism in Christ, the telos of the torah. It is only in this way that peace is truly made.

In v. 16 the notion of two being made one in Christ's body reiterates ideas in vv. 14–15. This verse elaborates on vv. 14–15 by reminding readers that Jews and Gentiles are reconciled to each other to the extent that they are reconciled to God. That is, the reconciliation of Jew and Gentile presumes that both have been reconciled to God through the cross. The mention of the cross helps to resolve any ambiguity in the claim in v. 14 that Christ has nullified the enmity "in his flesh." Indeed, in v. 16 Paul reaffirms that it is the enmity, rather than the law, that is "put to death."

The Ephesians' remembered Gentile past was characterized by hostility and alienation from God. Verse 17 reminds them that both they who were far off and the Jews who were near needed to hear Christ's good news of peace. The language of this verse draws heavily upon two verses in Isaiah. There is a fairly direct allusion to the LXX of Isa 57:19, which yields a translation like this: "Peace upon peace to those who are far and those who are near, says the Lord; and I will heal them."[26] In Isaiah both the far and near are Jews who are within the grasp of God's saving reach. Here that image of being far away is turned to apply to "you," meaning Gentiles (including the Ephesians) and their reconciliation with those Jews who are near. At the same time, the notion of Christ's coming to proclaim good news of peace can be taken as a christological interpretation of Isa 52:7 (cf. also the allusion in Eph 6:15; Lincoln, *Ephesians* 147). At this point it seems clear that the reconciliation of Gentile and Jew in Christ is predicated on and enabled by their prior reconciliation with God in Christ.

This is because, as v. 18 asserts, through Christ both Jews and Gentiles "have access to the Father in the one Spirit."[27] Thus the basis for the "new person" created out of two hostile parties is the reconciling work of Christ. Participation in Christ's reconciliation enables both Jews and Gentiles to have a common access to the one Father, access through the work of the Spirit.

The emphasis on the one Spirit parallels the emphasis on the one body in 2:16. This combination is also taken up again in 4:4 ("There is one body; there is one Spirit"). The Trinitarian structure so clear here is also present in 1:17 and 4:4–6 (Lincoln, *Ephesians* 150). Although there is no attempt to unpack the specific relations between the Trinitarian persons and their common essence, it is clear that Ephesians, like other NT passages, provides the material for later Trinitarian reflection.

[19–22] "Hence" introduces a section that recalls what has just been said and then builds upon it. Paul has called on the Ephesians to remember their past— a Gentile past characterized by alienation from Israel and its God. Paul has already indicated how Christ has enabled a new situation (cf. "now" in 2:13). He has also articulated an account of Christ's reconciling work (2:14–18). At this point Paul reconnects the Ephesians to this work in which Christ has gathered together the two into one through the Spirit for the Father. In these verses Paul deploys a series of images: architectural, domestic, and anatomical. The metaphors are mixed, to be sure. Instead of confusion, however, the combination of these images forms a relatively clear picture of Paul's views about the Ephesians' participation in Christ.

To begin, the Ephesians, in their "Gentileness," are "no longer strangers and aliens, but . . . fellow citizens with the saints." The language of "alien" and "stranger" hearkens back to the alienation described in 2:12. That alienation has

---

26. Dahl ("Christ, Creation" 432) calls vv. 13–18 a midrash on Isa 57:19.

27. The claim here is reminiscent of Rom 5:1–2: "Having been justified by grace, we have peace with God through our Lord Jesus Christ, through whom we have access to this grace" (AT).

been reconciled. This much is clear from the preceding verses. It is less clear what this entails for the Ephesians. They are citizens together with the saints, or holy ones. The political images of aliens and strangers are countered by the political image of citizenship. The country or city of citizenship is not noted. One would expect, perhaps, that based on 2:12, Paul would assert that the Ephesians have been incorporated into Israel. Paul certainly seems to think that in Christ, Jews and Gentiles are incorporated into a reconstituted and redeemed Israel (Rom 9–11). That is not his point here, however. Rather than describe the national identity of the Ephesians' fellow citizens, Paul describes their status: they are holy.[28]

Holiness certainly is God's primary desire for Israel (Exod 19:6; Lev 11:44–45; 19:2; 20:26; Deut 7:6; 14:2, 21; 26:19; Jer 2:3; Ezek 37:26–28 [on this, see below]). Yet it is interesting that when talking about the transformation of the Ephesian Gentile believers, Paul uses political images to speak of them as once strangers and aliens relative to Israel and Israel's God. When he continues with a political image to speak of the Ephesians' reconciliation with God and Jewish believers, he does not refer to the political entity Israel. Rather, Paul characterizes this group according to the purpose for which God brought the people of Israel out of slavery in Egypt: holiness. The allusions here are therefore more complex. The connections hinge on the fact that liberated Israel is free to be holy to God. Gentiles and Jews are liberated by Christ from their slavery to Sin, to powers hostile to God, and to the hostility generated by the torah under Sin's captivity and now are also free to be holy to God as one body in Christ.

This deeper set of connections is initially foreshadowed in the blessing that Paul pronounces at the beginning of the epistle. Recall that one of God's blessings on believers is choosing them to be "holy and blameless before him in love" (1:4). Holiness is God's choice for believers. Here Paul is indicating that in Christ the Ephesians have had their Gentile past (what could be less holy?) transformed. They are now fellow citizens with all the other holy ones. As will become clearer, God's intentions as laid out in 1:3–14 are being brought to fruition in that political space called the church.

By the end of v. 19 the image shifts. In addition to being fellow citizens with the saints, the Ephesians are members of the household of God. The image of citizenship connects the Ephesians to other believers. The image of the household connects believers to God. "Gentile Christians, once refugees, are now neither homeless nor stateless" (Best, *Ephesians* 279). Yet this language can operate at a fairly high level of abstraction unless it receives material embodiment in real communities in the world. The Gentile past, which Paul calls on the Ephesians to remember, requires them to see themselves outside of Christ

---

28. Yee (197) suggests that this shift is because "Israel" was too narrowly identified with an inward-looking Judaism. The problem here is that this is an exercise in mirror-reading, for which Yee can only deduce evidence by mirror-reading other passages in Ephesians.

as "strangers and aliens" to God and to Israel. Those who take on the task of remembering their past as a Gentile past cannot then be left bereft of a home. Moreover, they must not simply be relocated in some sort of notional sense. They must have a material setting in which to live out their new life in Christ.

Before speaking about how and in what ways the Ephesians might inhabit the household of God, Paul shifts the image to describe the building itself. The building metaphor here is used rather widely in the ancient world. There is little reason to seek its source in any particular text. In the NT both Col 2:7 and 1 Cor 3:10–11 use the image, albeit somewhat differently. In Eph 2:22 the present tense of the verb and its passive voice indicate that this building is already under construction and that God is the builder (unlike 1 Cor 3:10–11, where Paul is the builder). The "apostles and prophets" provide the foundation for this building. Although Paul uses only one definite article here ("the apostles and prophets" rather than "the apostles and the prophets"), Eph 4:11 makes it clear that he sees these as two separate groups. In 4:11 apostles and prophets refer to two of the variety of ministerial gifts given by the resurrected Christ to the church. Thus Paul is not here speaking directly of OT prophets. We do not know much more about the precise nature of this prophetic office. Ephesians 3:5–6 declares that God has revealed the place of Gentiles in the economy of salvation. They are the ones appointed to bring the gospel to Gentiles. In this respect one can see them as the foundation of the church.

The final clause of v. 20 situates Christ in relation to both believers on the one hand and the prophets and apostles on the other hand. Christ clearly has a distinct and irreplaceable role in this building. The vocabulary here, however, is open to two differing interpretations: Christ is either the "capstone" (Lincoln, *Ephesians* 155–56) or the "cornerstone" (McKelvey 195–204; MacDonald, *Ephesians* 249; Schnackenburg 124). With regard to vocabulary, the term *akrogōniaios* used here in 2:20 appears in the LXX only in Isa 28:16, where it clearly refers to a cornerstone, the key element in the foundation. Similar stone images (though with different vocabulary) appear in Ps 118 (117 LXX):22 to speak of a stone rejected by the builders, but which God renders precious, using it to cap off a pillar. Romans 9:32–33 combines parts of Isa 28:16 and Ps 118:22 to speak of Christ. Although the term "cornerstone" does not appear, the stone in Rom 9 must be a stone lying on the ground. The NT text closest to Eph 2:20–21, however, is 1 Pet 2:4–8. There Christ is referred to as a "living stone," a "cornerstone" (quoting Isa 28:16), the "capstone" (NIV; quoting Ps 118:22), and "a stone" that makes the disobedient stumble (quoting Isa 8:14). Moreover, 1 Pet 2:5 speaks of the incorporation of believers as stones into a "spiritual house."[29]

---

29. Schnackenburg (125) thinks that Ephesians and 1 Peter are each taking up a common Pauline tradition and working with it in their own ways.

The easy manner in which "cornerstone" and "capstone" are read christologically and incorporated into an image of the church as God's building in 1 Pet 2 should indicate to modern readers that there is very little at stake in opting for "cornerstone" or "capstone."[30] That is so unless choosing one of these limits the sense in which Christ is both the distinct foundation of the church and its unsurpassed head.[31]

As 2:21–22 continue to unfold this image, it becomes clear that Christ is foundational for this building, its head, and also that which holds the whole building together, causing it to "grow into a holy temple in the Lord."[32] Much of the language here conveys the sense of an ongoing building project rather than a completed structure.[33] Indeed, the same vocabulary is used in 4:15–16 to speak of the ways in which a human body is knit together and grows.

The function of this building is to be a "holy temple in the Lord."[34] In 1 Cor 3, where the image of the church as God's building project also occurs, Paul identifies the church as "God's temple" (3:17).[35] Again, there is some resonance here with 1 Pet 2, where believers are incorporated into a Christ-formed structure in order to be a royal priesthood. More immediately, the image of a holy temple reiterates the image of becoming fellow citizens with the "saints" in 2:19. Each image reminds the Ephesians that holiness is their ultimate end in God.

Verses 20–21 combine a variety of construction images in order to assert the comprehensively Christ-centered nature of God's building project, the church. Christ is cornerstone, capstone, the one who holds the structure together, and the one who causes its growth into a holy temple. Finally in v. 22 we are told that "in him" the Ephesians are being built together into a dwelling place for God in the Spirit. There appears to be a parallel structure here between v. 21 and v. 22. Each begins with "in him"; the temple (v. 21) is often seen as God's

---

30. Luke 20:17–18 indicates that the corner/capstone is one on which one can stumble and under which one can be crushed.

31. In commenting on Christ the cornerstone, Thomas Aq. (115) says that the corner is the point of convergence where Jew and Gentile meet.

32. MacDonald (*Ephesians* 250) argues that because this building continues to grow, it rules out the idea of Christ as a capstone. This seems to take the collection of metaphors here in an overly strict fashion. McKelvey (117) states: "The entire construction comprising cornerstone, foundation and superstructure forms an indivisible whole."

33. The term *oikodomē* is used by Paul to refer to the act of building in Rom 14:19; 15:2; 1 Cor 14:3, 5, 12, 26; 2 Cor 10:8; 12:19; 13:10; and Eph 4:12. The participle *synarmologoumenē* appears only here and in 4:16, where it describes the way in which a human body is knit together and grows.

34. McKelvey (112) cites 1 Chr 22:8–10 as indicating that peace is a prerequisite for the construction of the temple.

35. In the Qumran literature the community is also referred to as the true spiritual temple (cf. 1QS 8.4–10; 9.5–6; 4QFlor [4Q174] 1.6–7). In these references, however, there is a strong contrast between the pure temple represented by the Qumran community and the corrupt temple in Jerusalem. This antagonistic contrast is absent in Ephesians.

dwelling place (v. 22); the phrase "in the Lord" in 2:21 is paired with "in the Spirit" in 2:22. The point of these parallel structures is to tie the Ephesians directly into God's construction project in Christ. The building work described in vv. 20–21 in somewhat abstract ways is now made concrete for the Ephesians: they themselves are intimately part of this building project as they are incorporated into the church.

One interesting way of approaching 2:20–22 is through Ezek 37:24–28. Immediately before this passage, in 37:15–23, God promises to reunite Judah and Israel. The image here is of two sticks, one representing Judah and one for Israel. The stick of Judah is joined to the stick of Israel, making one stick in God's hand.[36] Then in 37:24–28 God promises to make an eternal covenant of peace with the children of Israel (cf. Eph 2:14, "Christ is our peace"). At that time God will establish "my sanctuary" or holy place (*ta hagia*) among the Israelites. As a result, "the nations will know that I, the Lord, am the one who sanctifies [*ho hagiazōn*] them when my sanctuary [*ta hagia*] is set in the midst of them forever" (Ezek 37:28 LXX). There is a fruitful ambiguity in the LXX here. In the MT the text reads, "The nations will know that I, the LORD, am the one who sanctifies *Israel*" (AT). In the LXX we simply have the relative pronoun "them." The most obvious antecedent for this pronoun is "the nations." If one follows this ambiguity, then the LXX of Ezekiel seems to be claiming that when the covenant of peace is made and God's sanctuary is established among the Israelites (and the Israelites are, by implication, sanctified), then the Gentiles also will know that God sanctifies them too. Holiness is thus the proper end of Israel and the proper end of Gentiles. This sanctification is achieved when the covenant of peace is established with Israel. If this is the prophetic thrust of the LXX of Ezek 37:24–28, it finds its fulfillment in Christ as detailed in Eph 2:11–22. Christ, our peace, makes Jews and Gentiles fellow citizens with all the saints[37] and builds them up into a holy temple in the Lord, achieving the purpose laid out in 1:4 that "we should be holy and blameless before him in love." This is not a claim that Paul wrote Eph 2:19–22 with Ezek 37 in mind.[38] We simply cannot know this. It is a claim that Christians with a two-Testament Scripture might well find both edification and a deeper understanding of God's purposes by reading these two texts together.

In this section Paul has challenged the Ephesians to remember their past as a Gentile past. Paul wants the Ephesians to see that they are not simply pagans redeemed by Christ. Rather, their past must be remembered as a past in

36. R. Martin (190) makes this connection.
37. See Yoder Neufeld, *Ephesians*, 125.
38. R. Martin (190) sees fewer connections here than I do: "We are left to wonder whether the sequence 'resurrection'—renewal—'one nation'—new 'covenant of peace'—God's dwelling place—his shrine in the Spirit in Eph 2:1–22 does not run artistically and theologically along lines already set in the Ezekiel prophecy as the author's fertile imagination meditated on it."

relation to Israel and Israel's God. They were strangers and aliens. Now through Christ the Ephesians have been liberated from their slavery to sin. This much was already implied in 2:1–10. Here Paul shows that Christ's redeeming work frees the Ephesian Gentiles from the things that alienated them from Israel and Israel's God. Thus freed, Jews and Gentiles in Christ are reconciled in Christ's single body. Moreover, just as Israel released from slavery in Egypt is liberated to be a holy people, so also Jews and Gentiles in Christ are freed from the things that alienated them from God and from each other and are joined in a common citizenship of holiness.

There are two further elements to reflect on here. First, unlike the churches in Rome or Galatia (as indicated above), there does not seem to be any conflict in Ephesus between Jewish and Gentile believers. The church in Ephesus was overwhelmingly if not exclusively Gentile. It even appears to have had little direct contact with non-Christian Jews. Why then does Paul challenge the Ephesian Christians to remember their pagan past as a Gentile past? Why emphasize Christ's reconciling work in joining the two groups into one new humanity? Why speak of the hostility generated by the torah under Sin's captivity? To the extent that one can discern answers to such questions, they go to the heart of Christian identity. It appears that whether or not Christians in Ephesus or elsewhere are subject to Judaizing pressures, they must understand themselves as Christians in relation to Israel and Israel's God. They must understand their past as a Gentile past because that is God's understanding of their past. Moreover, this understanding makes sense only in the light of God's call of Israel; if there are no Jews, then there are no Gentiles. Christian identity requires the taking on or remembering of Gentile identity because Christian identity is always tied to Israel. This is not to say that Jewish identity is untouched by the life, death, and resurrection of Christ. Far from it. Jewish identity is also radically reconceived in the light of Christ. Paul's accounts of the call of Israel, the place of the torah, and the inclusion of the Gentiles within redeemed Israel—all these are accounts that most of Paul's Jewish contemporaries rejected. Nevertheless, only in the light of this reconception can there be true reconciliation between Jew and Gentile.

It thus seems that the point of pressing these issues in Ephesians is not to respond to particular Judaizing forces within the church. Rather, the point of pressing the Ephesians to understand their relationship to Israel properly is because such an understanding is essential to Christian identity for both Jewish and Gentile believers. The Gentile Christians in Ephesus cannot rightly understand their place in God's drama of salvation until they understand their past as a Gentile past and until they understand their redemption in the light of God's reconciliation of Jew and Gentile in Christ. The striking message of Ephesians is that this is true even in a church without Jewish believers.

Second, it is important for an understanding of Christian mission that the message of reconciliation in Ephesians retains its particularity. The church in our current world is ever more composed of believers from diverse ethnic, national, and cultural backgrounds. Much of the best theological reflection on the global composition and global mission of the church looks to Eph 2:11–22 as a central text. One of the key elements taken from this text is its emphasis on the reconciliation of previously hostile groups into the body of Christ in ways that transform but do not require the erasure of national, ethnic, or cultural identity. In the face of centuries of Christian mission that tied being a Christian to abandoning one's ethnic and cultural heritage in favor of a European heritage, this is a needed antidote.[39]

Ephesians also makes it clear that although becoming a Christian does not require the erasure of one's ethnic or cultural past, it also requires the remembering of that past as a Gentile past. It demands an understanding of one's past and present in relation to Israel and the God of Israel. In these respects the formation of Christian identity will require a reevaluation, but not an erasure, of one's ethnic and cultural past. One of the challenges facing theological reflection on Christian mission, then, seems to lie in the area of addressing the necessary relationship between Christian identity relative to God's call of Israel and the variety of issues one confronts when the world's cultures are confronted with the stories and doctrines surrounding God's gracious call of Israel. Specifically, one must reckon with the Creator of all peoples choosing a particular people from among the nations, making everlasting covenants with them, taking on Jewish flesh in order to redeem the world, and reconciling Jews and Gentiles in one body in Christ.

Despite their obvious theological importance, many of these issues raise concerns that go beyond the scope of a commentary. Nevertheless, one may find some resources for addressing these issues by reading further in Ephesians. This is particularly true as one moves on to examine chapter 3, where Paul articulates his own call to be an apostle to the Gentiles.

---

39. For a historical overview of the way this passage has functioned in regard to racial reconciliation, see Rader.

Ephesians 3:1–13
Paul, Interpreter of the Grace of God

Think of Eph 2 as Paul's account of the Ephesians' status, a status that has been transformed by the life, death, and resurrection of Christ. Verses 1–10 present in cosmic terms the Ephesians' status, both before and after Christ. Verses 11–22 account for the Ephesians' status, both before and after Christ, relative to the people of Israel. Although in each case the Ephesians are the subject of Paul's account, God is the primary actor. God is the one who graciously transforms the Ephesians, liberating them from their slavery to Sin and bringing about their reconciliation with the people of God. The Ephesians are called to recognize this state of affairs, but they did not bring it about. Thus Paul invites the Ephesians to adopt a perspective on their past and present that they may not have held, but which Paul presents as indubitably true. The Ephesians do not bring about their salvation. That is the result of God's grace in Christ (2:8). Nevertheless, they must now come to see themselves and their past in the light of Paul's account in Eph 2.

As Eph 3 begins, Paul shifts from an account of the Ephesians' situation to an account of his own situation. Although Paul is the focus of the discussion in 3:1–7 and 8–13, this is really a discussion of God's grace and Paul's relationship to that grace. As in chapter 2, there are elements of a contrast between former times and the present. Yet these are not as clearly pronounced as in chapter 2.

Several commentators refer to this section as a digression. Some (e.g., Lincoln, *Ephesians* 171) see this as a *digressio* in the formal rhetorical sense of the term. Others (e.g., Best, *Ephesians* 293) think that this section is not sufficiently well organized to count as a formal *digressio*. Instead, they treat the passage as a digression in the more colloquial sense of the term. In each case it is common among modern commentators to treat this passage as only indirectly relevant and not logically necessary in the light of what precedes and what follows.[1] One cannot demonstrate that the claims of 2:11–22

---

1. Kirby (129–31) says this passage is a "long parenthesis" with no discernible connection to what follows. Gombis ("Ephesians 3:2–13") seeks to counter this view, though in ways different from those outlined above.

logically necessitate those of 3:1–13. The discussion below will, however, try
to tease out the reasoning that might relate 2:11–22 to 3:1–13. The connections between these two sections lie in the strong interpretive work that Paul
does in chapter 2, locating and accounting for the Ephesians' past and present
in very particular ways. The bold interpretive moves Paul makes in chapter 2
call forth an equally bold account of Paul's authority as an interpreter of God's
gracious activity in chapter 3.

Perhaps more than any other passage in the epistle, the stylistic peculiarities
of 3:1–13 are often taken to be indications of the epistle's pseudonymity (cf.
Lincoln, *Ephesians* 168). Readers with an interest in this issue, however, would
be well advised to avoid making overhasty judgments in this regard. As with
many of the arguments about authorship in Ephesians, what one commentator
finds to be a patent imitation of Paul is taken by another commentator to be
acceptably within the range of Pauline variation.

Formally, 3:1–13 is composed of two long sentences (vv. 2–7 and 8–12),
a short sentence (v. 13), and an introductory clause (v. 1).[2] The introductory
thought in v. 1 is not really completed until, perhaps, v. 13. Moreover since both
3:1 and 3:14 begin with "For this reason," it appears that the thought introduced
in 3:1 is taken up again in 3:14 more concisely.

3:1 For this reason,[a] I, Paul, the prisoner of Christ for the sake of you
Gentiles—**2** for surely[b] you have heard of the stewardship of the grace of
God that has been given to me for you, **3** namely,[c] that the mystery was
made known to me by revelation, just as I have written in the preceding[d]
words. **4** Accordingly, when you have read these, you will perceive my
insight[e] into the mystery of Christ. **5** This mystery was not made known
to previous generations,[f] but now it has been revealed by the Spirit to his
holy apostles and prophets **6** that the Gentiles have become fellow heirs,
fellow members of the body and fellow participants in the promise in
Christ Jesus through the gospel. **7** I have become a servant of this gospel
according to the gift of God's grace that was given to me according to
the working of his power.

8 This grace has been given to me, the very least[g] of all the saints, to
bring the good news of Christ's unimaginable[h] riches to the Gentiles and
9 to bring to light the plan of the mystery that was hidden from the ages in
God, the one who created all things, **10** so that now through the church the
manifold wisdom of God might be made known to the principalities and
powers in the heavenly realms, **11** according to the eternal purpose accomplished in Christ Jesus our Lord, **12** through whom we have boldness to
enter[i] with confidence[j] before God[k] through faith in him [*or* through his

---

2. Hoehner (417) treats 3:1–13 as one long sentence. This is possible.

faithfulness]. 13 Therefore I ask[l] that you not become discouraged[m] at my tribulations for your sake; they[n] are your glory.

a. The Greek *toutou charin*, "for this reason," only appears here, in 3:14, and in Titus 1:5.

b. Although this phrase is constructed as conditional, it is one of those expressions where it is clear that Paul has no doubt about its truth (see Thrall 87–88). Hence the translation begins "surely."

c. The Greek word *hoti* is omitted by numerous MSS. There is, however, ample evidence to think it original (see Hoehner 425–26). It often follows verbs of sense perception (cf. hearing in 3:2). In this case it introduces an appositional comment about Paul's stewardship and has been translated "namely."

d. The Greek might more literally be rendered "a few words written beforehand." Some interpreters treat this either as a reference to an earlier epistle to the Ephesians (Chrysostom, *Hom. Eph.* 6) or a reference to one of Paul's other Epistles that the Ephesians may have read (Bruce 312). The great majority of modern commentators, however, take this as a reference to the prior discussion of the "mystery" earlier in the letter (cf. 1:9). Since I follow this line of interpretation, I have translated the phrase as "preceding words."

e. The Greek word here translated as "insight" (*synesis*) occurs in Col 1:9; 2:2. In Col 1:9 the term refers to a more general discerning disposition (cf. also 2 Tim 2:7). In Col 2:2 it is used in connection with the phrase "God's mystery, that is, Christ himself." Nevertheless, it still reflects a general disposition that Paul desires for all Christians rather than to any particular gift. In Luke 2:47 and Dan 1:17 (also Theodotion: Dan 1:4, 17; 9:13, 23; 10:1, 11) the term is used more of a specific gift that an individual possesses. This is much closer to the usage in Eph 3:4.

f. The Greek text here has "of the sons of men." The phrase is a general reference to humanity in the LXX of Gen 11:5; Pss 11:2, 9 (12:1, 8 Eng.); 44:3 (45:2); 52:3 (53:2); and in Mark 3:28.

g. The Greek word translated here as "the very least" is actually in Greek the comparative form of the superlative "least." A literal translation might be something like "leaster." The form here seems to be used to indicate emphasis rather than comparison (BDF §§60–61). This would account for other translations such as "less than the least" as in NEB, TEV, JB, NIV, et al.

h. The Greek term translated here as "unimaginable" also appears in Rom 11:33 and the LXX of Job 5:9; 9:10; 34:24 to speak about the inscrutability of God's ways and the fathomless wonders of God's mighty acts.

i. The two Greek terms *parrēsia* (boldness) and *prosagōgē* (access) share a single definite article. Thus commentators treat this as a form of hendiadys, "boldness to enter."

j. The term translated "confidence" occurs only in Paul in the NT (2 Cor 1:15; 3:4; 8:22; 10:2; Phil 3:4).

k. The Greek does not have "before God." It is assumed based on the context and has been added to the English for the sake of clarity.

l. The verb "ask" is in the middle voice, which is generally used in the NT for making requests in a commercial context. The active voice is more commonly used of requests to God. (See BDF para 316; Best, *Ephesians* 330–31; Hoehner 467–68.)

m. The verb *enkakein* often has the meaning "to treat badly." In the NT the verb also occurs in Luke 18:1; 2 Cor 4:1, 16; Gal 6:9; 2 Thess 3:13. In each of these verses the verb conveys the idea of becoming weary or discouraged and losing heart.

n. The relative pronoun *hētis* refers back to "tribulations" even though it agrees in number and gender with "glory." A similar construction can be found in Phil 1:28.

[1] It is possible to treat this clause as a sentence by supplying the verb "to be." This yields a complete sentence, which might be translated, "For this reason I, Paul, am a prisoner of Christ for the sake of you Gentiles" (cf. NRSV). Although this yields a complete sentence, it seems to indicate that the previous verse, 2:22, which mentions the building up of the Ephesians into a dwelling for God through the work of the Spirit, is the cause of Paul's imprisonment. One might extrapolate from this that Paul's gospel of reconciliation of Jew and Gentile in Christ is what led certain Jews to arrest him—in order to make more sense of the assertion. This, however, is quite a stretch and does not really reflect the motives of those in Acts 20.[3] It is simply better to follow the vast majority of interpreters from Origen to the present and treat this verse as a sentence fragment, which seems to provoke (or is interrupted by) a related set of thoughts that are taken up in vv. 2–13.

Even so, it is important to attend to Paul's assertion that he is a prisoner of Christ for the sake of "you Gentiles." There is a built-in ambiguity to the claim the Paul is a prisoner of Christ. On the one hand, it reflects the notion that Paul is a prisoner because of Christ. That is, Paul's Christian convictions and apostolic mission, rather than any base crime, have landed him in jail. In this light, Paul mentions his imprisonment so that the Ephesians might see that being in Christ is not incompatible with being in chains, so that they would not be discouraged by Paul's sufferings (cf. 3:13). It is not so much an apology for his apostolic status despite being in chains (cf. 2 Cor 10–12) as it is a confident assertion of God's providential care of the gospel, of which Paul is an emissary. In this respect Paul's rhetorical aim here is more like that reflected in Phil 1:12–19.

On the other hand, being a prisoner of Christ reflects the idea that Paul has been captivated or even captured by Christ. Having had the mystery of God's saving purposes revealed to him, Paul is now compelled to preach the gospel. In this respect one might think of Paul as Christ's prisoner. Yet it is more common for Paul to make a point like this by speaking of being a slave of Christ (e.g., Rom 1:1; 1 Cor 7:22; Phil 1:1; Col 4:12).

Having indicated the importance of the Ephesians' Gentile identity in 2:11, Paul declares that he is the prisoner of Christ for the sake of "you Gentiles." Recognition of the Ephesians' Gentile identity is not only essential for them to

---

3. In addition, as Abbott (76) notes, if this were a complete sentence, one would not expect the article with the word "prisoner."

understand themselves properly before God; it is also the rationale for Paul's apostolic activity.

[2–7] By v. 2 Paul's imprisonment is no longer the focus of his comments. Rather, it is Paul's authority as an interpreter of God's drama of salvation. Although the Greek begins with a conditional expression that might be translated "if indeed," the conditional aspect of this phrase seems rhetorical. Hence many English translations use terms like "Surely you have heard," or "You have, of course, heard." A similar form is used in the same way in 4:21. This is also like the series of conditional statements that Paul makes in Phil 2:1, which are not really conditional at all.[4]

Paul assumes that the Ephesians already know that he has been given a trust or has been made a steward of the grace of God. The same word used here to speak of Paul's stewardship (*oikonomia*) appears in 1:10 and 3:9 to speak of God's plan or administration of the plan of salvation. Here in 3:2 the term indicates both Paul's status as steward and his activity of administering God's grace for the sake of "you Gentiles."[5] On its own this verse contains a variety of ambiguities, which the following verses help to resolve. The core of Paul's assertion here is that his place and his activity within the drama of salvation are initiated and sustained by God (rather than Paul's own initiative), and Paul plays this role for the sake of the Gentiles (rather than for his own aggrandizement; Best, *Ephesians* 299).

In the next verses Paul elaborates on the nature and content of the stewardship or mission given to him by God for the sake of the Gentiles. First, Paul asserts, the mystery that God has made known to him is "by revelation." As Lincoln (*Ephesians* 174–75) observes, it is important that "revelation" is not simply taken as the means by which Paul learns about his mission. Rather, the Greek makes it clear that Paul is saying both something about himself as the one who receives his gospel and that this gospel is normative. In this respect the argument presented here in a verse or two is very similar to the argument presented in Gal 1. Thus, to say that the mystery made known to Paul is "by revelation" (*kata apokalypsin*) is to contrast it with, for example, a gospel "of human origin" (*kata anthrōpon*, Gal 1:11). Paul in Galatians contrasts the single gospel, of which he is a servant, with alternative gospels more pleasing to humans. Alternatively, Paul in Ephesians asserts that he is really a steward rather than an inventor. Paul's gospel is something given to him by God. He

---

4. If Ephesians is pseudonymous, then the conditional element may be stronger. Lincoln (*Ephesians* 173) says, "The remark becomes more understandable when it is seen as part of the device of pseudonymity." Lincoln's point here is that a Paulinist is using this, as well as the repeated self-references in this passage, to tie himself strongly to Paul. Yet if the point of the passage is to assert Paul's authority to interpret the drama of salvation for the Ephesians in the ways he has just done, then the focus of this passage is explicable.

5. Reumann 165. The language here is very similar to Col 1:25.

is an authoritative interpreter because it comes to him by revelation; it is not something Paul could have invented or imagined on his own.[6]

Paul's reference to his previous writing is not a reference to other epistles. It is simply pointing back to his exposition of the mystery of God's drama of salvation relative to the Ephesian Gentiles in the previous two chapters.[7] As the next verse indicates, Paul assumes that upon reading his account of the reconciliation of Jew and Gentile in Christ, the Ephesians will perceive Paul's insight into the "mystery of Christ." Paul is not speaking here of a cultivated interpretive skill or of a general discerning disposition. Rather, this is an insight that has been given to Paul as part of his stewardship of God's grace.

To those familiar with Gal 1–2 or 2 Cor 10–12, it will seem odd that Paul seems to be asserting his credentials in the absence of specific types of opposition to his gospel. Alternatively, as in Galatians, Paul is offering a bold interpretation of God's plan for the salvation of the world. Under such circumstances it is reasonable to expect some account of Paul's interpretive credentials.[8] Paul is not particularly defensive in Ephesians. He does not provide an extensive account of his life as a whole (as in Gal 1–2; Phil 3:2–12) or of his ministry (as in 2 Cor 10–12). He does not assert his credentials over those of others as in Galatians and Philippians. Rather, he straightforwardly asserts his role as steward of God's grace for the sake of "you Gentiles" as if he expects it to be accepted at face value.

Paul makes it clear that insight into the "mystery of Christ" was not revealed to previous generations. This raises some sharp questions. Is the implication here that there is absolutely no knowledge of this mystery in the OT? In answering this question, much depends on the way one takes the conjunction linking the "before" and "after" parts of this verse. Most premodern along with some modern commentators treat the Greek conjunction *hōs* as introducing a contrast of degree. That is, what was known dimly in the OT has now been made clear in the NT.[9] Such interpreters are concerned that claims such as Jesus' claim in John 8:56 that Abraham "rejoiced . . . [to] see my day" not be falsified by this text. In addition, they want to make sure that the authors of the OT texts that are read as

---

6. If this must be tied to a particular moment of revelation, then it is probably the Damascus road experience. This verse, however, is not really interested in locating a moment in time. Rather, it is concerned with asserting the source of Paul's gospel. For even after the revelation on the road to Damascus, Paul himself admits that he spent quite some time contemplating the nature and scope of his gospel (Gal 1:15–22).

7. This is the position of the vast majority of modern commentators: Best, *Ephesians* 302; Hoehner 428; Lincoln, *Ephesians* 175; MacDonald, *Ephesians* 262; Schnackenburg 132.

8. Lincoln (*Ephesians* 176) considers this manifest evidence of pseudonymity. Clearly, there does not appear to be the sort of opposition to Paul that one finds in Galatians or 2 Corinthians. But Paul also does not defend his character here in Ephesians as he does in Galatians and 2 Corinthians.

9. Chrysostom, *Hom. Eph.* 6; Origen, in Heine 144–48; Thomas Aq. 121–23; Calvin 160; also Caragounis 102.

prefiguring Christ were not utterly ignorant of the content of their prophecies.[10] As important as these theological concerns are,[11] the syntax of the phrase seems to pose an absolute contrast between "other generations" and "now."[12]

At the same time as one must affirm that Paul here draws an absolute distinction between prior generations and "now," one should also carefully attend to the nature of the "mystery" that Paul is talking about in Ephesians. Unlike Col 1:24–29, where the "mystery" is understood as a more general reference to salvation in Christ, Paul here focuses on the reconciliation of Jew and Gentile in Christ in the particular ways outlined in Eph 2:11–22.[13] Thus, even though one might grant that a variety of OT texts such as Gen 12:1–3; Isa 2:1–4; and Isa 49:6–7 speak relatively clearly about the blessing of the nations, it is also true that the inclusion of the Gentiles within the redeemed people of God in Christ in the ways that Paul argues for throughout his writings does not seem to have been anticipated in earlier generations. Indeed, many of Paul's Jewish Christian contemporaries often did not see things in quite the way Paul does.

As Eph 3:5 makes clear, Paul is not the only recipient of this revealed mystery. Through the Spirit, God has made this mystery known to "his holy apostles and prophets." As with 2:20, it appears that Paul is referring to Christian prophets. The use of a single definite article for "apostles" and "prophets" shows that they are being considered together as a group. If that is the case, it may explain why the adjective "holy" is used for "apostles" and not prophets.[14] It seems that the use of the adjective "holy" here is not to preclude the sanctity of others, but to link the apostles and prophets back to their role in building God's holy temple (2:20–21). Paul here seems concerned to counter any idea that the interpretation of God's mystery, such as he has offered in 2:11–22, is idiosyncratic. Paul's understanding of the divine mystery is not unique to Paul. In this respect the argument is analogous to Gal 1:11–24, where Paul emphasizes that his gospel has a divine origin. Nevertheless, due to its recognition by the "pillars" in Jerusalem (Gal 2:9), his gospel is not idiosyncratic.

Finally, the substance of the mystery is recapitulated in Eph 3:6. The Gentiles have become "fellow heirs, fellow members of the body and fellow participants

---

10. Origen, 145, in particular is worried about Montanist claims here.

11. A comparative reading of this conjunction does not really protect against Marcionism. Even if one grants that the OT has a dim knowledge of the mystery of salvation in Christ, that in itself is not a reason to retain it once the revelation of that mystery in its fullness has occurred.

12. See Best, *Ephesians* 305–6; Hoehner 439–40; Lincoln, *Ephesians* 177; Schlier 150; Schnackenburg 132.

13. The connection between Col 1:26 and Eph 3:5 is far less striking than Lincoln (*Ephesians* 178–79) imagines. As Best (*Ephesians* 310–11) notes, there is very little overlap in vocabulary here.

14. Best (*Ephesians* 307–8) and Lincoln (*Ephesians* 179) see this as evidence against Pauline authorship because the term "holy apostles" does not appear elsewhere in the Greek NT and is quite common in Christian literature of the next generation.

in the promise in Christ Jesus through the gospel." As this verse indicates, this mystery is no longer hidden. Rather, it has become a primary component of Christian proclamation. The gospel may have required divine revelation in order to be made known, but it is now no longer hidden.

The notion of the Gentiles being fellow heirs takes its significance from 1:11–12, 18. In those verses Paul uses language that reflects God's choosing of Israel to speak of the Gentiles' incorporation into the divine plan of salvation. Becoming fellow heirs means becoming fellow heirs with Jewish believers. The idea of Jews and Gentiles in Christ being fellow members of the same body reflects the claim in 2:16 that the reconciliation of these two groups takes place in Christ's body.[15] Being fellow participants in the promise picks up a theme from Romans and Galatians that in Christ the promise to Abraham to bring a blessing to the nations is fulfilled, thus rendering a reconciled body of Jews and Gentiles in Christ.

Ultimately, Paul wants to assert that he is a servant of this gospel. He did not devise it. Rather, God has graciously made it known to him and given him the task of making it known to others. The previous verses establish Paul's power as recipient and interpreter of the mystery of salvation; now v. 7 indicates that the power really resides in God, who graciously works in Paul and of whose gospel Paul is a servant.

[8–12] This sentence continues to develop the relationship between the unfolding of God's purposes of bringing Jews and Gentiles into friendship with God and each other through Christ and Paul's role as interpreter and proclaimer of those purposes. It begins with Paul's further identification of himself as the "very least of all the saints."

Although Paul doubtless considers himself an apostle (cf. 1:1) and one of the "holy apostles" to whom God has revealed the mystery of salvation (3:5), he does not identify himself that way here. Instead, he is the very least among "all the saints." Although the language here is reminiscent of 1 Cor 15:9, Paul's aims here are slightly different. He is not, as in 1 Cor 15, concerned to situate himself properly among the apostles. There is no sense in Ephesians that Paul's status as apostle, or Paul's status relative to other apostles, is in dispute. Unlike in 1 Corinthians, Paul in Ephesians does not give a reason for his evaluation of himself as the very least among all the saints.[16]

Despite Paul's negligible status, God has graciously given him the task of evangelizing the Gentiles. More precisely, he is to proclaim the unimaginable

---

15. This is the first time (3:6) the word *syssōma* appears in Greek. It may have been coined by Paul, but we have no way of knowing this.

16. Lincoln (*Ephesians* 183) and Best (*Ephesians* 316–17) consider that the differences here indicate pseudonymity. Hoehner (454) assumes that a Pauline disciple would never identify Paul as the very least of the saints.

riches of Christ to the Gentiles. In identifying Christ's riches as unimaginable, Paul is further emphasizing the point that neither he nor anyone else could have reasoned their way to such an understanding of God's purposes.[17] Further, this language (as in 3:6) points back to 1:18, where Paul prays that the Ephesians may know the "riches of the glory of his inheritance among the saints." There in 1:18 Paul prays that the Ephesians may be given the insight to perceive what here in 3:8 Paul has been commissioned to proclaim.

This thought is carried over into 3:9, where Paul speaks of his commission as "bringing to light" or "enlightening" (cf. 1:18 again). The focus of that enlightenment is the plan of the mystery. Although Paul uses the Greek word *oikonomia* in 3:2 to speak of his stewardship, the term here in 3:9 reflects the usage in 1:10, where the term speaks of the plan or the unfolding of the plan of bringing all things to their proper end in Christ. In this case, Paul probably intends the more narrow focus on the reconciliation of Jews and Gentiles in Christ in the particular ways he has laid out in Eph 2. Rather than the content of the "plan of the mystery," Paul here emphasizes that God had hidden this plan from prior ages. That is, when the text says that this plan has been hidden "in God," it indicates that the hiding was part of God's purpose and not simply the result of human ignorance or sin. The additional identification of God as the Creator of all things is designed to undermine the possible inference that this plan was a haphazard device or reaction on God's part (Best, *Ephesians* 321). This plan is part of the eternal purposes of the one who created all things. Thus, to the extent that Paul or we might use language about planning analogously to speak of God's work, it is equally important to remember that God's planning is not reactive, always adjusting to human events. Therefore, the Ephesians and all believers can rest assured that God has providentially ordered this plan for good. It also further separates God's plan and its proclamation and exposition from Paul's own capacities and invention. Moreover, Lincoln (*Ephesians* 185) is right to assert that the emphasis on God's comprehensive creative power ensures that God is able to bring this plan to completion despite the rebellious desires and actions of the powers.

Verse 10 begins with a clause that indicates one of the purposes for which Paul has been given his grace of evangelizing the Gentiles:[18] that "through the church the manifold wisdom of God might be made known to the principalities

---

17. Origen, whose views on this are only available to us through Jerome (in Heine 148–49), says, "It is one thing by one's own curiosity to attain to a secret which ceases to be unsearchable as soon as it has been learned. It is another to be totally unable to understand by one's own diligence but by God's grace to know that which, once you know it and even made it known to others, continues none the less to be unsearchable. Although the mystery was made known to you, it continues to be as great as it was formerly."

18. The Greek *hina* is, ultimately, dependent on the verb "given" in v. 8 (with Best, *Ephesians* 322; Lincoln, *Ephesians* 185).

and powers in the heavenly realms." As indicated above (cf. comments on 1:21), these principalities and powers are created by God. Like Christ and the church, they are located in the heavenly realms. However, they are not yet completely under Christ's dominion (1:22). They are not fulfilling their purpose of participating in and enhancing God's good ordering of creation. According to this verse, the church is the means by which these powers might be restored to their proper relationship to God and the rest of creation. Paul does not go into great detail about how this is to happen. One can imagine this happening through the church's preaching or its engagements with earthly powers, but there is nothing specific in the text. In this context, the upshot of Paul's claim is that the very existence of the gathered body of Jews and Gentiles reconciled to God and each other in Christ makes known the manifold wisdom of God. Further, it is this precise witness to the manifold wisdom of God that will draw the powers back to their proper relationship with God and the world. Many modern commentators devote a great deal of space to reflection on the nature of the manifold wisdom of God and parallels with Hellenistic Jewish reflection about God's wisdom. The danger with this scholarly tendency is that it runs the risk of treating the notion of God's wisdom in 3:10 too narrowly (Lincoln, *Ephesians* 188).

Rather than simply seeking conceptual precedents for Paul's claims here, Christians may also find that passages such as Isa 2:1–4; 60:1–7; and Ezek 37 help in unpacking the implications of Paul's assertions in these verses. In particular one might see Paul's claims here as a further unpacking of Isa 2:1–4. When the redemption of Israel happens, according to this text, the nations will be so attracted to the renewed people of God and their relationship to God and each other that the Gentiles will be drawn to God. The result will be the peace characteristic of the garden in Genesis. The church, the body of Christ, is the place where the redemption of Israel is made manifest in word and deed, where Gentiles are welcomed and reconciled to God and to the renewed people of God, according to God's purposes. It should come as no surprise, then, that the attractiveness that first drew Gentiles to God should be made even more attractive in the light of the reconciliation of Jew and Gentile in Christ. Indeed, it may appear attractive enough to compel the powers to return to their proper place.

It is not my claim that Paul consciously reflected on Isaiah as he thought about his own commission. Rather, if Isaiah thinks of the reconciliation of the nations with redeemed Israel as having significant social consequences for the world, it is not unimaginable that Paul and others might see that the reconciliation of Jew and Gentile to God and to each other in Christ would have social and even cosmic consequences. Thus it is striking that although these powers are located in the heavenly realms, their understanding of the wisdom of God and any subsequent reconciliation is dependent on the material presence of communities such as those Paul seeks to form in Ephesus and elsewhere. Of course, Paul has already located believers, to some extent, in the heavenly realms. It seems equally likely that the powers in the heavenly realms might also have some direct engagement with the earthly realm.

Although one might wish that Paul had explored this issue in much more detail, he instead returns to the eternal nature of God's purposes in Christ. Making the wisdom of God known to the powers by means of the church requires the temporal and material presence of the church in the world. Further, this is not a contingent part of the church's mission. Rather, v. 11 indicates that this is part of God's eternal purpose accomplished in Christ Jesus our Lord.

This sentence concludes by declaring that through Christ, believers have boldness to enter into God's presence with confidence. The image of access to God first appears in 2:18. Here in 3:12 the issue is not who has access to God, but the manner in which believers have access. The Greek here conveys the impression of freedom and unrestricted access, of the confidence that one will be received and welcomed.

Verse 12 closes by stating that this confidence is by means of faith in Christ or by Christ's faithfulness. To those familiar with scholarly debates in Pauline studies, this is a case where we find *pistis autou*, standing for the ambiguous phrase *pistis Christou*.[19] Here are the basic interpretive options: First, one can take this as an objective genitive, where the emphasis is on faith in Christ. Thus faith in Christ is the basis for believers' bold, confident access to the Father. Second, one can take this phrase as a subjective genitive, where the emphasis is on Christ's faithfulness. Thus Christ's faithfulness in accomplishing the eternal purposes of God enables believers to have bold, confident access to the Father. To adjudicate this conflict, one might look to the analogous passage in Rom 5:1–2. Unfortunately, there each option is hotly contested, without much resolution.[20] In the case of Eph 3:12, very little hangs on making a sharp distinction between these two options. Both are possible, both fit the larger context, both convey theological truth, and both can be understood here.

[13] This section concludes with a sentence that helps bring the two long expositions of God's mystery and of Paul's role in proclaiming that mystery into clearer perspective. The sentence begins with "Therefore." This conjunction brings to completion the conditional sentence that began in 3:2. It summarizes the point or aim for which Paul has discussed the stewardship that God has given to Paul, about which the Ephesians have already heard. Because Paul has now discussed at some length the nature of his stewardship, the Ephesians

---

19. In Eph 3:12 the antecedent of *autou* is clearly Christ.

20. There are few neutral introductions to this issue. Nevertheless, Dunn (379–84) will give a student a fair list of the major scholarly voices in this debate.

are in a position to assent to a request.[21] That request is that they not lose hope in Paul's tribulations on their behalf. Presumably these tribulations find their current focus in Paul's status as a prisoner (cf. 3:1).

If Paul were simply addressing the fact that he is a prisoner in 3:13, then 3:2–12 seems more like conceptual wandering than a digression. It is hard to see why it is introduced here at all. Moreover, the logic is hard to follow whether it is from Paul or a Pauline disciple. One would expect something much more like the apologetic account of Paul's status found in 2 Cor 10–12 or the christologically dense account of apostolic suffering such as in Phil 1:12–26. If, however, Paul's imprisonment "for the sake of you Gentiles" (Eph 3:1) raises questions about Paul's gospel and particularly his bold account of the Gentiles' place in God's drama of salvation, then 3:2–12 appear as relevant considerations.

Verses 2–12 remind readers of God's eternal purpose to bring together Jew and Gentile in Christ, reconciling them in one body through the cross. Moreover, such a purpose was hidden from previous generations and unimaginable apart from the life, death, and resurrection of Christ. Even so, God graciously revealed this "mystery" to Paul and to others for the establishment of the church of Jews and Gentiles, a church that is capable of bearing witness to the powers of God's manifold wisdom in Christ. Thus any suffering that comes Paul's way in the course of fulfilling this commission must be understood in the light of God's providence. This account establishes Paul's credentials as an interpreter of God's gracious activity on behalf of the Gentiles. At the same time such an account makes it clear that Paul is no more than a servant of this gospel, whose revelation and acceptance is ultimately in God's hands. In this light, Paul's imprisonment is not a crisis. Rather, it simply represents a further episode in the drama of salvation.

We need to recognize that the association between Paul and the Ephesians would mean that the shame that accrued to Paul would also accrue to them. An increase in his status or glory would have also reflected well on them. For most within the empire, imprisonment represented a significant loss of status and honor. Association with someone in prison would have generally been taken as shameful. Contrary to this popular cultural assumption, Paul argues that being imprisoned for proclaiming the gospel to the Gentiles actually redounds to the Ephesians' glory. As Lincoln's comments (*Ephesians* 192) indicate, such an evaluation may await eschatological confirmation. Nevertheless, the way for the Ephesians not to become discouraged is to adopt this eschatological way of looking at things in the present and to live in the light of its truth.

21. Beginning with Jerome (in Heine 152), there is a long tradition of interpreting this verse as Paul's prayer to God that he himself might not lose heart in his tribulations. Although this is an adequate account of 3:13, it tends to lose sight of the fact that 3:13 is the apodosis of the conditional sentence in 3:2, which already has the Ephesians as its object.

In 2:11–22 Paul presents an audacious interpretation of the drama of salvation and the Ephesians' place within that drama. This requires the Ephesians to reconceive of their past in new ways, just as Paul needed to rethink his Judaism in the light of Christ. Moreover, as will become clear, participation in this drama of salvation will require the Ephesians to adopt a variety of practices and habits. In 3:1–13 Paul presents an account of himself that secures his role as interpreter of God's drama of salvation for the Ephesians. Although this is a position of power, Paul makes it clear that the real power lies in the gospel, of which he is merely a servant. What Paul seeks to balance here, as in Gal 1–2 and Phil 3, is the boldness and authority needed to articulate the fathomless mystery of God's plan for the salvation of the world and the self-effacing disposition of one who interprets, but in no way anticipates or devises, this plan. Paul's position is always relative and subservient to the role of the gospel in God's drama of salvation. Paul is always the gospel's servant and not its master. In the light of this account of Paul's role as interpreter of God's mystery, in 3:14–21 he will pray that the Ephesians will be given the spiritual and moral resources they will need to hold fast to this gospel.

Ephesians 3:14–21
Paul's Requests to God on Behalf
of the Ephesians

This passage picks up with the same phrase, "For this reason," found in 3:1. Some think that this prayer is really what Paul wanted to offer before the "digression" of 3:2–13. Just as it is not possible to offer an account of the logically necessary relationships between the beginning of Eph 3 and the end of Eph 2, it is also not possible to demonstrate how the prayer at the end of Eph 3 must necessarily follow from the claims at the beginning of the chapter. Nevertheless, as with 3:2–13, it is possible to show that there is a fitting relationship linking the claims of 2:11–22, Paul's account of himself as interpreter of God's grace in 3:2–13, and Paul's prayer for the Ephesians in 3:14–21. Although these three paragraphs do not follow each other in the ways that the points of a demonstrative argument might, it still is possible to see how each of these paragraphs might generate the types of claims in the following paragraphs.

One way of making this connection is to see 2:11–22 as an account of the mystery of God's drama of salvation, reconciling both Jew and Gentile in Christ. Paul admonishes the Ephesians to "remember" that they are Gentiles so that they can properly fit themselves into this drama. This account of God's grace contains a number of audacious and surprising claims about God's gracious activity. As a way of supporting these claims, Paul offers an account of himself as interpreter of God's grace in 3:1–13. Thus one can then view 3:14–21 as Paul's prayer, hope, and expectation that the Ephesians, too, will be given the grace to understand and participate in this mystery, which seems to have been his goal from at least 2:11. Indeed, one might go so far as to say that this would be Paul's desire and prayer for the church universal, past, present, and future, because he recognizes that understanding and participating in this mystery is foundational for faithful worship and faithful action.[1]

Further, Paul's prayer makes it clear that even his interpretive work as steward of God's mystery requires God's action for the Ephesians to receive it properly and to live in the light of this mystery. At the same time, Paul has no serious

---

1. This desire is clearly expressed in Philippians, but it is also, though less explicit, crucial to Romans and Galatians in particular.

doubt that God has and will continue to act on the Ephesians' behalf. Indeed, Paul's initial intercession in 1:17–23 makes it clear that God has already initiated such work in the Ephesians. Further, as chapter 4 will show, an understanding of God's action also entails a set of responsibilities, actions, and practices on the part of the Ephesians.

Formally, the passage begins with Paul situating himself relative to God (3:14–15). Paul then makes a series of requests to God on behalf of the Ephesians (vv. 16–19). There are three separate sections, each expressing a particular request and introduced by the Greek *hina*. Finally, the passage concludes with a doxology (vv. 20–21).

3:14 For[a] this reason I bend my knees before the Father,[b] 15 from whom every "family"[c] in heaven and on earth is named, 16 so that according to the riches of his glory he might grant you to be strengthened with power through his Spirit in your inner being, 17 so that Christ may dwell in your hearts through faith. Since you have been rooted in and grounded in love,[d] 18 I desire that you may be strengthened to comprehend with all the saints what is the breadth, length, height, and depth, 19 and to know the love of Christ, which surpasses knowledge, so that you may be filled[e] up to[f] all the fullness of God.

20 To the one who is able to do abundantly more[g] than we can ask or imagine,[h] according to power that works in us, 21 to him be glory in the church and in Christ Jesus in all generations forever and ever. Amen.

a. This is a single sentence in Greek. It has been broken up into several sentences in English for ease of comprehension.

b. There is a textual variant here. Many manuscripts have "the Father of our Lord Jesus Christ." The reading "Father" has earlier attestation $\mathfrak{P}^{46}$, ℵ*, A, B, C, et al. The reading "the Father of our Lord Jesus Christ" is attested in texts from a wider geographic area (ℵ[2], D, F, G, et al.). Hoehner (473) argues that this wider geographic distribution, along with the fact that this is the only time where this form is used instead of "God the Father of our Lord . . ." or "the God and Father of our Lord . . . ," leads him to take it as original. Metzger (535) argues that the longer form is a gloss on 1:3 and that the shorter form is more likely to be original. Clearly, taking the shorter form as original does not negate the assertions contained in the longer form.

c. In the LXX the Greek word *patria*, translated here as "family," normally designates a social grouping (tribe, clan, household) with a common ancestor (e.g., Exod 12:3; Num 32:28; 1 Chr 23:11). The term can also refer to social groups that are not related by blood (e.g., Ps 21:28 [22:27 Eng.]); in Jdt 8:18 *patria* appears as one of a list of social groupings beginning with *phylē* (tribe), then *patria*, then *dēmos* (people), and finally *polis* (city). Thus *patria* means something more than a nuclear family. In Acts 3:25 Peter gives a rough quotation of Gen 12:3 and uses *patriai* (families) instead of *ethnē* or *phylai* (nations or peoples). Hence, "family" is translated with scare quotes so that readers do not impart too narrow a meaning to the term.

d. There are several ambiguities in this phrase. The Greek *en agapē* must go with the two participles in this phrase and not as a further description of the dwelling of Christ in the hearts of believers. Some see the phrase as a further request under the first *hina* clause (e.g., Lincoln, *Ephesians* 197). The problem in that case is that the perfect tenses of the participles imply a state already achieved and continuing, not part of a request for the future. Others take the phrase to express the result of Christ's dwelling in the hearts of believers (Caragounis 75). Again, the perfect tense might make this a more difficult but not impossible reading. The alternative is to tie this phrase to the second *hina* clause, which begins in 3:18. This is equally problematic since one wonders why the *hina* does not precede rather than follow these participles (Hoehner 482). This latter option is probably best if taken as expressing the already-established condition of being grounded in love, from which Paul offers a request for an ever deeper comprehension of this love. Such a view also allows one to assume that being rooted and grounded in love is a result of the Spirit's and Christ's work in 3:16–17a.

e. The Greek here is a bit obscure. Thus it is not surprising that there is a textual variant in the final part of the verse. The variant is read by $\mathfrak{P}^{46}$, B, et al. and would be translated as "that all the fullness of God may be filled." The text as translated above has ample early witnesses (ℵ, A, C, D, F, G, et al.). It can hardly be said to be a less difficult reading, and there is little doubt that it is original.

f. The Greek preposition *eis* indicates that toward which something is directed. In this case, it is the point toward which the filling up of the Ephesians is directed. It should not be translated as "with," thereby indicating that with which the Ephesians are filled—as in the NRSV, RSV, and AV.

g. The adverbial combination of the Greek *hyper* and *hyperekperissou* works here to assert the infinite abundance of God's ability and willingness to act on our behalf. Hence, I use the translation "abundantly more."

h. Technically it is correct to translate the Greek word *nooumen* as "we think." The translation follows the NRSV here and uses the English word "imagine." If one is reflecting on a power that exceeds the limits of our conceptual powers, then "imagine" conveys this better than "think."

[14–15] This passage is generally referred to as a prayer or "prayer report." This is not incorrect. Indeed, by 3:16 Paul is making a request of God on the Ephesians' behalf. Using a term like "prayer report," however, can obscure some important issues around vocabulary and other matters. For example, Paul does not actually use a term for "prayer" as in, for example, 1:16.[2] Instead, Paul "bends his knees." There are a few references in the LXX to kneeling for prayer (Dan 6:11, Theodotion; 3 Kgdms [1 Kgs] 8:54; 1 Chr 29:20). In each of these cases, however, there is a verb indicating that the subject is praying.

2. For "praying," Paul's Letters often use the verb *proseuchomai* or its cognate noun, *proseuchē* (cf. Rom 1:10; 12:12; 15:30; 1 Cor 7:5; 11:4, 5, 13; 14:13, 14; Phil 1:9; 4:6; 1 Thess 1:2; 5:17, 25; et al.). Paul also uses *deomai* (beg or make request), which often appears in relation to prayer (Rom 1:10; 2 Cor 5:2; 8:4; 10:2; Gal 4:12; et al.).

Simply being on one's knees does not necessarily signify prayer. The more common Jewish and early Christian posture for prayer is to stand (cf. Mark 11:25; Luke 18:11, 13).[3] The terms referring to bending one's knee or knees (without a specific mention of prayer) appear only three other times in Paul's writings (Rom 11:4; 14:11; Phil 2:10). In these three other cases, Paul is pointing to OT texts. In Rom 11:4 Paul alludes to Elijah's complaint that he is the only prophet left and then quotes God's response that God has kept "seven thousand who have not bowed the knee to Baal" (cf. 1 Kgs 19:18). In Rom 14:11 and Phil 2:10–11, Paul quotes Isa 45:23 and declares that every "knee shall bow" and "every tongue confess . . ." (AT). Without question, the image of bending the knee is primarily one of recognition of and submission to another's lordship. This is more like an act of worship rather than a direct petition.

From these contexts it is clear that identifying the one to whom one bends is equally important as the act of kneeling itself. Submitting to a greater authority is only natural. The real key is where one locates that authority. In this case Paul bends his knee to the Father, from whom every family is named. Clearly this is the same God who speaks to Elijah and Isaiah and Jesus. Here, however, Paul emphasizes his submission to the Father "from whom every 'family' in heaven and on earth is named." The central act of the Father here is "naming." This seems to refer to God's activity in creation (cf. Ps 147:4; Isa 40:26; Eccl 6:10). In this sense the name identifies the Creator, perhaps in the same way potters or smiths identify their works with a particular mark. The image here is of God's comprehensive power and control over all social formations, whether in heaven or on earth.[4] This emphasis on God's power is fitting, given the nature of the requests that follow in vv. 16–19.

[16–19] Having indicated that Paul does not use the language of prayer here, it is important to see that there seems to be a connection between the act of bending the knee and the making of a request to God.[5] Paul, the powerful interpreter of God's grace, the steward of the mystery of salvation, is also the one who submits to the Father (unlike the powers). He intercedes for the Ephesians, asking for the gifts that he thinks they will need to faithfully negotiate their place in the drama of salvation that is unfolding before them.

---

3. In the NT Jesus falls on his knees to pray in the garden in Luke 22:41. In Acts 9:40; 20:36; 21:5 various people kneel to pray. In each case, however, there is a specific verb to indicate that prayer is happening. The kneeling on its own is not sufficient to signify prayer.

4. Schnackenburg claims (147) that the mention of "families" in heaven is a reference to good angels since God cannot be the father of rebellious heavenly powers; this view seems to miss the crucial assertion of Ephesians that God will ultimately subject all heavenly powers to Christ, returning them their proper relation as servants of God.

5. Grammatically, the *hina* in v. 16 is dependent upon the verb *kamptō* (bend) in v. 14.

The first clause asks that God would strengthen the Ephesians. Moreover, Paul asks that God would give "according to the riches of his glory." This phrase hearkens back to Paul's earlier intercession in 1:16–19 and to 1:18 in particular. There he boldly reminds the Ephesians that God's giving is unbounded just as God's glory is. God gives from a superabundance, so God is in no way diminished or lessened in the act of giving. The economy of God's giving is ruled by excess rather than lack, by grace rather than reciprocity and indebtedness.

The "riches of his glory" speaks to the character of God's giving. The gift that Paul particularly requests here is strength with power from the Holy Spirit. Rather than physical strength or political power, which can be acquired through human actions, the power Paul seeks for the Ephesians is a gift mediated by the Spirit. The Spirit is seen as the agent of God's strengthening. The power that Paul requests here is the same power that raised Jesus from the dead (1:19), that empowers his apostolic ministry, and that will enable the Ephesians to resist evil (6:10; see Lincoln, *Ephesians* 205).

The location of this strengthening is the inner person. In 2 Cor 4:16 (AT) the "inner person" is the site of God's renewing activity, which persists even though the "outer person" is wasting away. Later, in 2 Cor 5:12, Paul poses a similar outward/inner contrast.[6] This time "the heart" is used to reflect the inner person. Similarly, in the case of Eph 3:16, idea of the "inner person" is further developed in 3:17, where the term "heart" is used to speak of that place in believers where Christ dwells. Thus the heart or the inner person stands for the seat or ground of a person's self. It is the place that generates and sustains the memories, thoughts, actions, and feelings that constitute who a person really is. This place may not be visible or revealed to others or even to oneself, but it is fully known and accessible to God (cf. 1 Cor 13:12).

The first clause of Eph 3:17, "that Christ may dwell in your hearts through faith," elaborates on the request to be strengthened with power through the Spirit in the inner person. From a Trinitarian perspective it is striking that an increase in the Spirit's powerful work in the lives of believers entails Christ's deeper dwelling in the hearts of believers. The actions of Spirit and Son are intimately tied here in 3:16–17.[7] When this is coupled with the claims in Eph 1 that locate Christ within the identity of the Father, the Spirit is thus also drawn into the identity of the one God.

As discussed above in the translation notes, the next clause, "since you have been rooted in and grounded in love," may not grammatically indicate the result of the work of the Spirit and Christ; it certainly is one of the logical results of

---

6. In Rom 7:22–23 the inner person is the place in the Jew under the law that delights in God's law but is ultimately in captivity to Sin, unable to follow the law to its proper telos.

7. Similar connections between Christ and the Spirit can be found in Rom 8:9–10. Also in Eph 2:22 the church is seen as the dwelling place of God in the Spirit.

God's working in the lives of the Ephesians in the ways Paul desires. The phrase combines botanical and architectural images in a manner that recalls 2:20–22. Nevertheless, it is crucial to recognize that these are images that speak about the beginning or the basis of the Christian life, not of its completion. Being rooted in God's love provides a stability or security from which to grow. Thus growth in love of God and love of neighbor is both the vehicle and the end of the Christian life.[8]

It is toward this end that Paul offers his next petition. The petition beginning with *hina* in v. 16 is for a gift from God; then the next *hina* clause (starting with v. 18) seeks to lay out the purpose for which Paul hopes God's gift will be used. Specifically, having been rooted in and founded on love, Paul wants the Ephesians to be able to comprehend the love of Christ. Moreover, this is not simply a matter of individual contemplation. This is the aim of "all the saints" (v. 18).[9]

There still is much more to be said about this verse. First, one finds here a list of spatial terms: breadth, length, height, and depth. It is misleading to think of these words as an attempt to delineate precisely all types of spatial extension. As Best (*Ephesians* 344) notes, there are only three spatial dimensions, and any educated first-century person would have known this. Moreover, there is only one article for these four nouns. Hence, they are to be taken as a whole, not as separate acts of measurement. The extensive attempts by many modern commentators to find a precise and relevant background for these terms have all failed (see Best, *Ephesians* 344–46; Dahl, "Cosmic Dimensions"). Job 11:5–9 uses similar imagery but different vocabulary to talk about the vast incomprehensibility of God's wisdom. Similarly, Rom 11:33–36 uses the term "depth" (but none of the others) to speak of God's incomprehensible wisdom. Despite our best scholarly efforts, here one simply finds a metaphor that requires no parallels to make its force intelligible. Further, the excessive, hyperbolic piling on of terms is quite typical of Ephesians. The force of this complex of terms is to speak of an object without measure, something infinite. The text does not directly identify this object. Is it "knowledge" or "love"? The context indicates that it is the love of Christ.[10] Indeed, if one requires a conceptual parallel here, it would be Rom 8:38–39: "For I am convinced that neither death, nor life,

---

8. This notion is nicely expressed in Catherine of Siena's (36) letter to her confessor and friend Raymond of Capua: "The love a soul sees that God has for her, she in turn extends to all creatures. She sees how fully she herself is loved by God when she beholds herself in her source, the sea of God's being. She then desires to love herself in God and God in herself, like a person who, on looking into the water, sees his or her own image there; and in this vision loves and delights in self."

9. "The true understanding of Christ's love is not then an individual experience but takes place in the community" (Best, *Ephesians* 344).

10. Best, *Ephesians* 346–67; Hoehner 488. In addition, if "knowledge" in v. 19 were to have been the subject, then the Greek should have had *tēs gnōseōs* instead of *gnōnai*.

nor angels, nor rulers, nor things present, nor things to come, nor powers, nor height, nor depth, nor anything else in all creation, will be able to separate us from the love of God in Christ Jesus our Lord."[11]

Thus Paul asks that the Ephesians, being rooted and grounded in love (based on the work of the Spirit and Christ in their lives), be given the gift of comprehending Christ's love, a love that surpasses[12] knowledge. Here several things should be said about the immeasurable, infinite love of Christ, which "surpasses knowledge." First, although immeasurable and infinite, Christ's love can provide the root and foundation of the Christian life. This foundation is necessary but is not the end or goal of the Christian life. Further, as the end of the Christian life, this love must remain infinite, beyond measure. Otherwise one can imagine some point at which one would fully comprehend and be inhabited by that love. Growing in the knowledge and experience of God's love never reaches an end. This love has no limit; we cannot exhaust it.

Second, because knowledge of this love "surpasses knowledge," our comprehension of it can only be given as a gift from God. It must be revealed. Hence it is important to recall that this discussion is cast in terms of Paul's request to God on behalf of the Ephesians. Paul does not admonish the Ephesians to sharpen their faculties so that they may comprehend what a talented, ordered, and properly trained mind might comprehend on its own. Rather, he asks God to give it to the Ephesians.

Finally, it is clear that the phrase "love of Christ" here must refer to Christ's love and not human love directed to Christ. Yet it would be extremely odd if growth in knowledge of Christ's love did not deepen and enhance believers' love of God, love of neighbor, and following Chrysostom, love of enemy.[13]

The final clause of this section (also introduced by *hina* in v. 19) represents the climax of the intercessions Paul has offered thus far. He asks that the Ephesians may be strengthened by the workings of the Spirit and the indwelling of Christ so that, being rooted in and founded on love, they will be further enabled to know the infinite love of Christ, so that they might be "filled up to all the fullness of God." It is tempting to see Col 2:9–10 as a direct parallel to this notion. As Best (*Ephesians* 348) notes, however, the Colossian text differs

11. In the light of this passage, Christians have traditionally seen the fourfold dimensions here in Ephesians as a reference to the fourfold dimensions of the cross (i.e., heaven/earth and east/west, joining the whole world), that most incomprehensible sign of Christ's love. See Origen, in Heine 162; Augustine, *Doct. chr.* 2.4.1; Thomas Aq. 145–46.

12. The Greek participle *hyperballousan* is a form of the same verb used in 1:19 to speak of the "surpassing/limitless greatness of his power," and 2:7 to speak of the "surpassing/unlimited riches of his grace."

13. See *Hom. Eph.* 7, where regarding these verses Chrysostom says, "Thus, we ought to love our enemies. This is to love God, who has enjoined it, who has given it as His law. To imitate Him is to love our enemy." Thomas Aq. (145) also mentions this, but not in as much detail.

from Ephesians in one important respect. Colossians speaks of the fullness of God inhabiting believers; Ephesians speaks of being filled with a certain goal in mind. Thus "all the fullness of God" is that end point toward which knowledge of Christ's love should fill believers. The notion of being filled also indicates that this is an ongoing process. It is a process that awaits its final eschatological completion, but it is also a filling that happens now in the lives of believers. Thus this final clause sets the stage for the emphasis on action and formation in chapters 4–6.

The final end is to be filled with that which fills God. Given the current context, it is precisely God's love that is in view. Thus the end of the Christian life is to be filled up with God's love, that which is the very essence of God, that which characterizes the relations of the Triune persons, that which will make us one with God (cf. Best, *Ephesians* 348).

[20–21] These intercessions result in a doxology that concludes Eph 3. The first part of the doxology identifies God in terms directly relevant to the petitions Paul has just offered on behalf of the Ephesians. Verse 20 confirms the two elements crucial to the appropriate fulfillment of Paul's petitions. God is both sufficiently powerful to bring these things about and disposed to grant this petition because of God's care for us. The verse goes further to indicate that God is disposed to grant even more than humans can ask or think.

Having identified God in this way, v. 21 goes on to ascribe glory to God. Of course, humans do not actually increase the amount of God's glory. God is the "Father of glory" (1:17), the one who already has a wealth of glory (3:16). Instead, humans properly reflect back the radiance that God's goodness and power generate. The ascription of glory here is offered as the proper human response to the God who grants the Ephesians (and all believers) comprehension of the love of Christ, filling them with the fullness that fills God.

The closing part of this doxology locates the ascription of glory in the church and in Christ. Already in Ephesians we have learned that the church is Christ's body, "the fullness of the one who is filled in every way" (1:23); the church is God's dwelling place in the Spirit; and Christ is both its head and cornerstone (1:22; 2:20–22). We will also read that Christ is the head of the church (4:15) and her bridegroom (5:23). Throughout Ephesians, Christ and the church are closely linked through a variety of images. It is hardly surprising, then, that both the church and Christ are listed together here. It also reminds us that "the glory that is seen in the Church is not its own glory but derives from Christ" (Best, *Ephesians* 351).

Finally, the use of "in all generations" seems superfluous when followed by "forever and ever." Most commentators simply ascribe this to the pleonastic style typical of Ephesians and caution against drawing too much significance from this. The use of "Amen" at the end of doxologies is found in Matt 6:13 KJV; Rom 1:25; 9:5; 11:36; 15:33; 16:27. It carries the sense of "truly" or "yes."

In this section Paul wraps up his account of the gift that God has revealed and given to him: his gospel. He has subsequently reordered his life in the light of that gift. As chapter 3 ends, Paul prays that the Ephesians, too, may be granted their particular measure of this gift. At its core, what has been revealed to Paul as God's plan for the ages in 3:1–13 is precisely the comprehension of the immeasurable bounds of Christ's love. Paul's reception of God's revelation required him to reorder his life in a decisive way. If God grants Paul's request for the Ephesians (a gift Paul assumes God has already and will continue to give), the Ephesians will need to reorder their lives in particular ways. It is to this discussion that Paul turns in Ephesians 4.

Ephesians 4:1–16
Christian Unity and a Life Worthy
of God's Call

Chapter 4 begins a distinct section in Ephesians. It is quite common to treat chapters 1–3 as doctrinal and chapters 4–6 as moral instruction (paraenesis). This distinction is sometimes characterized as the difference between indicative (chs. 1–3) and imperative (chs. 4–6). As will be clear, this distinction is not absolute. There are several significant passages in Eph 4–6 (e.g., 4:4–6, 21–22) with doctrinal material, and several imperative demands are laid on the Ephesians in chapters 1–3 (e.g., 2:10–11; 3:13). In addition, as noted below, the connections between Eph 3 and 4 are much closer than many commentators grant. There are far more continuities between chapters 3 and 4 than differences. Nevertheless, this distinction can serve as a useful rule of thumb to see one of the central formal divisions in Ephesians.

At various points in time, scholars have treated what is clearly a formal distinction as a conceptual and theological distinction that needed to be explained. At a general level this distinction generates questions about how Paul relates doctrine and ethics.[1] These questions take on a special urgency if one holds a particular theology of grace that vigilantly tries to rule out any apparent admonitions to do particular works in order to "earn" one's salvation. Alternatively, if one takes Ephesians to have a fully or nearly fully realized eschatology, then moral admonition and exhortation seem superfluous.

Without determining this question for all Pauline texts, it seems fairly clear that in Ephesians the early parts of the epistle function to construct and to help the Ephesians to construct a particular identity as believers. Among other things, this requires an understanding of the end toward which God is moving all things (e.g., 1:10, 18–23); it requires an account of God's action in Christ as it relates to both the Ephesians and the cosmos (1:4–14); it requires an account of the Ephesians' alienation from God and how God works to overcome that alienation (2:1–10); and it calls the Ephesians to learn to think of themselves as Gentiles, in a particular relationship to Israel both before and after Christ (2:11–22; 3:1–13). In this light, having offered an account of the Ephesians' identity in Christ, it is certainly logical to assume that identity entails actions.

---

1. Jeal (ch. 1) surveys these matters quite well.

It is unproblematic to assume that having identified an object as a watch, one naturally expects that watch to perform certain tasks (such as keeping time); likewise, it is equally unproblematic to assume that having identified the Ephesians as the saints and faithful ones in Christ Jesus (1:1), Paul goes on to explicate the actions appropriate to that identity. Of course, both the articulation of the Ephesians' identity in Christ and the actions appropriate to that identity are much more complex and contested matters than the identity and actions of a watch. The point is that there is no inherent problem in assuming that a specific identity entails certain actions.

Formally, 4:1–16 breaks into two sections. Verses 1–6 begin the exhortation and focus on unity. Verses 7–16 build on this, asserting that this unity is maintained and enhanced by the exercise of diverse gifts. This section of the epistle is introduced by means of an almost formulaic phrase, "I exhort you therefore . . ." Very similar language also appears in Rom 12:1 and 1 Thess 4:1 to introduce paraenetic sections of the letters.[2] As usual, commentators often point to either similarities or differences between Ephesians and the other Paulines with authorship issues in mind. If authorship were not at stake here, I suspect most would not be bothered by any stylistic differences or variations between these epistles.

It is clear that in Eph 4 Paul begins moving in a new direction. Yet it is also important to identify some lines of continuity between chapter 3 and chapter 4. For example, chapter 4 begins with Paul, "a prisoner in the Lord," urging the Ephesians to "walk in a manner worthy of your calling." This calling is a call to unity, but is also tied to the diverse gifts God has given the church for the proper conduct of its life and mission. In chapter 3 Paul, "the prisoner of Christ," gives an account of the gracious gift that God has given him to preach to the Gentiles and how he has conducted himself in the light of that gift. Hence, while some scholars note that in Ephesians Paul uses the Greek word *charis* to refer to these gifts rather than *charismata*, as in Rom 12 and 1 Cor 12, they neglect to point out that it is precisely the word *charis* that Paul uses in Eph 3:2, 7 to speak of God's gift. Thus, in both chapters 3 and 4, Paul is concerned to discuss God's gracious call to him and to other believers. Whether one uses the language of revelation, as in chapter 3, or calling, as in chapter 4, it is clear that the initiative behind both lies with God. The revelation or the call comes from outside believers; it is not generated by believers. Both revelation and call, however, require particular forms of life and action from believers. Large portions of chapters 3 and 4 are devoted to articulating more precisely the nature and shape of those forms of life and action. Seen in this light, the transition

2. See Rom 15:30; 16:17; 1 Thess 4:1, 10; 5:14; 1 Cor 1:10; 4:16; 16:16; 2 Cor 2:8; 6:1; 10:1. See also Bjerkelund 34–74, 140, 170, 189; and Lincoln's corrective comments in *Ephesians* 227.

between chapters 3 and 4 is not the transition from doctrine to ethics. Rather, it is the transition from Paul's reflection on his own calling and how he views the world and conducts himself in the light of that call—to Paul's reflection on God's call to the Ephesians and how they should see the world and conduct themselves in the light of that call. Thus, much in chapter 4 depends on the work Paul does in 3:1–13 to establish himself as a faithful interpreter of the grace of God, so that what he has done in respect to his own life, he can now offer to the Ephesians with respect to their lives.

Because this section of Ephesians begins to offer concrete moral prescriptions, it is tempting to infer from Paul's particular admonitions that he is addressing distinct flaws in the life of the Ephesian congregation. John Barclay has nicely identified this scholarly practice as "mirror-reading." There are some cases when such inferential moves can be justified, but they are few and far between. For the most part, we should avoid the assumption that Paul's stress on unity, as in 4:1–6, indicates that there was a particular fractiousness in the Ephesian church.

4:1 I, a prisoner in the Lord, exhort[a] you, therefore, to walk in a manner worthy of the calling with which you have indeed been called, 2 with all[b] humility and gentleness, with patience, bearing with one another in love, 3 zealous[c] to maintain the unity of the Spirit in the bond of peace. 4 There is one body and one Spirit, just as you have been called in one hope of your calling, 5 one Lord, one faith, one baptism, 6 one God and Father of all, who is over all and through all and in all.

7 But[d] to each of us he gave grace according to the measure of the gift of Christ. 8 Therefore, it[e] says, "When he ascended on high, he captured the captives, and he gave gifts to humans." 9 What is the meaning[f] of "he ascended" except that he also descended[g] to the lower parts[h] of the earth? 10 The one who descended is indeed the one who also ascended high above all the heavens so that he might fill all things. 11 It was he who gave apostles, prophets, evangelists, and pastors and teachers, 12 for bringing the saints to completion, for the work of service, and for the building up of the body of Christ, 13 until we all come to the unity of the faith and knowledge of the Son of God, to the complete person,[i] the measure of the stature of the fullness of Christ. 14 We must no longer be like children, being tossed about by the waves, carried this way and that way by every wind of doctrine, by human cunning, by trickery and erroneous scheming. 15 Rather, speaking the truth[j] in love, we must grow up together in all things into him who is the head, into Christ, 16 from whom the entire body is joined and knit together[k] by every supporting connection[l] according to the activity appropriate to each part.

a. The verb *parakalō* carries a variety of meanings. It can be used to offer consolation (e.g., Matt 2:18; 2 Cor 1:4; Eph 6:22) or to request aid (e.g., Matt 8:5; 2 Cor 9:5). Here, however, it is clearly used to mean "exhort."

b. The use of "all" here is parallel to that in 6:18 ("in all perseverance and petition"). It is used here to denote the highest degree (Hoehner 507).

c. Often the Greek verb *spoudazō* means "to make haste," or "be eager." In passages such as Gal 2:10; 1 Thess 2:17; 2 Tim 2:15; Heb 4:11; 2 Pet 1:10, 15; 3:14 and here in Eph 4:3, the verb connotes extreme effort, diligence, or zeal rather than speed.

d. The term "but" here is probably the appropriate way to translate the Greek conjunction *de*. It should not be taken to introduce too sharp a contrast between the preceding discussion of unity and the discussion of diverse gifts that follows (Best, *Ephesians* 75).

e. The antecedent of "it" (or possibly "he") in this verse is unclear. Paul often uses the verb "to speak" to introduce a scriptural quotation. Thus it is best to take it as a reference to Scripture as in "Scripture says" (cf. Rom 4:3; 9:17; 10:11). Alternatively, it could refer to God (cf. Rom 9:14–15; 2 Cor 6:16) or David (cf. Rom 4:6).

f. A strictly literal translation of the Greek here might read something like "Now what is the 'he ascended'?" The point of the question is to raise the issue concerning the meaning or implication of "he ascended" (Hoehner 530–31).

g. Some MSS add the word "first" after "descended." If this is taken to be original, it decisively shapes the interpretation of the text. There is, however, ample evidence for treating the word as a later addition.[3]

h. Many MSS omit the Greek word *merē*, "parts." Harris (43–46) gives a convincing case for taking it as original. How one interprets the phrase "lower parts of the earth," however, depends on several factors noted below.

i. The Greek here could be translated "the mature man [*andra*]." It is a less generic reference than the new person in 2:15.

j. Although it may be tempting to translate the Greek verb *alētheuein* here as something like "speaking and doing the truth," there is a preponderance of LXX passages using this verb to mean speaking the truth (Lincoln, *Ephesians* 259).

k. The Greek of this verse is somewhat obscure. The two participles *synarmologoumenon* (also in the mixed metaphors of 2:21) and *symbibazomenon* (see the close parallel usage in Col 2:19) work to present a picture of constructed and maintained unity. Hence they are translated "joined and knit together."

l. The Greek phrase *haphēs tēs epichorēgias* describes that which joins and knits together the body. It is unclear, however, what particular means of connection or contact is meant here. Hoehner (570) translates the phrase "through every supporting connection." Lincoln (*Ephesians* 262) translates the phrase "every ligament which gives supply." The NRSV uses "every ligament with which it is equipped." The phrase is probably a medico-scientific term. This makes "ligament" perhaps a more precise translation of *haphē*. Alternatively, ligaments do not supply the body with anything. Hoehner's translation, while not conveying the scientific character of the language, does convey the overall sense of elements that connect and give life to a body.

---

3. Harris (32–40) gives a thorough evaluation of the manuscript evidence; cf. Metzger 536.

[1–6] Paul begins by reminding the Ephesians that he is a prisoner for Christ's sake. This is not to evoke pity from the Ephesians. It is rather a bold way to begin an authoritative exhortation. Prisoners are not normally in a position to make demands. Within the logic of the gospel, however, Paul's authority is sharpened because of his tribulations on behalf of Christ.

Paul's exhortation to the Ephesians is that they walk in a manner worthy of their calling. The use of the term "to walk" to characterize a way of life already appeared in 2:2, to refer to the Ephesians' moribund way of life outside of Christ. In 2:10 it is used to speak of the manner of life that God has prepared for believers, further connecting chapters 1–3 and 4–6. Here in chapter 4 the initial admonition to the Ephesians is to "walk in a manner worthy of the calling with which you have been called." The standard to which the Ephesians' common life should conform is the "calling with which they have been called." This calling is first mentioned in 1:18, but it is really in 2:1–10 and 11–22 where the shape of this calling is developed. Recall that in chapter 2 the Ephesians learn of their deathly state in God's purview and outside of Christ, yet also of how God has graciously delivered them from death into life in Christ so that they may walk in the good works that God has prepared for them. Hence, Paul is not setting some new standard for them. Rather, he is reminding them of what God has already done on their behalf. The use of the relative clause "with which you have been called" helps further refine the nature of the Ephesians' calling. This is not a call they have generated themselves. Rather, God has initiated the call. Moreover, we should not infer from this admonition that the Ephesians are inclined to walk in any other way.[4]

The idea of walking worthily (cf. Phil 1:27; 1 Thess 2:12) always entails acts of judgment. Although Paul will give more direct and concrete prescriptions to the Ephesians in the following verses and chapters, the task of walking worthily always entails the act of seeing the fit between one's actions or possible actions and some set standard. To do this, the Ephesians, and all other believers, will need to develop a set of habits and dispositions. Cultivating such habits and dispositions will enable the Ephesians to perceive themselves, their world, and the standard to which they aspire, thus to walk worthily in a manner that will lead them to recognize some actions as fitting or conforming to the standard and others as not conforming. Some of the habits and dispositions the Ephesians will need to cultivate in order to walk worthily are mentioned in the next verse.

In v. 2 Paul introduces two sets of characteristics needed to walk worthily. Each is introduced with the preposition *meta* (with). First, Paul notes

---

4. Hoehner (510) is merely the most recent commentator to infer from the discussion in 4:1–2 that "there was undoubtedly some tension between Jewish and Gentile believers even though they were now united into one body." In the absence of further evidence, this is precisely the sort of "mirror-reading" that one should avoid.

that walking worthily must be done "with all humility and gentleness." The Ephesians' pagan neighbors would not have considered "humility" a virtue. Epictetus (*Diatr.* 1.9.10; 3.24.56) lists it as a characteristic to avoid. For pagans, the word connoted a vile servility (see Josephus, *J.W.* 4.9.2). In the NT, when humility is commended as a virtue, it entails rightly recognizing one's status before God. Concomitantly, this will also lead one to situate oneself rightly relative to others. For example, in Acts 20:19 Paul indicates to the Ephesian elders that he has served the Lord with "humility" throughout Asia. In Col 2:18, 23 "humility" is also used to refer to a negative trait. Whatever practices might be in view in Colossians, it is clear that this sort of "humility" refers to badly or wrongly situating oneself relative to God. Paul contrasts this with the appropriate humility that he urges the Colossians to "put on" in 3:12. In Phil 2:3 "humility" is contrasted with seeking selfish advantages. Rather, humility lies in considering others better than oneself and seeking their interests rather than one's own. As Phil 2:6–8 goes on to declare, this is precisely the disposition displayed by Christ.[5] In Philippians, moreover, Paul treats humility as an essential virtue in maintaining the unity of the congregation (cf. 2:1–4). This is also a matter of some importance in this part of Ephesians.

In the NT "gentleness" is one of the fruits of the Spirit (Gal 5:23). Paul asks the Corinthians if they want him to come with a stick to beat them or with a "spirit of gentleness" (1 Cor 4:21). The context of 1 Cor 4 makes it clear that a spirit of gentleness is compatible with displays of God's power and the strength to offer correction. Indeed, this would also fit Jesus, who is described in Matt 11:29 as "gentle and humble in heart"; and Moses, who is described in the LXX of Num 12:3 as "exceedingly gentle," yet able to display God's power and to take corrective action against the Israelites.

A second use of the preposition *meta* (with) introduces another disposition needed to walk worthily. This is patience. Again, Gal 5:22 identifies patience as one of the fruits of the Spirit. In the OT this term is often used to describe God's practice of enduring human sinfulness with mercy (Exod 34:6; Num 14:18; LXX: Pss 85:15; 102:8; 144:8 [Eng.: 86:15; 103:8; 145:8]). In these cases the word is often combined with "mercy" and "compassion" as descriptions of God's character. In 1 Cor 13:4 Paul says that patience is one of the characteristics of *agapē*. In 1 Thess 5:14 and 2 Tim 4:2 it is a prerequisite for the common life of the church.

In v. 2 Paul further describes patience in terms of "bearing with one another in love."[6] Often the idea of bearing with someone means enduring their failures.

---

5. Hoehner (506) rightly characterizes humility as being cognizant of who one is "in God's program" (citing John 3:30 and Rom 12:3).

6. After using three singular nouns (in 4:2) to describe the dispositions needed to walk worthily, here Paul shifts to a participial phrase ("bearing with one another in love") that draws its grammati-

Jesus asks regarding those seeking a sign from him, "How long shall I bear with you?" (Matt 17:17 ASV par.). Paul uses it in 2 Cor 11:1, 4, 19, 20 in a similar way. The term is also employed to speak of Job's endurance (Job 6:11, 26 LXX). With the same word Paul speaks of enduring persecution in 1 Cor 4:12 and 2 Thess 1:4. All of these uses can give the impression of passive, grudging, almost fatalistic endurance. Here, however, Paul tells the Ephesians to bear one another *in love*. This can hardly be passive or fatalistic. Rather, it must entail both action and hope.

The call to forebear one another in love assumes several significant things about the life Christians share with each other. First, the notion of forbearance (as in all the examples above) presumes failure. Thus, for Christians to bear one another in love recognizes that Christians will sin against each other and fail one another from time to time. Such failures must be borne in love. This cannot mean either a grudging acceptance of sin and failure or a willed indifference to one another's sin and failure (Thomas Aq. 152). Love cannot abide either of these ways of glossing the truth. Hence, the call to bear with one another in love is implicitly a call to practice truthful confession; asking for and receiving forgiveness in the same manner in which God forgives; and creative and transformative acts of repentance.

Further, the first three of the dispositions listed in vv. 1–2 are relational in that they concern how one understands and lives with oneself and others in God. One cannot display these dispositions in the absence of others. The addition of "one another" to the command to forebear makes it clear that all of these dispositions are directed not simply to isolated individuals within the congregation. They are dispositions constitutive of the common life of a congregation walking worthily of the calling with which they have been called. It should be clear now, if it was not before, that Paul is not so much interested in personal piety here as in the common life of Christian communities.

Finally, the idea that believers are to bear with one another in love recognizes that believers in Ephesus (as well as believers today) were not all in the same place on the path to ever deeper friendship with God and each other.[7] The body of Christ is composed of people who have varying measures of maturity in their faith, varying experiences of God's love, and differing temperaments in worship. Within the single body of Christ, there are diverse members. Homogeneity is not and should not be one of the marks of Christ's body. The body of Christ is appropriately diverse and yet also harmonious in

---

cal form from the subject of the infinitive " to walk," that is, you, the Ephesians. Although there is a grammatical parallel between this participial phrase and the one following in v. 3, it seems clear that "bearing with one another in love" should be understood either as one of four dispositions needed for walking worthily (closer to Best, *Ephesians* 364) or as a further specification of "patience" (Lincoln, *Ephesians* 236). The differences here seem inconsequential.

7. Origen (in Heine 165) implicitly recognizes this in his comments on the verse.

its composition. Thus, bearing with one another in love does not mean that all things are acceptable in all times and places. It does, however, mean that within this diverse body, believers need to be able to bump up against very different sorts of people, equally committed to the faith, whose differences are to be borne in love.

In this light, it is not that surprising that in v. 3 Paul admonishes the Ephesians to do all they can to "maintain the unity of the Spirit in the bond of peace."[8] It appears that the clear emphasis on the "one Spirit" in v. 4 indicates that the Spirit in v. 3 is also the Holy Spirit and not the spirit of the Ephesian congregation (Best, *Ephesians* 365; Hoehner 512; Lincoln, *Ephesians* 237). The use of the verb "maintain" reminds the Ephesians and contemporary Christians that the unity of the Spirit is already given, not created by humans. That is, unity is a gift given by the Spirit already and not some subsequent achievement of believers. Alternatively, however, this admonition might imply that believers could somehow break the unity of the Spirit. If unity is given by the Spirit and premised on the unity of the Godhead (cf. vv. 4–6), then God might withdraw the unity of the Spirit in judgment against the church. In some sense humans might damage or deform this unity, but they cannot destroy it.

At the same time, the admonition to maintain the unity of the Spirit "in the bond of peace" seems to imply that the unity given by the Spirit must be demonstrated visibly.[9] The term translated here as "bond" is used to refer to various types of fasteners. It also has a wide metaphorical usage covering the unity of a citizenry that keeps a state together (Plato, *Resp.* 7.5.520a), the bond between children and parents (Aristotle, *Eth. Nic.* 9.12.7), and "the bonds of injustice" (Isa 58:6, 9). In each of these cases the metaphorical sense of "bond" indicates that which holds individuals together (for better or worse). In Ephesians, then, peace is that which binds believers together as the visible manifestation of the Spirit's unity.[10] The peace that Paul speaks of here is the peace that comes from lives properly related to God, to creation, and to each other.

This admonition raises serious questions for contemporary Christians within divided churches. First, in the face of the Spirit's already-delivered gift of unity, Christian division simply is a contradiction of the Spirit's unity (Root 106–7). Division does not so much destroy unity as mock unity, thereby bringing the name of the Lord into disrepute among nonbelievers (cf. Ezek 36:20–22; Rom 2:24). Church division must count as one of the primary examples of "grieving

8. Stylistically, this clause is parallel to the preceding one in that each begins with a participle and concludes with a prepositional phrase using *en* (Lincoln, *Ephesians* 237). We should not infer from this that the two clauses are simply appositional.

9. Origen (in Heine 167) declares, "The unity of the Spirit is preserved when love binds those together who are united in the Spirit and brings them together into the 'one body' of Christ."

10. Both Best (*Ephesians* 365) and Hoehner (513) take the phrase this way, minimizing the similarities with Col 3:14.

the Spirit" (cf. Eph 4:30). Christian division must also be seen as God's judgment on believers' desire to live separated lives. That is, Christian division is one of those examples of God's judgment where God gives people precisely what they ask for (cf. 1 Sam 8). Finally, Paul's admonition to be zealous to maintain the unity of the Spirit reminds believers that, for the most part, they are indifferent to the divisions within Christ's body. Believers in the United States have largely blunted the sting of division. As Ephraim Radner (ch. 4) declares, in a divided church the Eucharist should taste bitter in our mouths. All too often this is not the case.

Verses 4–6 are a dense and concise explication of the bases for the dispositions and the unity advocated in 4:1–3. These verses are not directly admonitions in themselves. Rather, they are part of the rationale for those admonitions. These verses also provide the bases from which Paul will discuss the diversity of gifts within the life of the congregation.

The shift in style leads some scholars to argue that Paul is drawing on (or quoting from) an early Christian hymn (Barth 429), a creed or confession (Wengst 141), or liturgical material (Schnackenburg 160–61), or from parts of various different creedal or liturgical material (Lincoln, *Ephesians* 228–29). This may or may not be the case. Further, without a great deal more information, it is not clear how any of these speculations should shape the way one should read the text as it now stands.

The assertion that there is one body has already appeared in 2:16. There it reflects the idea that in the body of Christ, Jew and Gentile have been reconciled to God and to each other. The two groups are made into one. Thus 2:16 focuses on the act of making the two into one. Here in 4:4 the focus is on the singularity of the body. The singularity of the Spirit mentioned in the next clause is what one would expect in light of the emphasis on the unity of the Spirit in v. 3. The subsequent clause, "just as you have been called in one hope of your calling," has already appeared as part of Paul's prayer for the Ephesians in 1:18. There Paul prays that the Spirit of wisdom will reveal to the Ephesians the hope of God's calling. That calling is directly related to God's choosing of believers to participate in the drama of redemption so that believers would be brought to their proper end of standing holy and blameless before God (1:4). This is the substance of Christian hope. Because that drama has yet to be completed, because all things have yet to come under Christ's lordship, hope also is the appropriate disposition of the faithful. It is hope that God's call will ultimately be consummated. The basis of this hope is not the inner emotions of believers; rather, it rests on the faithfulness of God to bring the good work that God started in believers to completion on the day of Christ (Phil 1:6). Here in Eph 4:4 Paul emphasizes the singularity of that hope. Presumably those sharing a common hope will act in concert as together they are drawn toward their ultimate end in God (Thomas Aq. 154). A single hope will thus help maintain the bond of peace.

Verse 5 continues in this vein by asserting that there is one Lord, one faith, and one baptism. Baptism here presumes the confession of faith that Jesus is Lord (cf. Acts 8:16; 19:5; Rom 10:9). Indeed, baptism is the act in which believers are joined with Christ in his death and resurrection (Rom 6:1–11). Moreover, as Gal 3:27–28 indicates, a common baptism is capable of breaking down divisive barriers between Jew and Greek, slave and free, men and women (cf. also 1 Cor 12:12). Thus the one baptism serves to unite believers with their Lord and to found their unity with each other.[11]

In this light, it is likely that the mention of one faith has some connection to the baptismal confession "Jesus is Lord." Earlier Paul had already mentioned the Ephesians' "faith in the Lord Jesus Christ" (1:15). It is most likely that the faith mentioned here in 4:5 is primarily a reference to the content of a profession of faith (e.g., Rom 10:9) rather than a common subjective attitude of trust (with Lincoln, *Ephesians* 241; Best, *Ephesians* 369; against Hoehner 516; Muddiman 184). Although one should be careful of drawing too sharp a distinction between an attitude of belief and the subject matter of that belief, in this particular instance the singularity of faith could really only be manifested in the content of a common confession.

This verse begins with the assertion that there is one Lord. The term "Lord" is a reference to Christ (cf. 1:15; 1 Cor 12:3; Rom 10:9). Jesus is shown to be Lord most decisively in his resurrection and exaltation (1 Cor 8:6; Phil 2:9–11). The Greek word translated here and throughout the NT as "Lord" is *kyrios*. This is the word used in the LXX to translate the Hebrew four-letter name for God: YHWH. It appears that the very earliest Jewish Christians applied this title to Christ, boldly drawing Christ into the identity of the one God of Israel.

In 4:5–6 it is particularly striking that Paul asserts that there is only one Lord and that there is one God and Father of all. In just a few words Paul lays out the set of assertions that provide the conceptual tensions driving later Trinitarian reflection. The God of Israel, the God and Father of all, is one. Paul's assertion about the one Lord includes Jesus within the identity of the God of Israel, apparently without compromising God's singularity. The precise ways of parsing this Trinitarian logic take some time to develop. The pieces, however, are already laid out in the NT and very succinctly so in these verses.

In vv. 3–4 we are presented with the singularity of the Spirit. In v. 5 we learn that there is one Lord, Christ. This Trinitarian reflection is completed in v. 6 with the assertion that there is one God and Father of all. This verse most clearly mirrors 1 Cor 8:6. Lincoln (*Ephesians* 240) claims that particular verse is itself a Christian modification of the Shema of Deut 6:4. More directly, however, this claim picks up images from 3:14–15. In chapter 3 the idea that God is the Father from whom every group is named works to assert God's ultimate supremacy.

---

11. Paul makes the same sorts of claims about the Lord's Supper in 1 Cor 11.

Here the coloring is different. Paul looks to the singularity of God as a way of founding the unity of believers that he advocates in vv. 1–3.

The prepositional phrases "over all and through all and in all" have a built-in ambiguity. The Greek word translated here as "all" can either be masculine, referring to all believers (Schnackenburg 167; Hoehner 521), or neuter, refer-ring to all things (Best, *Ephesians* 371; Lincoln, *Ephesians* 241). If this verse comes from a creed or liturgy, it may have one meaning in that context and another meaning here. Within the current context, several considerations may tip the balance here in favor of a masculine reading of "all." First, when Paul speaks of God as Father, he means the Father of believers (Rom 8:15; Gal 4:6; Col 1:2; 2 Thess 2:16; Phlm 3) or the Father of our Lord Jesus Christ (Rom 15:6; 2 Cor 1:3; 11:31; Eph 1:3; Col 1:3). He never refers to God as the Father of creation. Second, the context of 4:1–6 is about the unity of individuals within the Ephesian church. Moreover, the transition to 4:7 begins by speaking of individuals. Hence, there is a consistent focus on believers in these verses.

Alternatively, 3:14–15 uses the term "Father" to speak more broadly than just believing individuals.[12] Further, the term "all" is used with cosmic connotations in 1:10, 21–23; 3:9. In each of these cases, however, the term is clearly neuter.

Perhaps one should simply treat this as a fruitful ambiguity. Taken as a reference to all things, the verse asserts that amid the manifest diversity of all things, they are all united in their common origin and dependence upon the one God. Taken as a reference to believers, the image conveys both the dependence of all believers on God (over all) and the intimacy between God and believers (through all and in all). It concludes the focus on unity of 4:1–6 and leads into the focus on diverse gifts in 4:7–16.

Two particular issues emerge from this section. First, although it is his-torically accurate to distance Paul (or even later Pauline disciples) from the Trinitarian debates of the third and fourth centuries, it is also striking that he grounds this discussion of the unity of the church in such Trinitarian terms. As anticipated in earlier verses of Ephesians, Paul in 4:3–6 draws Father, Son, and Spirit together in ways designed to underwrite the unity of the church. This call to unity will only have force to the extent that Paul (and then the Ephesians) imagine Father, Son, and Spirit to be united. Yes, Paul does not articulate the nature of this unity in the manner of later conciliar writings. His argument here, however, requires a robust understanding of the unity of Father, Son, and Spirit if it is to provide the basis for the type of Christian unity Paul desires.

Second, Christian unity is the gift of the Spirit and not an achievement of the church. Nevertheless, it becomes clear that unity is not a homogenizing process

---

12. In 3:15 God is mentioned as the one from whom every *patria* is named. This might pre-sume that God is Father (*patēr*) of all *patria*. Even in this case, God is not thought of as the Father of all things.

in which believers all learn to march in lockstep with each other. Rather, it depends on the character of relationships between persons. Most significantly, these relationships depend on bearing one another in love, which results in the bond of peace.

[7–10] This is a complex and intriguing passage on a variety of levels. These verses mark a shift from the discussion of unity to the gifts given to the church for the preservation and maintenance of unity. Moreover, Paul shifts from an emphasis on "one" in 4:4–6, to "each of us" in v. 7, and then to specific groups in v. 11. Explaining this as a shift from unity to diversity, however, misses certain important elements in the discussion. For example, the shift to "each of us" indicates a grace that has been given to all believers. In some ways this recalls the specific "grace" God gave Paul to proclaim the gospel, mentioned in 3:7. As in chapter 3, the nature of this grace requires some explication and interpretation. It appears that the grace given "to each of us" is the grace needed to "maintain the unity of the Spirit in the bond of peace" (4:3). This rightly reminds believers that unity is God's gracious gift to the church and not their own achievement. As 4:11–16 indicate, although the grace of unity is given to all, specific people have been given particular gifts that will help build up the body of Christ. Although these gifts seems to take individual capacities and proclivities into account, they are not earned by people based on their talents or activities. They are gifts from Christ, the gift-giver (cf. Best, *Ephesians* 375). More will be said about the relationship between grace, gifts, and unity in the course of discussing 4:11–16.

Verse 7 concludes with the notion that Christ has apportioned grace "to each of us," in a distinctive way, "according to the measure of the gift of Christ." Although this idea may irritate modern egalitarian sensibilities, Paul introduces the notion of individual believers having a specific measure of faith apportioned to them by God in Rom 12:3. The idea in both Romans and Ephesians is not that God is stingy or that there is a fixed supply of either faith or grace that needs to be rationed. Rather, the point in each of these verses is to recognize that God's gifts to believers are appropriately fitted to our individual capacities and proclivities (Origen, in Heine 171). Rather than thinking of grace as a supply (either limited or unlimited) of undifferentiated cloth, this verse encourages us to think of God's gift of grace as a precisely tailored suit that fits each of us perfectly.

As a further way of explicating the nature of Christ's gift of grace, v. 8 moves to present a rough quotation from Ps 68:18 (67:19 LXX) along with a set of interpretive comments in 4:9–10. These verses pose a number of textual puzzles as well as several interpretive possibilities. The first puzzle is related to the text that Paul cites. The LXX of Ps 67:19 can be translated this way: "You ascended on high; you captured the captives; you received gifts from humanity" (cf. NETS). The LXX sticks closely to the MT. Paul's citation is different from the LXX in several respects. Instead of the finite verb "you ascended," Paul uses a participle translated as "When he ascended."[13] Instead of the second-person singular verbs "you captured" and "you received," Paul uses the third-person singular. Instead of the verb "received," Paul uses "gave."

Although it does not fully resolve this puzzle, it is worth noting that the Targum on this passage reads as follows: "You ascended to the firmament, Prophet Moses; you took captive captivity, you learned the words of the Torah, you gave them as gifts to the sons of men" (Harris 65). The Targum shows that at least some Jews interpreted this psalm in terms of Moses' reception of the law from God. Moses returned with those words and offered them as gifts to the Israelites.[14] In this light, there seem to be some parallels here to Paul's christological interpretation of this psalm. Scholars have diligently tried to establish some sort of direct continuity between Eph 4:8 and this Targum or other rabbinic traditions. Given the highly contested dating of so much of this material, it is unlikely that one could convincingly argue that Paul was directly dependent on it. It is as likely, if not more likely, that some of this material was influenced by Paul as the other way around. We can, however, see that Paul's pattern of reading and interpreting Ps 68 is similar to the ways that at least some other Jews interpreted the Psalm. Similarly, in both texts there is no clear and distinct line between quotation and explication. They are seamlessly woven together. So, although one cannot locate a line of textual dependence from the Targum or some other text to Eph 4:8, one can say that Paul's treatment of this text is less idiosyncratic than one might think at first.

The second set of puzzles concerns the imagery of the passage and how Paul applies it in Ephesians. The notion of "capturing captives" has distinct military overtones. In the light of Ps 68, the image here is of a conqueror, returning after a victory over a foe. The victor is leading back prisoners. In the case of the psalm as it stands in the OT, Yahweh, the conqueror, not only brings back prisoners; Yahweh also receives spoil or tribute from the vanquished. Alternatively, Paul's treatment of the imagery is thoroughly christological. According to the interpretation Paul offers in Eph 4:8, Christ can either be leading his enemies, meaning Satan and Satan's minions, captive (Chrysostom, *Hom. Eph.* 11); or Christ can be leading back those who had been captivated by Satan and are now liberated (Origen and Jerome, in Heine 172). Thomas Aquinas (159) in particular reads this phrase in the light of Isa 49:24–25: "Can the prey be taken from the mighty, or the captives of a tyrant be rescued? But thus says the LORD: Even the captives of the mighty shall be taken, and the prey of the tyrant be rescued." In addition, Paul's citation shifts the action from receiving gifts to

---

13. The Vaticanus (B) text of the LXX indicates that such a change had already occurred by the fourth century.

14. See Harris (ch. 3) for a full discussion of various rabbinic textual traditions associating Moses with Ps 68.

giving gifts. In this way, receiving spoil is transformed into the distribution of plunder. One could expect either outcome after a great victory.

Although it is rather clear that Paul is offering a christological interpretation of Ps 68 (67 LXX), it is not precisely clear how that interpretation should be unpacked. Verses 9–10 are devoted to such an explication. Verse 9 raises the question What does "he ascended" mean except that he also descended to the depths of the earth? This links descent and ascent in some particular way. It is not clear, however, which comes first: descent or ascent? The conjunction "and/also" (*kai*) simply does not provide a clear way of adjudicating this. The psalm itself presumes descent and then ascent. The Mosaic interpretation of the Targum presumes ascent and then descent.

Verse 10 asserts that the one who descended is the same one who ascended to the highest heights, filling all things. This seems to provide a brief recapitulation of the assertions about Christ's supremacy and dominion over all things in 1:19–23.

Given these considerations, there are three basic ways Christians have interpreted this text. A variety of interpreters ranging from Chrysostom to James D. G. Dunn interpret this passage as a reference to Christ's descent into hell. Following Ps 68's logic of descent preceding ascent, this passage would then stand with 1 Pet 3:18–21 as one of the two NT witnesses to Christ's descent into hell during the period between crucifixion and resurrection.[15] In terms of addressing the details of this passage, this interpretation leaves several problems unresolved. For example, in the original psalm, descent precedes ascent; but in the best manuscripts of Eph 4:8, ascent appears to precede descent. Further, it is not clear how Christ's descent to hell would be tied to the giving of gifts to humans. Moreover, in the context of Ephesians, it is not clear what place a reference to Christ's descent into hell has in the argument. The "powers" mentioned in 2:2 are not located beneath the earth. Thus, although the assertion that Christ descended into hell is part of the standard Christian confession of faith, it is not likely that such an event is in view here.

The second interpretive option treats Paul's christological interpretation of Ps 68 as a reference to the incarnation. This verse takes Christ's descent to the earth as a reference to the incarnation, which ultimately leads to Christ's ascent after the resurrection, where he is above all the heavens and fills all things (vv. 9–10). In this respect the interpretation of Ps 68 follows the general pattern of Phil 2:6–11: The Son of God willingly humbles himself and takes on flesh. He is obedient to the Father, even to the extent of dying on the cross. Therefore, the Son is exalted (Hoehner 531–33; Thomas Aq. 160–62). This interpretation

---

15. Donelson, *I & II Peter and Jude* 112 gives reasons for taking 1 Pet 3:19 as a reference to Jesus' proclamation to those rebellious spirits first mentioned in Gen 6:1–6 and later imprisoned (cf. *Jub.* 7.21; 10.1–9; *1 En.* 6–16; 13.6; 15.4–7; 18.12–19.2).

keeps to the original psalm's ordering of descent followed by ascent, which does not appear to be the case in Ephesians. Further, although this seems to offer a perfectly acceptable christological interpretation of Ps 68:18, it is less clear how this interpretation fits into the context of the giving of grace and the receiving of gifts in Eph 4:7–16.[16] Thus both of these interpretive options (above) work best as christological interpretations of Ps 68:18 and not as interpretations of Eph 4:8–10.

Given the context of Ephesians, it seems more likely that the interpretive explanations of 4:9–10 seek to present a christological reading of Ps 68:18 in terms of Christ's ascension and the subsequent sending of the Spirit at Pentecost.[17] If one takes the term "lower parts" as original to v. 9, then this interpretation requires one to read "of the earth" as appositional to "lower parts." Thus the term "lower parts" should be taken as lower parts of the cosmos, that is, the earth.[18] The claim in v. 10 that the one who descended is the same as the one who ascended then becomes an extraordinary assertion of the identity of Son and Spirit. Moreover, since the assertions in 4:10 seem to recapitulate those of 1:19–23, it may also be significant to observe that the assertions about Christ's superiority in 1:19–23 come as part of Paul's prayer for the Ephesians in 1:17 that "the God of our Lord Jesus Christ . . . may give you a [the] Spirit of wisdom. . . ."

Within the argument of 4:7–16, the idea that Christ's ascension leads to the descent of the Spirit and the giving of gifts for the proper ordering of the life of Christ's body seems to be the most fitting interpretation of 4:8–10. Making this judgment does not rule out the incarnational interpretation of 4:8, nor even the descent-into-hell interpretation — in the sense that all three views (descent into hell, incarnation, ascension/sending) assert truths about Christ that have some textual support. Nevertheless, seeing 4:8 as an interpretation of Ps 68:18 that connects it to the pouring out of gifts through the Spirit's descent at Pentecost seems to address more fully the details of Ephesians.

16. See Abbott's (116) comment, "But, in fact, this ascension is not what is in question, but the giving of gifts; what had to be shown was, that a descent was necessary, in order that He who ascended should give gifts."

17. The major proponents of this view are Abbott 116; Caird; Harris; Lincoln, *Ephesians* 243–47. If Caird is right that Ps 68 and its interpretation in the light of Moses' reception and giving of the law was already closely tied to the Jewish feast of Pentecost, all the better. This aspect of Caird's position, however, is speculative, as explained by Gombis, "Cosmic Lordship" 368–71. Lincoln (*Ephesians* 243–44) offers the most evidence for the connection between Mosaic reception of the law and Pentecost. Yet it is not clear from this evidence that Ps 68 played a role in this connection. Noting the speculative nature of this proposal, however, is far less consequential than Gombis seems to think.

18. Harris 46–54; Lincoln, *Ephesians* 245. This use of the genitive is found in 2:2, 15; 3:7; 6:14, 16, 17. There are a number of reasons against treating this as a partitive genitive. Hoehner (*Ephesians* 534–35) outlines these.

The purpose of Christ's ascension is "that he might fill all things" (4:10). This clause, too, recalls 1:22–23. In the light of those verses, this clause reaffirms the assertion that all things reach their proper end under Christ's rule (1:10). This is as true of the church, which is the focus of 4:7–10, as it is of the rest of creation. Christ's ascension enables him to fill all things and thus bring them to their proper end. This also enables the gifts sent through the Spirit to bring about their desired result, the preservation of the unity of the Spirit in the bond of peace.

[11–16] Verses 11–16 represent a shift from 4:7–10. In vv. 7–10 Paul asserts that each believer has been given "grace according to the measure of Christ's gift." In vv. 11–16 Paul shifts his attention to focus on specific offices or ministries. If one reads 4:7–10 as a description of the Trinitarian origin of the gifts given to the church to enhance its unity, then 4:11–16 articulates more precisely the nature of those gifts and their ultimate purpose. It is crucial to keep in mind that whatever else one wants to say about them, "apostles," "prophets," "evangelists," "pastors" and "teachers" are offices or ministries given by Christ through the Spirit to enable the church to grow into the unity that is already given to the church in 4:3. These offices or ministries are gifts for a purpose.

Verse 11 begins by stressing that the one who ascended and descended is also the one who gives the apostles and prophets and so forth. Many translations treat the Greek words for "apostles," "prophets," "evangelists," and "pastors and teachers" as predicates. This yields a translation such as "He gave some as [*or* to be] apostles, some as [*or* to be] prophets," and so forth (e.g., Hoehner 538–39). There is little reason to do this. Such a translation places the emphasis on the group or individuals who receive a particular gift, such as being prophets. This fits better the discussion in 1 Cor 12, where Paul emphasizes a view of the church as a single coherent organism, with many differing parts all functioning for the betterment of the whole. That is, the point of 1 Cor 12 is to rightly understand how individuals with distinct charisms are all needed for the proper functioning of the body of Christ.[19]

In Ephesians the emphasis is not on the individuals or groups who receive "apostleship" as a gift. Rather, apostles, prophets, evangelists, pastors and teachers are *themselves* the gifts given by the ascended Christ through the Spirit.[20] This shifts the focus from discerning which individuals have which gift to understanding the proper function of these gifts. As it becomes clear that the chief role of apostles, prophets, evangelists, pastors and teachers is to enable the church to better grow into the unity and maturity that Christ desires for the church, there is no sense in which these offices compete with each other. It is

---

19. Moreover, 1 Cor 12 primarily relies on the term *charismata*. In Eph 4, the key term is *domata* (v. 8).

20. See Best (*Ephesians* 388): "The gifts are not made to people but gifts of people." He holds this view even though he relies on the traditional translation, "He gave some as apostles, others as prophets . . ."

also not obvious that there are clear distinctions between these offices. It seems quite possible that one could be both evangelist and teacher, for example.

In 2:20 and 3:5 Paul has already introduced apostles and prophets as central figures in the building of the church and as ministers, interpreters, and proclaimers of the mystery of God's economy of salvation. The term "evangelist" (*euangelistēs*) is not very common in the NT. It refers to Philip (Acts 8:26–40; 21:8), and Timothy is urged to do the work of an "evangelist" in 2 Tim 4:5. In these cases the term refers to the activity of proclaiming the "good news." Certainly Philip's work in Acts 8:26–40 involves preaching to someone outside the church. Alternatively, his preaching to the Ethiopian eunuch seems primarily directed toward opening the Scriptures of Israel to him in such a way that he can see Jesus as the fulfillment of Isaiah's prophecy. In Eph 3:6 and 3:8 *euangelion* specifically refers to the good news about including the Gentiles in God's promises to Israel through Christ. This also seems to be the way the term is used in 6:19. Thus, if there is any special significance to the term "evangelist" in Ephesians, it probably refers to the act of proclaiming this particular message, which Paul himself has been given. Further, Eph 4:12–16 directs all of these gifts toward the formation of believers with the aim of living into the unity of the Spirit. Thus "evangelists" here may not so much be addressing outsiders as further proclaiming the mystery of the gospel to believers, helping to open the Scriptures to believers and nascent believers, as Philip did with the Ethiopian in Acts 8.

The use of only one definite article to cover "pastors and teachers" indicates, at the very least, that these are closely associated roles, though probably not one single group.[21] The Greek term translated as "pastors" is a metaphorical use of the term for "shepherds." These pastors play a role in leadership, protection, guidance, care, and oversight (e.g., 1 Sam 17:34; Ps 23:1; Jer 23:2; Ezek 34:11; etc.). Jesus is the Good Shepherd, who gives his life for the sheep (John 10:11–18) and guards their souls (1 Pet 2:25). The image of the shepherd here is clear enough when it is extended to people in the church. It is not as clear that such an image is tied to a particular office in Eph 4:11. Interestingly, Acts 20:28 connects these shepherding functions to those appointed as "bishops" or "overseers" (*episkopoi*) of the church in Ephesus.

Teachers are listed after apostles and prophets in 1 Cor 12:28. Their role seems to be connected to the passing on and explication of doctrines and traditions of the church (cf. Rom 6:17; 1 Cor 4:17; Col 2:7). Teachers appear to be central in the growth in wisdom and knowledge that Paul desires for the Ephesians in 1:17–19; 3:18–19.

Verse 12 begins to unfold the precise purpose for which Christ through the Spirit gives these particular gifts to the church. Here are three specific, though

---

21. The single article is used of apostles and prophets in 2:20, where they are not treated as a single group.

related, activities.[22] First, Paul declares that Christ gave these particular gifts to the church, a body in which each has been given grace according to the measure of Christ's gift (cf. Lincoln, *Ephesians* 253–54). Thus one aim of giving apostles, prophets, evangelists, pastors and teachers is "for bringing the saints to completion, for the work of service, and for the building up of the body of Christ." The term translated here as "bringing to completion" has a wide range of meanings often associated with repair or restoration (see Hoehner 549–50). Given the emphasis on completion, stature, and fullness in 4:13, it seems best to see this term in v. 12 as a reference to the process by which believers reach their proper goal. Thus this activity would be most closely allied with the formation of Christians.

Second, those receiving these gifts are to engage in the "work of service." Paul uses the same terminology in 2 Cor 3:6, 8, 9; 4:1 in an extended discussion of his own ministry (see also 2 Cor 5:18; 6:3; Rom 11:13; and 1 Cor 16:15, where it refers to the ministry of Stephanas and his household, who serve the saints). In these cases it appears that rather than delimiting a specific activity or activities, the work of service depicts a disposition toward these gifts given by Christ. They are best displayed in service rather than self-aggrandizement.

Finally, when displayed in the proper way, these gifts will lead to the building up of the body of Christ. This phrase similarly relies on the combination of physical and architectural images such as those used of the church in 2:20–21. The body of Christ is a physical body composed of other bodies. Nevertheless, it can be built up like a structure.

Verse 13 explicates this point further. The work of those given the gifts mentioned in 4:11 is directed toward all believers' attaining "the unity of the faith and knowledge of the Son of God. . . ." One of the striking things about this goal is that it applies to "all." That is, this is a corporate attainment. In 4:5 Paul has already made the point that there is "one faith." Moreover, in 1:17 Paul prayed that the Ephesians might be given the Spirit of "wisdom and revelation in knowledge of him." In 1:18–19 Paul further explicates this knowledge in terms of understanding the mystery of salvation. In 4:13 the focus of unified faith and knowledge is the "Son of God." Given that "knowledge" in Ephesians is already tied to revelation of the mystery of redemption, the unity of faith and knowledge of the Son of God must be directed toward the proper understanding of God's mystery of salvation of both Gentiles and Jews in Christ.

---

22. Paul discusses each by means of a prepositional phrase. Yet he uses two different prepositions. This has led some commentators to reflect about how these phrases should be related to each other. Page has made a strong case for arguing that these are all coordinating prepositions, as reflected in the translation above. Thus each office mentioned in v. 11 is covered by each of the purposes mentioned in v. 12. Hoehner (547–49) covers several different interpretive options. His primary criterion for selecting one interpretation, however, seems to depend on which reading does the most to dissolve any distinction between clergy and laity (although he admits that such a distinction did not exist at this time).

The next clause is quite brief. One can translate it in a variety of ways: "the complete person" or "the mature person." Both are quite common. Given the context, it is quite clear that Paul's expression is a way of speaking of attaining one's ultimate goal in Christ. Paul explicates this more fully in the next clause, "the measure of the stature of the fullness of Christ." The images in these last two clauses reflect the idea of growing toward adulthood, reaching one's proper goal.

Verse 14 makes this clearer by contrasting this mature state with childhood. The Ephesians are to leave behind instability and inconstancy with regard to faith and knowledge of the Son of God.[23] Further, they are to avoid human cunning, "trickery and erroneous scheming." Paul gives no specifics here. He may have a particular set of teachings or teachers in mind, but there is no way to discern this from the text. Moreover, given the relatively strong commendation of the community in 1:15–16, it seems unlikely that Paul thinks of them as being in this childish state. Rather, after setting out the goal of maintaining the unity of the Spirit and moving toward the church's ultimate end in Christ, Paul contrasts this movement with the disruptive instability that would impede the Ephesians as they make their way ever closer to Christ. It does not seem that Paul is primarily interested in contrasting the Ephesians' childish state with a mature state so much as he wishes to warn against a set of constant hazards and temptations that threaten the Ephesians' progress toward their proper end in Christ.

The alternative to the allure of crafty and erroneous teaching seems to be "speaking the truth in love." This is the "means of the Church's growth" (Lincoln, *Ephesians* 260). For Paul and all Christians, truth and love cannot be seen as separable components that are only occasionally joined. The test by which one discerns how well truth and love are joined is that we "grow up together in all things into him who is the head, into Christ." Truth spoken in love results in ever-closer conformity to Christ. Within this image, the notion of Christ as head provides the rationale and direction for the body's growth and the coordination of its movements. This is the upshot of 4:16. Here at the end of this section, one finds some of the same emphases that mark 1 Cor 12: the image of a body with ligaments and joints, in which the various components working together promote the growth of the whole.

Although the image of a body with various components working each in its proper way to achieve the growth of the whole is relatively clear in this verse, the discrete vocabulary and their connections are quite obscure at points. The verse begins by asserting that Christ is the source of this body's cohesion and coordination. The participles used to speak about the joining together of the various elements of the body are relatively clear. The next clause, "through every supporting connection" (Hoehner 570), is an approximation of what

---

23. Lincoln (*Ephesians* 257) insightfully notes that the contrast between child and adult here is also a contrast between the plural children and the singular unified adult.

the Greek seems to express. Alternative translations such as "through every ligament which gives supply" (Lincoln, *Ephesians* 262), or "through every ligament of supply" (Best, *Ephesians* 411–12), or "through every contact of supply" (Barth 449)—all can be defended (see translation notes). The result of this obscure physical imagery is presented at the end of the verse in architectural terms similar to 2:21–22. The body is built up in love.

There is a great temptation for commentators to read their preferred ecclesial polity into this passage. On the one hand, this makes some sense. Who would want a church to be ordered in a way that contradicts Eph 4:1–16? On the other hand, such moves tend to obscure the deep connections between the account of the unity of the church in 4:1–7 and the provision of gifts such as apostles, prophets, evangelists, pastors and teachers, whose role is to enhance and enable this unity. In the light of the manifest disunity among the churches, arguments over whether these are ministries, offices, or orders and how these fit with the threefold order of ministry of the early church—all such debates seem to miss the point.

In the absence of such unity, what is one to make of gifts from Christ through the Spirit, gifts designed to bring and maintain the unity of the Spirit in the bond of peace? As mentioned above, unity is already the Spirit's gift to the church. Alternatively, the gifts provided for maintaining that unity have clearly fallen into disuse or disrepair. At the very least they are not functioning properly. Such a situation must surely grieve the Spirit. The first challenge of this passage to Christians in the present is not about the relation of orders to offices or ministries. Rather, the first challenge to Christians today is to become as grieved by our disunity as our disunity must grieve the Spirit. If believers are satisfied with and even desirous of a fractured body of Christ, then we have failed to understand this passage at a much deeper level.

It is important to recall that Paul began this passage with an admonition to the Ephesians to walk in a manner worthy of their calling. He then discussed several habits, practices, and dispositions essential to walking worthily. The cultivation of these dispositions and practices also serves one of the larger aims of walking worthily. Walking worthily works to maintain the unity of the body of Christ through the exercise of various ministerial gifts given to the church by Christ through the Spirit. As chapter 4 moves on, Paul discusses practices that the Ephesians need to avoid in order to walk worthily.

Ephesians 4:17–24
Breaking Free from a Pagan Past

In 2:11 Paul emphasized the importance for the Ephesians to remember their past as a Gentile past so that they could conceive of their life in Christ in its proper relationship to Israel. Eph 2 makes it clear that Gentiles who become followers of the crucified and resurrected Messiah of Israel do not need to erase their Gentile identity and become Jews in order fully to participate in Christ. Nevertheless, 4:17–24 makes the point that the Ephesians must likewise make a decisive break with their pagan past.

Recall that in 4:1–3 Paul urges the Ephesians to walk in a manner worthy of their calling. In the same verses Paul displays some of the communal practices that he considers essential for the Ephesian church if they are to walk in a manner worthy of their call. This leads to further comments about the unity of the church and the gifts given by God for the proper ordering of the body of Christ.

Now in 4:17–24 Paul emphasizes the importance of walking in a way that avoids various practices conventionally associated (at least by Jews) with Gentiles. In this respect walking in a manner worthy of their calling will require the Ephesians to live in a way that clearly distinguishes them from their pagan Gentile neighbors.[1] Verses 17–19 in particular describe the non-Christian Gentiles' fundamental and comprehensive alienation from God in a manner that recalls 2:1–5. Here in 4:17–19, however, Paul focuses on the behaviors that flow from such an alienated position. From this description Paul in vv. 20–24 proceeds to articulate the importance of being renewed in Christ, putting off the old person and putting on the new.

4:17 I,[a] therefore, insist[b] on this in the Lord: You must not walk as the Gentiles do, in the futility of their minds. **18** They reason in the dark.[c] They are alienated from the life of God because of the ignorance that is in them, because of the hardness[d] of their hearts. **19** Having become calloused,[e] they gave themselves over to wanton behavior for the practice of every kind of impurity with covetousness.

---

1. Darko (31–38) reminds us that these verses are directed to distinguishing the manner of life of the Ephesian Christians from that of their non-Christian neighbors.

20 But this is not the way you learned Christ. **21** If (as is most certainly the case)[f] you have heard about him and were taught in him, just as the truth[g] is in Jesus, **22** you[h] were taught that you have put off the old person, along with its former way of life, corrupted by deceitful desires, **23** and that you are being renewed by the spirit of your minds, **24** having clothed yourselves with the new man, created according to [the desires and plan of] God[i] in the righteousness and holiness that come from the truth.

a. As is common in Ephesians, verses 17–19 are a single complex sentence in Greek. They are here rendered as several English sentences.

b. This verse begins with two main verbs in Greek: "I say" and "I testify." The combination of these two seems designed to stress the seriousness and urgency of Paul's demands (Lincoln, *Ephesians* 276, noting similar usage in 1 Thess 2:12; Josephus, *Ant.* 10.104). Thus the translation uses the more conventional English verb "insist."

c. Here two participial phrases extend the sentence that began in v. 17. I have rendered them as separate sentences in English. The first clause could be translated as "They are darkened in their understanding" [NRSV]. This is formally accurate but tends to miss the sense of moral and rational blindness that affects unbelieving Gentiles, according to Paul. Hence the translation "They reason in the dark."

d. In the 1960s there was a brief scholarly dispute about whether the Greek term *pōrōsis* (hardness) reflected a copying error, that an earlier text included the Greek word *pērōsis* (blindness). There now seems to be little doubt that "hardness" is the appropriate term (see the discussions in Hoehner 588; Best, *Ephesians* 420–21).

e. The Greek perfect participle *apēlgēkotes* does not appear elsewhere in the NT or LXX. Although it can mean "despondent," it can also designate becoming insensitive or calloused. This latter meaning fits the context best (with Hoehner 589).

f. The syntax of this verse is conditional, but as in 3:2, there is no doubt about Paul's conviction that they have heard and been taught.

g. Although the Greek text does not use the definite article "the" before "truth," it is inserted here. Paul will omit the article from abstract nouns, or alternate using it and leaving it out (cf. "grace" and "the grace" in Eph 2:5, 8. See also BDF §258; Lincoln, *Ephesians* 281). Moreover, the idea that (just) some truth or a truth among other truths was in Jesus would have been foreign to Paul.

h. This verse contains three infinitive verbs, the first followed by a second-person plural accusative pronoun (*hymas*). There are several scholarly views about how to account for this grammatically. Yet there is little interpretive difference between the grammatical options. The translation above takes the infinitives as dependent upon the verb "you were taught" and as further explicating the content of the teaching. The pronoun reintroduces the subject of the main verb following the parenthetical remark "Truth is in Jesus." This is the position of Best (*Ephesians* 430) and is quite similar to Hoehner's (601–2) preference. Numerous scholars, including Lincoln (*Ephesians* 283–4) and Schnackenburg (200) take the infinitive verbs to have an imperative force. This would yield a translation emphasizing the fact that because the Ephesians have been taught certain things, they should therefore "put off the old person. . . ." Although the subsequent section invokes several moral imperatives, verses 20–24 seem to be laying out the conceptual bases for the admonitions that follow.

i. The Greek translated here as "created according to the desires and plan of God" could be formally rendered as "created like God" or "created according to God." Either of these possibilities could refer to the godlike manner in which God creates. This says very little since God can only create in a godlike manner. The Greek implies more here, and that needs to be expressed in English. The context indicates that this new person is created according to the will and plan of God so that such new creatures can attain their proper ends (purposes) in God. In a closely parallel passage in Col 3:10, Paul describes the new person (lit., man) as "in the image of the one who created him." In this light several translations and commentators opt for "created according to the image [*or* likeness] of God" (see NRSV, NIV, TEV; Lincoln, *Ephesians* 286; Best, *Ephesians* 436–37; Hoehner 611). As with the translation above, this reading adds more than is strictly in the text; although it can be supported, it also risks some confusion and has not been followed here (see comments below).

[17–19] Paul "insists in the Lord" that the Ephesians no longer walk as the Gentiles do even though they are in many respects still Gentiles. Although they are not required to become Jews in order to complete their faith in Christ, they are also not free to continue to live as their pagan neighbors do. Paul and the Ephesians now inhabit a realm ruled, ordered, and directed by the crucified and risen Christ. The Ephesians are bound to each other and to Paul because they are in the Lord. Being in the Lord, abiding in the space defined and ruled by Christ, is where the futility of the mind, the darkening of reason, and the hardening of the heart typical of Gentile life are all healed and renewed.

The depiction of Gentile life in these verses reflects many of the standard characterizations offered by Jews (cf. Wis 13–14) and is similar to those offered by Paul in Rom 1. In these standard Jewish accounts, the abominable behavior of the Gentiles is traced to prior failures of perception or judgment. If there is some sense of a chain of causes and effects here, it appears to move backward from hardness of heart to ignorance to alienation from the life of God to darkened reasoning to futility of the mind (Hoehner 588). It is not clear, however, that Paul is really trying to develop a chain of causation. Rather, he is providing a comprehensive set of reasons for the Gentiles' failure to "walk worthily."

The claim in vv. 17–18 that the Gentiles' reasoning is futile and their minds are darkened echoes Paul's claims about the Gentiles in Rom 1:21. In Romans these assertions seem to be directed to accounting for how Gentiles misperceive the natural world's testimony to God's glory and power. In Ephesians the imagery seems to explain the Gentiles' inability to tell right from wrong. They are incapable of discerning which actions will help advance them toward their proper ends in God. Their reasoning about how to "walk" is futile because they are alienated from the life of God, and their alienation from the life of God is the result of their ignorance and hardness of heart. Paul is describing a cycle or downward spiral that includes alienation from God, which leads to frustrated reasoning about how to walk according to God's desires, which leads to sinful actions, which lead to further alienation from God, which further frustrates reason, and so forth.

The description of the Gentiles as "alienated from the life of God" is both obscure in that it is a phrase not found elsewhere in the NT to describe Gentiles and full of interesting theological resonances. First, this phrase should be read in the light of Paul's earlier description of the Ephesians' state as once "dead" (2:1, 5) yet now made alive together with Christ (2:5).[2] The phrase may also indicate "an existence estranged from that holy living which comes through faith: 'I live, now not I; but Christ liveth in me' (Gal 2:20 [cf. KJV])" (Thomas Aq. 176).

Modern commentators are quick to assert that the phrase "the life of God" cannot refer to God's own life (Best, *Ephesians* 420; Muddiman 213); Hoehner (586) relies on arbitrary grammatical designations to make this point. Rather, it is a reference to the life that God gives. Thus, being alienated from the life that God gives is another way of speaking about spiritual death. The phrase is unusual, but it is by no means clear that it is a reference to the life that God gives. In addition, it seems that participation in the life of God is that very thing for which God made us. Indeed, 2 Pet 1:4 explicitly contrasts our sharing in the divine nature with the life of corruption and lust. Thus, if participation in the life of God is both God's desire for us and our proper end in Christ, there seems to be good theological justification for thinking that Paul is characterizing Gentile existence as fundamentally alienated from the life of God in just this sense. Gentiles outside of Christ are disconnected from the ends for which God made them, that is, participation in God's own life.

The source of Gentile alienation is ignorance and hardness of heart.[3] The combination of ignorance with hardness of heart makes it clear that the Gentiles' failing is not simply an intellectual error that might be corrected through further study. Rather, along with futile reasoning and darkened understanding, ignorance and hardness of heart all work together to present a picture of Gentiles as alienated from their true end in God in a comprehensive way, touching on the intellect, perceptions, affections, desires, and judgments.

The result of their comprehensive alienation from God is that the Gentiles have become "calloused," insensitive to what is good or evil (v. 19). In this light, it is only to be expected that they would give themselves over to all kinds of sin. Paul first characterizes this behavior as "wanton" (*aselgeia*). Quite simply,

---

2. In Eph 2:12 Paul uses the same Greek word to speak about the Gentiles as "excluded from the commonwealth of Israel." Although alienation both from the life of God and from the commonwealth of Israel are signs of the Gentiles' deathly state outside of Christ, it is probably saying too much to equate participation in the commonwealth of Israel with participation in the life of God.

3. In the OT, both Jews and Gentiles are subject to hardness of heart, a stubborn refusal to believe in and submit to God (see Exod 4:21; Ps 95:8; Jer 19:15; Isa 6:10).

this is acting as if there are no limits, as if one is completely unconstrained.[4] Lack of constraint frees Gentiles "for the practice of every kind of impurity." The range of meanings for the term impurity (*akatharsia*) runs from ritual impurity (cf. Lev 15) to moral impurity (Rom 6:19, where slavery to impurity is contrasted with slavery to righteousness) and to sexual impurity (Rom 1:24, particularly with regard to standard Gentile practices). This wide range of meaning in the phrase "all kinds of impurity" probably indicates deficiencies in all aspects of life. The final characteristic of Gentile behavior is covetousness. Dio Chrysostom called covetousness (*pleonexia*; coveter, *pleonektos*) both the greatest cause of evils and the greatest evil (*Or.* 17.7). In the LXX this term is used to refer to unjust gains taken by force (Judg 5:19; Ps 118 [119 Eng.]:36; Jer 22:17; Ezek 22:27; Hab 2:9); in the NT the term appears in lists of vices in Mark 7:22; Rom 1:29; 1 Cor 5:10, 11. In Eph 5:3, 5 the same term occurs in connection with sexual sins, impurity, and idolatry. Thus, without going into great detail, this verse makes it clear that Gentile ignorance and hardness of heart in relation to God result in comprehensively disordered lives.

One apparent difference between this description of the ways in which Gentiles "walk" and the description offered in Rom 1 is that in Romans, God is the subject who "gives over" the Gentiles to their corrupt lives because of their inability to recognize God in their hearts and minds. The corruption of Gentile lives, therefore, reflects God's judgment on their futile reasoning. In Ephesians, the Gentiles' ignorance and hardness of heart both alienates them from the life of God and leads them to "give themselves over" to corrupt living. Gentiles, because of their futile reasoning, willingly turn themselves over to lives characterized by excess. When faced with this contrast between Romans and Ephesians, John Chrysostom argues that these passages actually say the same thing (*Hom. Eph.* 13). They do not. Alternatively, they do not exclude each other. God can hand Gentiles (or anyone else) over to the very thing Gentiles willingly desire for themselves. This may well be one of those cases where God's judgment on humans is to give them exactly what they want. Nevertheless, Paul is clear that the Ephesian Christians are to distinguish themselves from the Gentile way of walking.

[20–24] In 4:17–19 Paul has made it clear that the lives of the Ephesian Christians are to stand as a sharp contrast to those of their Gentile neighbors. These verses articulate both the depravity of Gentile living yet also some of the reasons for it. Now as vv. 20–24 indicate in dealing both with Gentile vice

---

4. This term is used to describe Alcibiades' punching a rich man simply on a dare (Plutarch, *Alc.* 8.1), Ptolemy's political corruption (3 Macc 2:26), and the disordered sexual and marital relations of Gentiles (Wis 14:26). In the NT it describes sexual immorality (2 Cor 12:21) and is one of the works of the flesh (Gal 5:19). In Rom 13:13 it is linked with reveling and drunkenness. In 2 Cor 12:21; Gal 5:19; and here in Eph 4:19, *aselgeia* appears in a list with *akatharsia* (impurity).

and Christian virtue, Paul makes it clear that living one way rather than another depends upon a set of inner dispositions, affections, and habits of mind. In this respect Paul was no different from other ancient moral philosophers. Virtue, however defined, required the transformation and cultivation of particular patterns of thinking, feeling, and perceiving. Pagan Gentiles reason in futile, frustrated ways; their hearts are hard, and they are ignorant. Alternatively, believers have "learned Christ." They have put away the old person and put on the new.

Given that Paul assumes such transformation has already happened in the lives of the Ephesian Christians, he wants to ensure that they will not only continue to cultivate Christ-focused patterns of thinking, feeling, and perceiving, but that they will also begin to live differently, that they will walk in a manner worthy of their call.

Hence, after rehearsing the ignorance and hardness of heart of the Gentiles and their wanton way of life, Paul can begin v. 20 with a deceptively simple assertion: "But this is not the way you learned Christ." The use of a personal object with the verb to learn (*manthanō*) does not appear to have any precedent. Colossians 2:6, "As you have received Christ Jesus the Lord, so walk in him" (NASB), seems to offer the closest parallel, linking reception of Christ, presumably through some teaching, to a particular way of life (Lincoln, *Ephesians* 279).

What does this odd formulation mean? Does it refer to some point in the past, such as a time of conversion or baptism? Is this really just a shorthand way of referring to the passing on of traditions about Christ (Lincoln [*Ephesians* 279–80] asserts a close link with Col 2:6)? Does it presume some earlier catechesis that Paul has provided to the Ephesians and of which he now reminds them (cf. Hoehner 594–95)?

The implied logic of this assertion is that the Ephesians have already "learned Christ" to a sufficient degree that they can walk in a manner worthy of their calling, in contrast to their pagan neighbors. At the same time, the notion of renewal and of clothing oneself that is part of vv. 23–24 indicate that although one may have "learned Christ," there is still room for growth. Given that these seem to be the basic assumptions of this passage, one must admit that any of the options noted above could fit within such logic.

One of the best ways to think of this may be to understand the notion of "learning Christ" through the lenses that Paul uses to speak of his own situation in Phil 3:7–14. Here Paul is speaking of the transformation of his own patterns of thinking, feeling, and acting in the light of "knowing Christ" (3:7–8). He has abandoned his prior perceptions about his identity and how he should act in the world so that he "may gain Christ" and "be found in him" (3:9). The result of such a transformation is that Paul would "know Christ and the power of his resurrection and the sharing of his sufferings," and "may attain the resurrection from the dead" (3:10–11). As Phil 3:12–14 makes clear, Paul has in several significant ways already "learned Christ" (Eph 4:20). At the same time, learning Christ is also the end toward which he directs his future strivings. In Phil 3:7–14 and in Eph 4:20–24, Christ is seen as both the source of the transformations in Christians' dispositions and habits of thinking and perceiving as well as the goal toward which those transformations are directed.

Verse 21 explicates this notion further. Although the syntax of the sentence is conditional, Paul has no doubts that the Ephesians have indeed "heard about Christ" and "were taught in him."[5] The notion of hearing about Christ seems relatively straightforward. It does, however, remind modern Christians that early Christian formation was primarily conveyed orally. This demanded a different and much more complex set of relationships between teacher and student than between a reader and an author. The teacher was never a disembodied voice conveyed by means of words on a page. Instead, the teacher was someone known to the student, someone whose daily life, pattern of prayer, and habits of worship could be as instructive as anything conveyed in a classroom.

The second clause of this verse, "and you were taught in him," is less clear. Lincoln (*Ephesians* 280) takes "in him" to be another way of saying "about him." Most commentators, however, see something more here. For most commentators, the phrase "in him" indicates the sphere in which the Ephesians were taught (Hoehner 595; Best, *Ephesians* 428). This fits with the basic distinction between Gentiles and those who are "in Christ," a distinction that drives this entire passage. Indeed, Paul emphasizes this contrast in the concluding clause of this verse: "just as the truth is in Jesus." Recall that the Gentiles' reasoning is futile; they are ignorant, and their hearts are hard. In contrast, the Ephesian Christians have "heard about Christ"; they have been "taught in him," and "the truth is in Jesus." The contrast is clear and decisive. Christ has transformed the Ephesians' patterns of perception and habits of thinking and feeling such that they now know the truth and can "take every thought captive to Christ" (2 Cor 10:5), who is "the way, and the truth, and the life" (John 14:6), with the aim of living a life worthy of their calling.[6]

Verses 22–24 further elaborate the substance of what the Ephesians were taught. These verses rely on the image of putting off and putting on clothing to speak about the transformation that occurs when one enters the body of

---

5. Thrall (87–88) treats this verse (among others) as a place where Paul uses a conditional construction to express a conviction that is neither hypothetical nor tentative.

6. Several scholars see a sharp distinction between Paul's use of the terms "Christ" in 4:20 and "Jesus" in 4:21. This distinction was supposedly designed either to counter a separation between the exalted Christ and the earthly Jesus such as we find attacked in 1 John 1 (Schlier 216–17), or to draw attention to the moral example of the earthly Jesus (Schnackenburg 199; Best, *Ephesians* 430). In response: although the use of "Jesus" on its own is unique in Ephesians, neither of these options really seem to fit with the context and its interest in distinguishing between Gentile and Christian existence (Lincoln, *Ephesians* 282).

Christ.[7] The first step in this transformation is disrobing, putting off the old person and the way of life associated with that old self. The description of this old self recalls the earlier statements in Eph 2:1–5, where Paul recounts the Ephesians' morbid state outside of Christ. Moreover, it builds upon the description of Gentile life in 4:17–19. The old self with its attendant way of life is corrupted by deceitful desires. As has been the case throughout this section, Paul makes it clear that a corrupt pattern of behavior is preceded by and reinforces corruption in the ways one thinks and feels. In this case, he uses the phrase "deceitful desires" (or more lit., "desires that come from deceit"). It is important to recognize that the mere act of desiring is not a problem. Desiring is but one form of loving. If we were to extinguish all desires we would not be in a position to love God or our neighbor; we would not be able to know God's love for us. Nevertheless, given the description of the Gentiles' habits of mind and heart in vv. 17–19, it is not surprising that their desires are generated and driven by deceit rather than the truth that is in Jesus.

Paul continues his concern with habits of thinking and feeling as the source of action when he teaches that having put off the old person, believers are to be continually renewed in the spirit of their mind.[8] Although Rom 12:2 uses a different verb to speak about the renewal of believers' minds, the notion that being in Christ enables and requires the ongoing transformation of believers' habits of thinking, feeling, and perceiving is the thrust of both of these passages. Being joined to the body of Christ requires one to dispose of or unlearn old patterns of thinking, feeling, and perceiving; to learn and relearn the habits of thinking, feeling, and perceiving appropriate to one who is in Christ; and as a result to walk in a manner worthy of one's call.

Putting off the old person is accompanied by putting on the new person. This new person is described as "created according to [the desires and plan of] God in the righteousness and holiness that come from the truth."

Formally, "the righteousness and holiness that come from the truth" are in contrast to lives driven by desires that come from deceit (v. 22). This must also be tied to the notion in v. 21 that the truth is in Jesus. At the same time, the righteousness and holiness that come from the truth stand as alternatives to any other standard of righteousness, such as "my own righteousness found in the law" (cf. Phil 3:9). This christologically normed righteousness is the

---

7. Best (*Ephesians* 431) rightly notes that this image is so widely used in the ancient world that there is no point in trying to locate a precise source for Paul's use of the image.

8. Modern commentators are divided about whether the "spirit" spoken of here is the Holy Spirit (Schnackenburg 200; Gnilka 230–31) or a reference to the spirit of one's mind, where spirit and mind are used pleonastically (Hoehner 608; Best, *Ephesians* 435; Lincoln, *Ephesians* 287). The Greek clearly seems to indicate the latter. Moreover, this reading does not exclude, and may require, the conviction that the spirits of the minds of believers must be renewed by the operation of the Holy Spirit.

result of being clothed with the new person. As Paul has assumed throughout this section, a transformation of identity—of patterns of thinking, feeling, and perceiving—enables and entails righteous, holy living.

This new person is "created according to God." If Paul primarily intends to allude to Gen 1:26, he certainly could have been more explicit.[9] The text contains no mention of the image or likeness of God. Moreover, such a direct allusion would invite confusion. This is because it might then seem that only believers, those who have put on the new person, are bearers of God's image. One of the points of Gen 1:26 seems to be that all humans are created in the image of God. Hence this phrase must indicate something else.

Despite the logic of the metaphor of clothing oneself with the new person, this is God's work, not ours. In this scene, we cannot undress or dress ourselves. Thus a central claim of 4:24 is that this clothing is done according to God's plan and enabled by God's gracious action. Moreover, putting on this new person is sufficient for believers to attain their true end in God. Further changes of clothing will not be needed for us to reach our goal. The point here seems to be that whatever damage was done to God's image because of one's sin, that damage is now sufficiently healed to enable believers to carry on in the righteousness and holiness that come from the truth, so that they will ultimately reach that for which God first reached out to us. Thus being created "according to God" must primarily refer to this healing that will bring all "new persons" into that place where they can with hope live into God's desires for them.

Several scholars argue that vv. 22–24 reflect pieces from an early baptismal liturgy (see Hoehner 613 n. 3 for a list). Hoehner is right to observe that there is little evidence to support this claim. This does not mean, however, that one should not recognize that for the vast majority of the church's life, the transformation from old person to new was sacramentally and ritually marked by baptism. The vocabulary need not be from a baptismal liturgy for Christians to recognize the close links between the transformations that Paul elaborates here and the practice of baptism. Conversely, this close link is not really evidence that Eph 4:23–24 replicates language from a baptismal liturgy.

In this passage Paul has been at pains to make clear that walking in a manner worthy of their calling will require the Ephesians to distinguish their manner of life from their non-Christian Gentile neighbors. To do this, he contrasts the state of unregenerate Gentiles with the Ephesian Christians. Given that outside of Christ, Gentiles are comprehensively alienated from God and that the Ephesians have been transformed and renewed in the spirit of their minds, one should expect nothing less. As Paul continues into the next section, he begins to speak of specific practices that he expects the Ephesian Christians to adopt.

---

9. Gnilka (232) notes that the absence of "image" or "likeness" stands in opposition to the much clearer reference to Gen 1:26 found in Col 3:10.

Ephesians 4:25–5:2
A Common Life Worthy of the Gospel

In this section Paul urges specific practices on the Ephesians. These practices result from clothing oneself with the new person and continuing to cultivate the Christ-focused patterns of thinking, feeling, and perceiving that first began with the Ephesians' baptism. Manifesting the life of the new person in Christ serves as the appropriate testimony to the transformation that Paul has outlined in 4:17–24.

Scholars have devoted a significant amount of energy to identifying both the form and sources of these admonitions.[1] Formally, these verses share a great deal with contemporary texts. Both Jewish and Greco-Roman materials employ similar brief moral admonitions, using similar vocabulary. Despite these similarities, the day-to-day lives and behavioral expectations of first-century Jews and Christians, Romans, and others often differed substantially from each other. This indicates that the contexts in which these admonitions are offered and the larger ends toward which specific groups of people direct their lives will have a significant effect on the ways in which people embody such admonitions as "Speak the truth." Thus the best way to follow the discussion in 4:25–5:2 and beyond is to understand Paul's moral demands in the light of the christological and ecclesiological contexts in which they are offered.

4:25 Therefore, putting aside falsehood, let each of us[a] speak the truth with our neighbors for we are all members of each other. 26 Be angry, yet do not sin; do not let the sun go down on your anger, 27 neither give an opportunity to the devil. 28 Those who are stealing should stop. Instead, let them labor, working at some good with their hands so that they might have something to share with those in need. 29 Do not let any corrosive[b] talk come forth from your mouth, but whatever words are good for building up where there is a need,[c] so that they might give grace[d] to those who hear.

---

1. In his discussion, Lincoln (*Ephesians* 293–95) identifies these verses as a collection of moral *sententiae*, "sentences, frequently in the form of imperatives, which give a rule for conduct in daily life" (295). This form of writing is well known among Hellenistic moral philosophers (see Malherbe 105–20).

30 Do not grieve the Holy Spirit of God, in whom you were sealed for the day of redemption. **31** Put away from yourselves all bitterness, anger, wrath, shouting, and abusive speech, along with all malice. **32** Be kind toward one another and compassionate, forgiving each other just as God in Christ forgave you. **5:1** Therefore become imitators of God as beloved children **5:2** and walk in love just as Christ loved us[e] and handed himself over for us, an offering and sacrifice whose aroma is pleasing to God.

a. The translation above renders both clauses of this verse in the first-person plural. Literally, the subject of the first clause (which appears to quote Zech 8:16) is in the second-person plural (i.e., "Each of you must speak the truth with his neighbor"). Since the next clause indicates that "we are all members of each other," the injunction to speak the truth must apply to "us" as well (cf. NRSV).

b. Some English versions translate the Greek phrase *logos sapros* as "evil talk" (RSV, NRSV). The adjective *sapros* is used elsewhere in the NT to refer to things that are rotten (e.g., wood and fruit in Matt 7:17; 12:33; Luke 6:43) and thereby useless. Moreover, this verse contrasts *sapros* speech with words that "build up." Hence the translation "corrosive."

c. The use of the Greek word *chreia* in the genitive case here is ambiguous. Several later copyists (including D*, F, G, et al.) found the term so difficult to understand in this context that they corrected it to read "faith" (i.e., "whatever is good for building up the faith"). James A. Findlay argues that the term should be taken to mean "witty." The syntax of the sentence makes this unlikely. It is much more likely that this constructive component of v. 29 picks up the use of the terms "good/beneficial" and "need" from v. 28. Thus, just as the antidote to theft is good work so that the needs of the poor may be met, the antidote to corrosive speech is beneficial words that build up when the need arises (see Lincoln, *Ephesians* 306; Best, *Ephesians* 456).

d. Finally, the Greek phrase translated as "give grace" here can have the everyday meaning of "do a favor" or "confer a benefit" (BDAG 1079–80). In this case, however, Paul may well be playing on this idiom to refer to either a more general sort of benefit or a spiritual one (cf. Best, *Ephesians* 457). Hence the translation above opts for the more literal rendering "give grace."

e. There is textual variation regarding the plural personal pronouns in this verse. The first variation between "us" and "you" is fairly well balanced, with $\mathfrak{P}^{46}$, $\aleph^2$, D, F, G, et al. reading "loved us"; and $\aleph$*, A, B, P, et al. reading "loved you." It seems most likely that the text would have retained consistency between the two pronouns. Moreover, the evidence in the second case overwhelmingly favors "for us" ($\mathfrak{P}^{46}$, $\mathfrak{P}^{49}$, $\aleph$, A, D, G, K, et al.). Thus the first-person plural pronoun is used both places in this verse (see Metzger 538–39).

[4:25–5:2] This section begins with a conjunction that directly ties the subsequent admonitions and injunctions to the prior discussion about putting on the new person (4:24). Thus, having established that believers are indeed new people being renewed in their minds, Paul gives practical force to this renewal relative to the common life of the Ephesian church.

In this light, having put away falsehood, the Ephesians are to speak the truth with each other. The term "neighbor" is part of the quotation from Zech 8:16.[2] In Zechariah's context, neighbors would have been fellow Israelites. In Ephesians, in the light of the subsequent clause indicating that we are all members of each other, "neighbor" refers to fellow Christians. One should not infer from this that Christians are only obligated to tell the truth to other Christians and may lie to non-Christians. Rather, because Christians share a common turning away from the falsehoods of the world and because the Spirit of Christ, who is the truth, animates them, there is a degree of transparency and openness with each other that is distinctive. The common life of the Ephesian community (and contemporary churches) depends on and generates such truthfulness. Thus it is not strictly abandonment of falsehood that drives Christians to truthfulness. Rather, it is their communion and partnership with each other that requires truthfulness. As Paul has already insisted in 4:15, speaking the truth in love is a crucial element for growing into the body of Christ.

The second command is somewhat less clear (v. 26). Taken straightforwardly, the command to "be angry" seems to contradict the command in v. 31 to "put anger, wrath, shouting, and abusive speech, along with all malice away from yourselves." Moreover, the command cannot be taken as an admonition to be constantly angry. This leads some to argue that the imperative verb translated as "be angry" should be taken to have a concessive or conditional force.[3] Thus it could be translated, "When you are angry, do not sin." This would be similar to the injunction in Jas 1:19–20, "Let everyone be . . . slow to anger; for your anger does not produce God's righteousness." Whether one translates the imperative conditionally or not, it is important to recognize that this passage does not reflect a series of discrete admonitions as much as an interconnected complex whole. Anger cannot and should not be the Christian's constant disposition. Nevertheless, there are times when anger as an emotion simply comes upon us. Other times anger is the result of a more thoughtful accounting of a situation or set of actions. In either case, it is not sinful in itself. Anger does, however, provide the environment in which sin can flourish. Moreover, a state of anger can provide an occasion for the devil.

This passage recalls the conversation between God and Cain just before Cain kills Abel. The Lord says to Cain, "Why are you angry, and why has your countenance fallen? If you do well, will you not be accepted? And if you do not do well, sin is lurking at the door: its desire is for you, but you must master

---

2. Hoehner (618) notes that in Zech 8:15–16, God promises to do good to the remnant in Judah. The first command to this remnant is that they speak the truth to each other. This is also Paul's first command to the Ephesians.

3. See BDF §387; Best, *Ephesians* 449.

it" (Gen 4:5–7).[4] Anger is sometimes justified, but it is always disruptive. In that disruption, righteous anger can easily turn to sin. It is an emotion that can open oneself up to great acts of self-sacrifice. Alternatively, it can open one up to all manner of evil. The wise response to anger in 4:26 is not to let the sun go down on one's anger. The longer anger, righteous or otherwise, festers within us, the more likely it is to lead us into sin.

With its use of words for building up and tearing down, with the connections between inner dispositions and verbal practices, this paragraph is primarily concerned with speech. In this light, it comes as a surprise in 4:28, when Paul says that those who are stealing must stop and take up honest work. This is one of the most intriguing verses in the NT because of where it occurs. I have written on it quite extensively and do not want to repeat all of those arguments here.[5] Nevertheless, I point out several interesting elements of this verse. First, the types of things Paul is probably talking about include the numerous small-scale ways in which slaves might pilfer their master's goods (see Phlm 18). In addition, he might be referring to those in the marketplace who use unfair scales or engage in price fixing. Petty con artists might also fit the bill. Second, in the light of the manifest fact that this entire passage is addressed to the common life of the Ephesian church, one must entertain the likelihood that those stealing are stealing from other members of the congregation. This is not a notion foreign to the NT. The story of the "neglect" of the widows of the "Hellenists" in Acts 6 may serve as an appropriate example of the sort of stealing Paul has in mind. Alternatively, Paul might be talking about a scenario in which some members of the congregation, either through idleness or misplaced views about the Parousia, were living as parasites off the charity of the church, like those addressed in 2 Thess 3:6–15. One does not know exactly what type of behavior Paul has in mind here, but the Ephesians must have known.

Further, it is not difficult to imagine that certain Ephesians' stealing would be quite destructive of the trust and honesty needed to speak truthfully, and to engage in all of the other verbal activities that contribute to the building up of the church. Indeed, a quick look at the episode of Ananias and Sapphira in Acts 5 shows how closely linked issues of stealing and lying are. Ananias and Sapphira are not judged for stealing from the community. Peter asserts that their property and the proceeds from its sale belonged to them. It was their conspiracy to lie to God that brings about abrupt judgment upon them.

---

4. See also *T. Dan* 4.7–5.1, which links lying and anger in this way: "Anger and falsehood together are a double-edged evil, and work together to perturb the reason. And when the soul is continually perturbed, the Lord withdraws from it and Beliar rules it. Observe the Lord's commandments, then, my children, and keep his Law. Avoid wrath, and hate lying, in order that the Lord may dwell among you, and Beliar may flee from you. Each of you speak truth clearly to his neighbor."

5. See Fowl, *Engaging Scripture*, ch. 6.

As with theft in the preceding verse, Paul's admonitions about speech in v. 29 focus primarily on the impact that particular sorts of speech have on the common life of the church. Corrosive speech is not so much false as it is destructive of the bonds that help constitute the body of Christ. Paul's phrasing of the positive assertion of this clause indicates that he assumes there will be an ongoing need for edifying discourse among the Ephesians. This is not to impute bad will to them, nor does it provide evidence that corrosive speech was a particularly persistent problem for the Ephesians. Rather, this verse simply recognizes that any group as interdependent as Paul expects the Ephesian Christians to be will need to cope with occasions when words are spoken that threaten to undermine the common life of the church. Such situations require edifying speech that might provide the grace needed to repair the damage.

Although there may be numerous ways of grieving the Spirit, the context of Eph 4:30 offers a particular shape to this commandment to avoid grieving the Holy Spirit. Paul warns believers not to "quench the Spirit" in 1 Thess 5:19, and Acts 7:51 speaks of "resisting the Holy Spirit" (NASB). This is the only NT occasion where anyone speaks of "grieving the Spirit." In Isa 63:10 the MT speaks of the Israelites' grieving the Spirit as they successively resist God's purposes for them.[6] In this light, grieving the Holy Spirit is connected to God's people's resistance to God's purposes for them. Paul has already asserted that the Ephesians have been sealed by the Holy Spirit and that this is the sign of their acceptance into the people of God (1:13). Further, this sealing has its proper end in bringing believers to the "day of redemption." Thus the work of the Spirit cannot be separated from the ends that God aims to achieve in all believers. With this in mind, 2:22 claims that the church, of which the Ephesians are a concrete manifestation, is that reconciled body of Jews and Gentiles in Christ, a structure whose pieces are being joined together in the Spirit to be a dwelling place of God. Thus it appears that a primary purpose of the Spirit's work in the Ephesian church is building up the body into that which God intends. In the context of 4:25–5:2, then, grieving the Spirit refers to the practices of falsehood, theft, corrosive speech, and anything else that frustrates the Spirit's work of building up the Ephesians into one body (4:4), the work of strengthening them so that Christ may dwell in their hearts through faith as they are rooted and grounded in love (3:17), "until we all come to the unity of the faith and knowledge of the Son of God" (4:13).

When speaking of grieving the Spirit, it is useful to remember that from a theological perspective such language is always analogical. The grief that the

---

6. Fee (712–15) speaks of Paul's "echoing" or "citing" Isa 63:10. There seems to be little possibility that there is a linguistic connection between the MT of Isaiah and Ephesians. The LXX of Isa 63:10 reads that the Israelites' rebellion "provoked" (*parōxynan*) the Spirit. The key terminology here is different from that in Ephesians.

Spirit might be said to experience is not sadness that comes from being subject to the vagaries of circumstance. The Spirit, as God, is not subject to passions in the ways that we are. Human actions and the actions of believers in particular might contingently frustrate the work of the Spirit. These could be said to grieve the Spirit. The Spirit's work, however, cannot ultimately be frustrated. If grieving the Spirit is tied to resisting God's purposes, then believers are those who primarily suffer from grieving the Spirit in this way.

The next two verses (31–32) contain lists of vices to be avoided and virtues to be cultivated, without a great deal of elaboration or explanation. The use of virtue and vice lists was relatively common in the Greco-Roman world. The use of such lists presumes that the various practices enumerated as vices or virtues are already understood, as well as the reasons for avoiding or pursuing them.[7] In the case of Ephesians, the vices listed here are all related to anger in some way. This ties them back to the admonition "Be angry, yet do not sin" in v. 26. There are five particular components of vice here: "bitterness, anger, wrath, shouting, and abusive speech." These together seem to be taken to comprise "all malice." Bitterness seems to be the internal disposition that leads to the manifestation of the other four. Moreover, bitterness seems to generate the sort of anger that would open one up to sin. The words translated "anger" and "wrath" are common Greek terms for describing anger. The two terms are used in parallel in Rom 2:8 and Rev 14:10 (both times describing God's anger) and also in Col 3:8 (a passage similar to Eph 4:31). Although the term translated "shouting" can refer to shouting for joy (e.g., Luke 1:42, when Elizabeth recognizes Mary's baby; Matt 25:6, announcing the arrival of the bridegroom), in this context and when paired with "abusive speech," the shouting imagined here must be tied to anger.

The term translated "abusive speech" (*blasphēmia*) is used in the LXX to refer to Gentiles' harsh words spoken against God and God's people (Ezek 35:12; Dan 3:29; 1 Macc 2:6; 2 Macc 8:4; 10:35; 15:24; Tob 1:18). In the NT it is used more generally of abusive speech. In the cases of both "shouting" and "abusive speech," Paul is referring to speech among believers. All of these vices are summarized by the injunction to put them away from you, "along with all malice." All of these are taken to be particularly corrosive of the common life of the Ephesian church. Putting them away is crucial to walking in a manner worthy of the believers' calling.

The virtues described in v. 32 are not the antitheses of the vices of v. 31. Rather, 4:31 describes vices particularly destructive to the common life Paul desires for the Ephesians; then 4:32 describes virtues essential to the proper

---

7. The particular lists here in Eph 4 are quite similar to those found in Col 3:8, 12–13. It is less clear what to make of this, however. Best (*Ephesians* 460) notes that a variety of Stoic texts also use lists of words related to anger.

working of the Ephesians' common life. Paul emphasizes this through the prominence of the term "one another" in this sentence. All the virtues here can only be practiced in relation to others.

The term translated "kind" is accurate yet may also mislead modern readers. In our modern idiom, kindness can be anything from a random act to a small gesture of politeness, to an invitation to dinner, to housing the homeless.[8] Paul has already used this term in Ephesians to describe God's work among the Ephesians. In 2:7 the nominal form of this term describes God's saving work in bringing the Ephesians from death into life as God's "kindness toward us in Christ Jesus." Although Paul makes no direct reference back to 2:7, this passage closes (in 4:32–5:2) by urging the Ephesians to model their interactions with each other on God's interactions with them through Christ. In this respect, Paul here sets before the Ephesians a standard of kindness that is measured by Christ's self-willed offering of himself for the benefit of the Ephesians. This is quite similar to the dispositions that Paul calls the Philippians to demonstrate to each other in their common life in Phil 2:1–11.

The only other place the Greek term rendered above as "compassion" appears in the NT is in 1 Pet 3:8, where it also is in a list of virtues. Its context in 1 Peter is not, however, specific enough to provide a great deal of precision to the phrase. The term appears several times in the *Testaments of the Twelve Patriarchs* (*T. Sim.* 4.4; *T. Zeb.* 5.1; 7.2; 8.1). In each of these cases it appears that compassion is the disposition one displays when confronted with another's need, failing, or lack—and one extends mercy. Such a notion would fit well in this context, too.

Finally, Paul urges the Ephesians to forgive each other as God in Christ has forgiven them.[9] As noted above, all these virtues are relational: they are practiced and displayed in relation to others. Moreover, forgiveness and compassion in particular presume that sin, failure, and need are part of the day-to-day life of the Ephesian congregation. Thus, rather than emphasizing moral perfection as the key to the proper working of the common life of the Ephesian church, Paul stresses practices designed to repair and enhance relationships between believers. Even in cases where the Ephesians avoid anger, bitterness, abusive speech, and so forth, Paul assumes that they will still fall out with each other from time to time. The keys to a common life that is worthy of the calling to which the

---

8. There is also a significant breadth to the way the Greek term *chrēstos* is used. See LSJ 2007.

9. Hoehner (639) argues that the Greek term *charizomenoi* refers more generally to being gracious rather than to forgiveness. This is a possible reading. The more focused use of this term to speak of forgiveness can be found in 2 Cor 2:7, 10; 12:13; and Col 2:13; 3:13. The strongest argument in favor of "forgiveness" is that when Paul has previously spoken of God's work in Christ relative to the Ephesians, it has been in terms of forgiveness. Those, such as Lincoln (*Ephesians* 309), who argue for a strong dependency of Ephesians on Colossians let the clear use of the term in Colossians shape the meaning of the phrase in Ephesians.

Ephesians are called are practices that will generate restored, forgiven relationships rather than morally perfect souls, though that is to be encouraged, too.

The final two verses of this section comprise the beginning of chapter 5.[10] They serve to wrap up a larger discussion that began at 4:17 with the admonition to avoid walking as the Gentiles walk. Here at the end of that discussion, Paul concludes by constructively urging the Ephesians to be imitators of God and to walk in love.

In 4:32 Paul alludes to God's kindness to the Ephesians as the model for the kindness the Ephesians should show each other. At the end of v. 32 Paul urges the Ephesians to forgive each other as God in Christ has forgiven them. Paul then generalizes from these calls for divine imitation into a command to become imitators of God.[11] The Ephesians are beloved children incorporated into God's family. They should thereby seek to imitate the actions of the head of this family.[12]

Obviously, humans cannot imitate God in all respects. All human imitation of God must work on the basis of analogy rather than strict mimesis. At the same time, God's desire is that we participate in the divine nature (2 Pet 1:4). It is important, therefore, that on the one hand Christians avoid all attempts to transgress the boundary between Creator and creature, and on the other hand that they not sell short their calling to participate in the life of the triune God.

In 5:2 the demand to walk in a manner worthy of God's calling (cf. 4:1) is described as walking in love. Any chance of oversentimentalizing this notion is cut short by the next clause. The love in which Christians are to walk is modeled on Christ's willed self-offering on our behalf. In 5:25 we find the same description of Christ's handing himself over on behalf of the church. In both 5:2 and 5:25 the willed self-giving is a mark of Christ's love. In addition, here in 5:2 Paul describes Christ's self-giving as an offering and sacrifice. The further description of that sacrifice as having an aroma pleasing to God describes God's acceptance of the offering. The language here resonates with numerous texts from the LXX (e.g., Gen 8:21; Exod 29:18). In terms of illuminating Ephesians, the most interesting use of this language is in Ezek 20:41. There the Lord speaks of restored Israel, which God has gathered back to Zion from among

---

10. It is possible to follow Hoehner (643), who argues that the term "therefore" in 5:1 marks the beginning of a new section that covers 5:1–6. I have followed Best (*Ephesians* 467), Lincoln (*Ephesians* 310), and Schnackenburg (204), who argue that the repetition of the verb *ginesthe* (be/ become) in 4:32 and 5:1 ties these two verses together, thus drawing 5:1–2 into the orbit of 4:25–32.

11. On one level it is surprising that Jews and Christians would have adopted the notion of imitating God. This on the face of it seems to have been the root of Adam's sin. Wild has usefully accounted for how the Platonic view of imitating God worked its way into the writings of Jews such as Philo and later into texts like Ephesians. He is less clear about how to interpret this text as it stands. See also Best, *Ephesians* 466.

12. Wild 143 n. 60; Lincoln, *Ephesians* 310.

the nations to witness the display of God's holiness, as an acceptable offering whose odor is pleasing. In addition, Paul uses quite similar vocabulary in Phil 4:18 to describe the Philippians' financial gift to him as an acceptable display of their Christ-focused love for him.

Although Eph 5:2 speaks of Christ's death in sacrificial terms, there is no discussion here of the purpose and effects of that sacrifice. This may be because there was already a well-established view of the atonement operative in the Ephesian church, and that doctrine could simply be assumed. Although possible, there is no evidence to support such an assumption, nor would such an assumption really reveal what that particular presumed doctrine of the atonement was. On this score, 5:2 is appropriately silent. This silence is appropriate because the force of the verse is to describe a particular form of self-giving love that Christ has exemplified and that Paul wants the Ephesians to show toward each other. No matter how well they achieve this, it would never accomplish the soteriological significance of Christ's death.

This section of Ephesians has continued the focus on the common life of the Ephesian Christians that started in 4:1. Paul uses the image of "walking" to articulate the manner of life appropriate to those called to be disciples of Christ. He enjoins certain practices and admonishes the Ephesians to eschew other practices. Both in what he commends and in what he forbids, Paul is focused on the common life of the Ephesian church. He is not addressing isolated individuals. Rather, he is concerned with a community and the ways in which they can grow and advance together toward their common end in God. As the rest of chapters 5 and 6 unfold, Paul will continue primarily to address the practical life of the Ephesian church.

Ephesians 5:3–14
Walking Worthily with an Eye
on the World

This passage continues the general theme of walking in a manner worthy of one's calling that began in 4:1. In the first part of this section (5:3–7), Paul focuses on practices and patterns of life that the Ephesians are to avoid. These vices are often sexual in nature. Verses 3–7 are quite similar to Col 3:5–7, and also to lists of vices that would have been well known in both Judaism and pagan society. In the second part of the passage (vv. 8–14), Paul seems concerned with the ways in which the wider society may perceive the Ephesian Christians and with how the Ephesian Christians comport themselves in pagan society more generally. Although this concern becomes explicit in the discussion of darkness and light in vv. 8–14, the concern is also evident in vv. 3–7.

5:3 Do not let sexual misconduct or any kind of uncleanness or covetousness be noted[a] among you, as is fitting for those who are holy.[b] **4** Also, avoid indecency or[c] foolish talk or coarse jesting,[d] for these are also inappropriate, but rather let there be thanksgiving.[e] **5** Be certain of this: No one who is unchaste or unclean or covetous (that is, an idolater) has an inheritance in the kingdom of Christ and of God. **6** Do not let anyone deceive you with empty words. Because of such things, the wrath of God comes upon the children of disobedience. **7** You must not be participants with them.[f] **8** For you were once darkness, but now you are light in the Lord. Walk as children of light **9** —for the fruit of the light is found in all that is good and righteous and true— **10** being able to discern rightly what is pleasing to the Lord. **11** Do not participate in the unfruitful works of darkness. Instead, expose them.[g] **12** For the things they do in secret are shameful even to mention. **13** But all things exposed by the light become visible, **14** and everything that becomes[h] visible is light. Therefore it says, "Awake, O sleeper, and rise from the dead, and Christ will shine on you."

a. The same verb, "be noted" (*onomazesthō*, lit., "be named"), should apply to the nouns of vv. 3 and 4. The NRSV, Lincoln (*Ephesians* 321), and Hoehner (651) translate this term as "mentioned." This translation has some linguistic basis (cf. Jer 20:9 LXX) but also obscures some important points and ignores the way this verb is used in Eph 1:21 and 3:15. See the discussion below.

b. The absence of the definite article here indicates that Paul is not so much referring to a group (i.e., "the saints") as to an identity or state (i.e., "those who are holy").

c. There is some textual variation in the conjunctions used between these three nouns. The best textual witnesses favor the coordinating conjunction *kai* before the first noun (hence the translation "also"). The textual witnesses are almost evenly divided between reading a coordinating or a disjunctive conjunction before the noun translated as "foolish talk." Those reading "and" (*kai*) are 𝔓⁴⁶, 𝔓⁴⁹; ℵ¹, B, 𝔐, et al. Those reading the disjunctive "or" (*ē*) are ℵ*, A, D*, F, et al. The textual witnesses are not determinative here. Commentators and translators generally opt for a coordinating conjunction if they argue that the first noun, "indecency," is really a reference to "indecent speech." The translation above follows Best (*Ephesians* 478) among others in treating this as a reference to indecent acts of all sorts. Hence there is a disjunction between "indecency" and "foolish speech." Finally, the textual witnesses reading a coordinating conjunction before "coarse jesting" are not very strong. See also the arguments in Hoehner (654–55).

d. The Greek noun *eutrapelia*, translated here as "coarse jesting," is used by Aristotle to refer to "wittiness," that virtue between boorishness and buffoonery (*Eth. Nic.* 2.7.13). But in *Eth. Nic.* 4.8 Aristotle recognizes that the term has negative connotations as well and can be hard to apply properly. In addition, there are also instances where the term is used negatively (see LSJ 735). Moreover, the context here indicates that it must refer to some attempt at joking that transgresses the bounds of what is appropriate to "those who are holy."

e. "Let there be thanksgiving." There is actually only the Greek term for "thanksgiving" here. The verb "to be" has been added, as is often necessary in Greek.

f. The phrase translated here as "with them" (*autōn*) is a reference to people, not to the vices mentioned above. See also Lincoln (*Ephesians* 327), Hoehner (668), and Schnackenburg (221–22). This is against Gnilka (250) and Best (*Ephesians* 486).

g. In the second clause of this verse, there is no expressed object for the verb. The translation assumes that "unfruitful works of darkness" is the presumed object of the verb "expose." See below for further comments on the verb "expose."

h. Although the sense of this clause is fairly clear, the Greek is somewhat unclear. The translation above takes the participle *phaneroumenon* as passive rather than as a middle voice with an active sense. To treat this verb as a middle would make it inconsistent with the finite verb of the preceding clause and would also render the entire clause tautologous. The translation thus takes *pan to phaneroumenon* as the subject, "light" as the object. In particular see the discussion in Moritz (97–99).

[3–7] Paul admonishes the Ephesians to steer clear of all sorts of sexual misconduct. Two of these three vices (impurity and covetousness) also appeared in 4:19. The addition of "sexual misconduct" at the head of this list may color the particular types of unclean and covetous behavior in view here. For the most part, the pagan culture with which the Ephesians were familiar would have been much more sexually licentious than Judaism and Christianity. Paul would have censured any number of these pagan practices. Thus translations that use the term "fornication" are too narrow when it comes to describing the types of sexual misconduct Paul has in mind here.

Paul uses the term "uncleanness" alongside "sexual misconduct" in 2 Cor 12:21 and Gal 5:19 when talking about a list of activities that should have no place among believers. When these are further linked with "covetousness," which is both proscribed in Exod 20:17 in relation to the wife of one's neighbor, among other things, and later linked to idolatry in Eph 5:5, we can see that Paul means to describe the widest possible range of sexual misconduct (Best, *Ephesians* 476). Indeed, Paul already understands that sex is never really a separate category of activity. Then as now, sex was always tied up with issues such as purity, identity, power, and desire, which touch on most aspects of life. Thus misconduct in one's sexual practices reflects a wider and deeper level of disorder.

Two particular issues flow from this: First, as most commentators recognize, Paul wants the Ephesians to make a clear, decisive, and comprehensive break with their pagan past. The second point is connected to the idea that none of these vices should be "noted" among the Ephesians. Most contemporary commentators take this as an admonition for the Ephesians to avoid even talking about such practices (Lincoln, *Ephesians* 322; Best, *Ephesians* 477; Hoehner 653). This is a strange interpretation on several counts. First, it seems hard to imagine any sort of moral reasoning going on among the Ephesians if they cannot even talk about particular practices to avoid. Further, Paul mentions such practices himself in 1 Cor 5, for example. In addition, it is hard to understand how mentioning a practice is, in itself, problematic. Most important, this is not the way the Greek verb *onomazō* is used the two other times it appears in the epistle. In both 1:21 and 3:15 it refers much more precisely to naming something—recognizing something and identifying it.

It therefore seems much better to take this verse as not only admonishing the Ephesians to stay away from these practices, but also to make sure that nobody outside the congregation can observe the presence of these practices among them. Paul's concern here would not be about what the Ephesians mention among themselves, but how they are perceived by those outside the congregation. In this way Paul is reflecting both a concern for the integrity of the Ephesians' witness to their neighbors, and also a concern that the lives of the Ephesian Christians might bring God, Christ, and/or the gospel into disrepute needlessly.[1] This concern, however, presumes that there are sufficient interactions between the Ephesian Christians and the rest of society that such judgments might be made.[2] Moreover, this is consistent with Paul's concern

---

1. See the similar notion expressed in Ezek 36:22–24. Thomas Aq. (198) takes the verse this way.

2. Darko (48–58) makes similar points. This is contrary to MacDonald's presumptions in both *Ephesians* and the more recent "Politics of Identity," which stress the idea that Paul calls the Ephesians to a high level of separation from the surrounding society.

throughout 5:3–14 with the ways in which the Ephesian church interacts with and is perceived by the wider culture.

The immediate reason Paul gives for avoiding all sorts of sexual misconduct, uncleanness, and covetousness is that such things are not "fitting" for those called to holiness. Paul has already established that God has called the Christians in Ephesus to holiness (1:4; 2:19–22). Moreover, he has reminded the believers in Ephesus that they have been "sealed" by the Holy Spirit (1:13). Holiness is simply a constitutive part of Christian identity. In this light, certain ways of life can only be seen as inappropriate. Given Christian identity, particularly as narrated by Paul in Eph 2–3, certain practices are ruled out as fundamentally incompatible with that identity.

Verse 4 continues to list behavior inappropriate to the Christian's call to holiness. In this verse the behavior in question is related to speech. Each of the three terms used here occurs only in this verse and nowhere else in the NT. There may be some ambiguity concerning the first of these terms, "indecency." The noun *aischrotēs* normally refers to shameful behavior and is different from the similar but more explicit reference to indecent speech, *aischrologia*, found in Col 3:8. Since the following two terms, "foolish talk" and "coarse jesting," both refer to verbal practices, many commentators take the first term to be a more narrow reference to "indecent speech."[3] Rather than dissect each of these terms to find out which types of speech are implied here, it is probably better to see these three terms as working together to present a composite sketch of the types of speech Christians are to avoid. When taken as a group, these three terms outline a pattern of speech that stands in sharp contrast to the positive admonitions of 4:29, where the Ephesians are encouraged to speak in ways that edify and give grace to those who hear.

The single term "thanksgiving" stands as the sole counterweight to the six vices mentioned here. Throughout the NT, thanksgiving is always to be directed to the Lord. It should be taken this way in 5:4 as well. One finds a similar pattern in Ps 50. There in vv. 18–20 God indicts "the wicked" for making "friends with a thief," keeping "company with adulterers," giving their mouths "free rein for evil," framing deceit with their tongues, and slandering their own relations. In the light of this, the wicked in Israel face God's wrath. The alternative to this, as advised in Ps 50:23, is to bring "thanksgiving as their sacrifice to honor" God.

As Best (*Ephesians* 479) observes, the introduction of thanksgiving injects an interesting twist into the discussion. So far, the vices to be avoided here are all related to interactions with others. The antidote to all of these destructive patterns of behavior and speech is not renewed focus on improving interpersonal relations but thanksgiving to God. There seem to be several respects in

---

3. See Lincoln, *Ephesians* 323; Gnilka 247.

which this might be so. For example, each of these vices in one way or another reflects a level of disorder in one's desires and loves. Thanksgiving reorders a believer's loves so that they are focused on God. Further, cultivating the habit of thanksgiving also enables believers to love others in God properly. Thus, focusing believers' attention thankfully on God can also enable believers to apprehend their neighbors with the love God commands them to show.

One should not imagine, however, that cultivating the habit of thanksgiving is an easy achievement. The vices listed above always confront people through their attractiveness, through their ability to appear to be virtuous or to play upon some aspect of virtue without actually resulting in virtue. Thus they are able to distract believers' attentions and hearts away from God. Cultivating the habit of thanksgiving may first, then, involve rooting out and transforming distorted habits and affections with the help of the Spirit. It is also only with the Spirit's continued help that the habit of thanksgiving can take root and flourish within believers' lives.

Verse 5 returns to narrate the consequences of failing to have one's love and attention properly focused on God. We read that no sexually immoral person, no impure person, and no greedy person will have a share in the "kingdom of Christ and of God." The vices of v. 3 reappear in v. 5. In 5:5, however, the nouns are altered so that they refer to people who engage in these vices rather than the vices themselves. Paul appears less concerned with discrete moral lapses than with a regular habit of behavior.

In this verse Paul further defines "covetousness" as idolatry.[4] This specification should remind believers that idolatry at its root is a misdirection of love and attention away from God and toward something else that is not God. The material world as such—including such things as food, commodities, and works of art—need not draw our attention and love away from God. Indeed, in many cases they can further sharpen our vision of God and enhance our devotion. When and if they truncate or misdirect our attentions, however, our engagements with such things threaten to become idolatrous.

All commentators recognize the odd nature of the locution "the kingdom of Christ and of God." The phrase does not appear elsewhere in the NT. There is sufficient textual variation to confirm that ancient copyists also found the phrase strange. The variants are not sufficiently strong, however, to doubt the originality of the text we have. If the text seeks to make fine distinctions regarding the consummation of all things in the kingdom of God, it is not clear what those distinctions are. The closest formulation to this might be found in Rev 11:15 (cf. Rev 12:10), where the seventh angel blows his trumpet, and

---

4. Although texts such as 1 Cor 6:12–20 link temple prostitution and idolatry, and images of prostitution are often used to describe Israel's attraction to other gods, the syntax of this sentence limits the identification of idolatry solely to covetousness (see Best, *Ephesians* 481; Hoehner 661).

a great voice sounds in the heavens, saying, "The kingdom of the world has become the kingdom of our Lord and of his Messiah, and he will reign forever and ever."[5]

Verse 5 indicates that pagans, because of their habits of sexual misconduct, greed, and idolatry, cannot share in the kingdom of God; verse 6 goes on to declare that such people are not merely excluded from the kingdom but are also subject to God's wrath (cf. 2:3). The "empty words" proffered by such people probably refer to rhetoric that might misdirect the love and attention of believers away from God. A similar phrase is found in Col 2:8, but the Colossian context indicates that Paul is referring to specific false teaching. Such specificity is absent here. Rather than connecting "empty words" to false teaching, this verse connects empty words to their sources, "the children of disobedience." These characters also appear in 2:2, where they are part of a general description of the Ephesians' comprehensive alienation from God outside of Christ.

Although this discussion in v. 6 begins with warnings about "empty words," the introduction of disobedience at the end of v. 6, along with the notions of participation in v. 7, "walking" in v. 8, and "fruit" in v. 9—all show the intimate connection of practice and belief, words and deeds.

The Ephesians are urged not to become participants with "the children of disobedience." The Greek term *symmetochos* (participant) occurs only here and in 3:6, where it refers to the Gentiles being brought into the one body of Christ and becoming participants in the promise of the gospel. This indicates that the "participation" proscribed here is not a casual affiliation, but a wholehearted identification with a body of people.[6]

Given the ways this line of thought develops in vv. 6–7, it appears that Paul is not so much addressing a specific segment of the Ephesian congregation as he is speaking about the occasions and manner in which the Christians in Ephesus engage with the world around them. For reasons both practical and theological, Christians cannot simply abandon all contact and connection with the nonbelievers around them. At the same time, Paul's admonitions here indicate that believers must also be attentive to the differences between them and the nonbelieving world. Ephesians does not advocate withdrawal from the surrounding culture. Rather, Paul is concerned that the common life of

5. Ephesus is one of the seven churches addressed in Revelation. See Lemcio for more on this. It is not clear why Best (*Ephesians* 482) seems to think that reference to the kingdom here is a reference to the kingdom as present now rather than its eschatological consummation.

6. There is no obvious reason why the use of "participant" in 3:6 should count as evidence that the people referred to in 5:7 are members of the church in Ephesus, as Best (*Ephesians* 486) argues. The word could just as easily refer to two incommensurable realms in which one might participate.

the church in Ephesus should stand as a distinct witness and alternative to the wider pagan culture.[7]

[8–14] As he did in chapter 2, now in 5:8 Paul presents the Ephesians with another contrast between "then" and "now," what was once the case and what is now the case. Here the contrast serves to explain why the Ephesians must not become participants with the "sons [children] of disobedience." This explanation is relatively straightforward: "You were once darkness, but now you are light in the Lord. Walk as children of light." Although this reasoning is fairly clear, it is surprising in the light of the preceding verses.

In verses 5–6 Paul tells the Ephesians that those who think and live in particular ways come under God's judgment and have no place in the kingdom. One might think, then, that the reason for not participating in the words and deeds of the disobedient would be to avoid the wrath of God. Instead, Paul employs a form of reasoning he has used elsewhere, most notably in Rom 6:1–11. Given that one has been transferred from the realm of darkness into the kingdom of Christ, it is unintelligible for one to act as if one still participated in the realm of darkness. The Ephesians' allegiance, their citizenship, has been transformed and transferred into Christ's realm. It is only reasonable that they act accordingly. Their words and deeds are not driven by fear of God's wrath. Rather, because they now inhabit the body of Christ, they cannot live any other way. Of course, this does not rule out discrete failures and transgressions. Rather, in Paul's view such sins would now be deformations or aberrant activities of those who are now children of light.

Far too much scholarly effort has been directed at two issues in this verse. First, it is easy to overemphasize the lack of the preposition "in" to describe people as either "in" darkness or "in" light. Given that Paul has just been speaking about participation as a wholehearted commitment to a pattern of thinking, feeling, and acting in v. 7, the idea of being "darkness" or "light" should be seen as an image further specifying a wholehearted commitment to a realm defined either by darkness or light in the Lord. Second, the metaphorical use of darkness and light is so widespread in the ancient world and so immediately intelligible in specific contexts that little is gained by speculating about the particular source of this specific use of the image.

Verse 9 adds a parenthetical note that walking as a child of the light will generate goodness, righteousness, and truth. Paul calls these virtues "fruit," recalling the lengthier account of the "fruit" of the Spirit in Gal 5:22–23. Walking

---

7. Thus, contrary to MacDonald ("Politics of Identity" 424) et al., I see this passage as part of a strategy of engagement and not withdrawal. Although Darko (56) does not accept MacDonald's thesis about withdrawal, his own sociological emphasis on social differentiation does not give sufficient weight to the constructive agenda implied in Paul's argument.

in the light and/or walking according to the Spirit quite naturally forms and generates particular types of people, people whose lives are marked by a particular type of fruit. As with the fruit of the Spirit in Galatians, the fruit of light in Ephesians is characterized in fairly general and abstract ways. Presumably even the disobedient, whose lives are characterized in vv. 5–6, are in favor of "goodness, righteousness, and truth." To be opposed to these things simply means that you do not understand how to use such words. The larger struggle for Christians—who are called to form and maintain distinct communities amid larger social groups that are either hostile or indifferent to Christianity—lies in applying words like "goodness, justice, and truth" to patterns of thinking, feeling, and acting that are appropriate to being "light in the Lord." For example, consider those early Christians who gave up their lives rather than renounce their Christianity. To the Roman authorities executing them, these Christians were stubborn, irascible, and even irrational. To their brothers and sisters in Christ, the martyrs' faithful witness and obedience even unto death became the epitome of "goodness, righteousness, and truth."

In this light, 5:10 goes on to declare that as the Ephesian believers walk as children of light, they will develop the capacities to discern and enact patterns of life pleasing to the Lord. The pattern and style of Paul's admonition here is quite close to Rom 12:2, where he enjoins believers not to be "conformed to this age, but [to] be transformed by the renewing of your minds, so that you may discern the will of God, that which is good, pleasing, and perfect" (AT).

The corollary demand in Eph 5:11 is that believers not participate in the "unfruitful works of darkness." This much seems relatively clear. The next clause is less clear. The interpretive disputes hinge on two matters: the force and implications of the verb translated as "expose" (*elenchete*), and whether the deeds exposed here are those of believers or unbelievers.

It is clear that the Greek term can and often does express not simply exposure, but also confrontation with the aim of pointing out a flaw.[8] On the one hand, the same verb appears in 5:13 with a more neutral sense of exposure and bringing to light. On the other hand, it seems equally clear that the Ephesian believers are to expose the fruitless works of darkness with the aim of pointing out their deficiencies and making them appear unattractive and avoidable, in contrast with lives marked by the fruit of light. This is the nature of the confrontation that Paul imagines here (see also Engberg-Pedersen 102).

Although believers are called to confront and admonish one another regarding their behavior (cf. Matt 18:15–20; Gal 6:1; 1 Tim 5:20; 2 Tim 4:2; Jas 5:19–20; 1 John 5:16), this particular context in Ephesians is different. From the beginning of this section in 5:3, both Paul's constructive admonitions

---

8. This point is clearly made by Engberg-Pedersen 97.

and his warnings about what to avoid have been directed toward ensuring that the Ephesian congregation stands as what Gerhard Lohfink (ch. 2) calls a *contrast society*. This is a body of Christians whose common life and practice stand as a sharp yet appealing alternative to the surrounding world. Paul has not focused on matters internal to the Ephesian congregation. Rather, he addresses the borders and contrasts between the congregation and the world. Thus it is most likely that Paul is speaking about exposing the deeds of the world relative to what he hopes will be the deeds of the church. The primary aim here is not to cultivate a form of churchly, self-acquired goodness. Rather, the challenge to the church is to stand as an appealing alternative to the world. This appeal would not lie primarily in the moral superiority of Christians to any other people. Rather, the appeal would lie in the manner in which believers confront their sins, seek and offer forgiveness, and live reconciled and reconciling lives.

The last three verses of this section are more obscure,[9] but they can be read as building on this theme of how the Christians in Ephesus are to relate to their unbelieving neighbors. Verse 12 appears to be a further parenthetical comment about the unfruitful works of darkness. They are done in secret, and even mentioning them is shameful. These claims do not really help us discern what particular deeds Paul has in mind. Presumably the Ephesians had a good idea of what they were. Paul goes on to assert that everything exposed by the light becomes visible. On the logic of v. 8, believers themselves are light, thus reinforcing the notion that the fruitful lives of believers reveal the moral poverty of the surrounding culture. Here Paul seems to imagine a more general version of the process initially described in 1 Cor 14:24–25, where the deficiencies of the lives of individual unbelievers are exposed. This more general practice is also discussed in John 16:8, where the same Greek verb is used as here. There Jesus promises that the coming Paraclete will "expose the world with regard to sin, righteousness, and judgment" (AT). It appears, then, that Paul understands the Christian community to be the vehicle through which the Spirit plays that role described in John 16:8. Finally, when Paul says that everything that becomes visible is light, he seems to imply that as believers "shine as lights in the midst of a crooked and perverse generation" (Phil 2:15 KJV alt.), the quality of their common life will both display the poverty of alternative ways of living and provide a sufficiently fascinating and compelling alternative that those outside of the light will be drawn into that light.[10] J. B. Phillips's paraphrase of this verse catches this sense, "It is even possible (after all, it happened to you!) for

---

9. Gnilka (256) calls these verses the most enigmatic in the whole letter.

10. Yoder Neufeld (*Ephesians* 226) speaks of nonconformity as a means of transforming the world.

light to turn the thing it shines upon into light also." In this respect it is fitting for Paul in v. 14 to recall the Ephesians' own experience.

The concluding part of v. 14 begins with the phrase "Therefore it says." This is the same phrase that is used in 4:8 to introduce a quotation from the OT. There is no LXX text, however, that matches up well with this verse. The closest texts would be Isa 26:19 and 60:1. Even here the match is not very close. Nevertheless, the passage does seem to exhibit a sort of poetic structure that certainly distinguishes it both from the preceding and the following verses. As a result, scholars argue that Paul is quoting from a hymn or some liturgical phrase that would have been well known to the Ephesians. Although this may be the case, we are obligated to understand these clauses in the context of Ephesians and not in some prior, speculatively reconstructed context.[11]

By introducing these three concise clauses with "therefore," Paul ties this passage to the discussion that initially started in 5:8, reflecting on the Ephesians' conversion from darkness to light. In the first clause, "Awake, O sleeper," Paul is clearly using sleep in a metaphorical sense. Although sleep can be used as a metaphor for laziness or inattentive behavior (1 Thess 5:6–7), Paul is probably using it as a metaphor for death (also with a different Greek verb, as in KJV, NRSV mg.: 1 Thess 4:13; 1 Cor 7:39; 11:30; 15:6, 18, 20, 51). This fits best with the next clause, which speaks of resurrection. Further, according to the logic of 5:13–14a, the image of Christ as shining on believers would be a way of speaking about believers' conversion from darkness into light.

This final passage reminds believers that although they were once dead (2:1) and in darkness (5:8), they now are light because Christ has shone upon them. This means that even as they live in such a way as to display the darkness of the world around them, they must also live in the hope that just as Christ brought them into the light, Christ aims to bring all into the light.

In 5:8–14 Paul admonishes the Ephesians to avoid participation in the unfruitful works of the pagan culture that surrounds them. Paul's concluding recitation of Christ's enlightening work should also shape believers' dispositions to the world around them. They cannot despair over the pagan culture around them; they cannot despise it, and they cannot abandon it even as they eschew its ways. Instead, they are to shine a light on it. This is not primarily to condemn the world. Rather, to the extent that the common life of Christian communities offers a beautiful and bright alternative, such communities can

---

11. This is against Moritz (97), who asserts without arguing that "the complex issue of detecting and form-critically evaluating such 'hymns' cannot be circumvented." If one is interested in commenting on the text of Ephesians, rather than producing a history of a particular but nowhere else attested text, then one need not deal with these issues at all. For a fuller philosophical account of the reasons for this, see Fowl, *Story of Christ*, ch. 2.

expect that the world around them will be drawn to God by what the world sees in their lives.[12]

Understanding how to articulate the differences between the Ephesian church and the wider world and how to live as light, both exposing and attracting the wider world, will require a measure of wisdom from the Ephesians. In the following passage Paul takes up this idea, enjoining the Ephesians to walk as wise people.

12. Macdonald (*Pauline Churches*) offers an alternative account of the relationship between the church in Ephesus and the surrounding culture (see esp. 99–120). Without question, different dynamics are at work in the various "Pauline" Letters. I am not persuaded that an account of the growing institutionalization of the church is the best way to account for these differences. Moreover, there is a great temptation with sociological models to let the model drive the interpretation of the text, rather than inquiring whether the interpretation of the text fits the model or not.

Ephesians 5:15–20
Walking Wisely

This passage continues the theme of "walking," which Paul introduced in 4:1. In 4:1 Paul enjoins the Ephesians to walk in a manner worthy of their calling. In 4:17 they are admonished not to walk as the Gentiles do. In 5:2 Paul urges them to "walk in love." Most recently, in 5:8 he reminds the Ephesians that they were darkness, but now they are light; they should therefore "walk as children of light." Each of these uses of "walk" is tied to the conjunction "therefore," which links the manner of walking to a set of convictions about God, the world, and God's dealings with the world. Sometimes these convictions are clearly articulated in the immediately preceding verses. Other times they need to be inferred from things Paul has said previously in the epistle.

In the case of 5:15 the command to walk wisely is tied to the previous paragraph, where Paul's entire argument presumes the cultivation of wisdom with regard to how Christians comport themselves in relation to the wider culture. As this passage goes on, it will become clear that the wisdom Paul imagines here is a Spirit-directed habit cultivated as much in worship and thanksgiving as by improving the intellect.

> **5:15** Be careful, therefore,[a] how you walk, not as unwise people, but as wise, **16** making the most of the time,[b] for the days are evil. **17** On account of this, do not be foolish, but understand what the will of the Lord is. **18** Also do not get drunk with wine, which leads to dissipation, but be filled with the Spirit,[c] **19** speaking to each other in psalms and hymns and spiritual songs, singing and making melody in your hearts[d] to the Lord, **20** always giving thanks for everything in the name of our Lord Jesus Christ to God the Father.[e]

a. In the translation above, the Greek *blepete oun akribōs* (which may be translated as "Therefore, pay careful attention," is rendered with the more straightforward "Be careful, therefore." Second, the translation above follows 𝔓⁴⁶, ℵ*, B, et al. in placing the adverb *akribōs* with the imperative *blepete*. The alternative reading, which also has strong manuscript support, would place the adverb with the verb *peripateite*, resulting in a translation such as Hoehner's (690): "Therefore, look how carefully you are walking."

b. In the LXX of Dan 2:8, we find a Greek phrase (*kairon hymeis exagorazete*) quite similar to that used here. In that context, Nebuchadnezzar accuses his advisors of trying to "buy time" for themselves (i.e., stalling). Here Paul uses the notion of "buying time" with a positive sense of making the most of it (Lincoln, *Ephesians* 341, Hoehner 692, Mac-Donald, *Ephesians* 317). The notion of "redeeming the time," an alternative translation favored by several commentators (Schnackenburg 235; Robinson 202), is a bit awkward in that it requires one to think of time as a captive rather than a commodity. Even if one thinks in terms of things such as time being captivated by Satan, believers themselves would not be able to "redeem" time in any soteriological sense. The metaphor of humans as redeeming time must be a way of talking about making the most of the time.

c. Recently Heil ("Ephesians 5:18b"), among others, has questioned the traditional way of translating this verse as an admonition to be filled with the Spirit. The Greek preposition *en* here is admittedly flexible. It could be translated as "Be filled by the Spirit," or as Heil argues, "Be filled in the Spirit." Being filled in the Spirit means "being within the dynamic realm or sphere established and characterized by having been given the Spirit" (507). This requires Heil to argue that one should read the other occasions in Ephesians where the phrase *en* the Spirit appears (2:18, 22; 3:5; 6:18; and 4:30, where *en* is followed by a relative pronoun referring to the Spirit) in the same way. In each of these cases it seems quite clear that *en* the Spirit refers to the Spirit's work of confirming the movement of God's drama of salvation through the Spirit's presence in the one body of Christ. The phrase seems to indicate that the Spirit is both the one who fills and the filling itself (cf. Rom 5:5). Thus the translation above uses "with."

d. There is some textual variation with the phrase translated above as "in your hearts." There are three variations among the manuscripts. One reads "in your heart" (locative dative: *tē kardia hymōn*, in $\mathfrak{P}^{46}$, $\aleph$*, B, et al.), another reads "in your hearts" (*en tais kardiais hymōn*, in $\aleph^2$, A, D, F, G, P, et al.), and a third reads "in your heart" (*en tē kardia hymōn*, in Ψ, $\mathfrak{M}$, et al.). The reading "in your hearts" has wide distribution. It is also the reading found in a similar verses in Col 3:15, 16. Alternatively, "in your heart" is the more difficult reading and may therefore have generated subsequent corrections. Hoehner (712) opts for "in your hearts" as the original. The case for originality is quite closely balanced, but there is no doubt that the sense of the phrase is better captured by "in your hearts."

e. The final words of this verse in Greek might also be rendered "to God and the Father." As in 1:3, however, the second noun is in the same case as the first noun, has no article, and is preceded by "and," so should be seen as a further specification of the first noun (Hoehner 715).

[15–20] This passage begins with the now-familiar admonition to walk in a particular way. The upshot of the preceding passage is that the Ephesians need to cultivate a wise and discerning eye when it comes to the ways they look at and then engage the wider culture around them.[1] In the first instance, wise walking requires making the most of each opportunity.[2]

---

1. This is against Best (*Ephesians* 505), who assumes that because 5:15–16 does not explicitly deal with those outside the church, these verses are not concerned with how the church in Ephesus should engage the wider culture. The preceding verses establish this context.

2. See the similar use of the Greek word *kairos* to signify an opportunity in Gal 6:10.

The reason for making the most of each opportunity is given in the final clause of v. 16: "The days are evil." In 6:13 Paul speaks of a climactic, apocalyptic point in time as "the evil day." Here he seems to be offering a more general characterization about all days. This notion is not all that surprising given the use of light-and-dark imagery in the preceding verses to establish a contrast between believers and the surrounding culture (cf. 5:8–12). In addition, Ephesians offers the very clear impression that creation has been captivated by the "the ruler of the realm of the air," by the "spirit at work in the children of disobedience," and so forth (2:1–3). Alternatively, the world is God's creation; all things are being brought to their proper end in Christ, to which the Spirit gives ample testimony (1:10–14). Christians in Ephesus and elsewhere simply cannot treat the world as a place of unrelenting darkness. Neither should they blithely assume that because Christ has fully entered our world, therefore all aspects of our world are basically good. Just because the guidance systems of first-strike nuclear weapons employ the goods of electrical engineering, physics, and metallurgy, one cannot take them either to be testimony of the goodness of creation or suitable witnesses to the incarnation (example from Budde 99). Instead, Christians in Ephesus and elsewhere are called to cultivate the wisdom needed to discern when, where, and in what ways to affirm, criticize, or otherwise engage the world around them, making the most of each opportunity.

In v. 17 Paul further specifies what is involved in the cultivation of wisdom. He does this by contrasting foolishness with understanding "the will of the Lord." Paul is already confident that the mystery of God's will has been made known to the Ephesians (1:9). This will is to bring all things to their proper end in and through Christ. That is, the Ephesians already know the end, or telos, toward which God is moving all things. How and when will God do these things? How and in what ways might the Ephesians and other believers participate in these movements? Answering these questions amid the concrete circumstances of daily life calls for practical wisdom to discern how and in what ways any particular course of action might best fit with the end toward which God is moving all things. The rest of this passage can be read as offering a set of habits or practices that will aid the cultivation of such practical wisdom, and a contrasting set of habits and practices that will frustrate the cultivation of such wisdom.

Being filled with the Spirit is the first habit that Paul urges the Ephesians to cultivate. This immediately raises the question of whether believers can fill themselves with the Spirit. On the one hand, the answer is clearly no. The Spirit comes to believers as a gift. Believers might accept this gift and say with Paul in Rom 5:5 that "God's love has been poured into our hearts through the Holy Spirit that has been given to us." We cannot, however, "possess the Spirit by our own power" (Thomas Aquinas 213).[3]

---

3. Most modern commentators do not address the theological question posed by this verse.

On the other hand, if Paul admonishes the Ephesians to be filled by the Spirit, there must be some sense in which this is in their power. Thomas Aquinas (213) addresses this point: "Someone may be said to receive the Holy Spirit, and nonetheless not be full of the Holy Spirit. He has the grace of the Holy Spirit in reference to certain aspects of his life, but not in reference to every one of his actions. Then he is said to be full of the Holy Spirit when he avails himself of the Spirit in all he does." In this way being filled with the Spirit entails bringing the gift of the Spirit to bear on all aspects of one's life.

In contrast to being filled with the Spirit, Paul admonishes the Ephesians to avoid drunkenness. We should not infer from this that drunkenness was a particular problem in the Ephesian church. Rather, drunkenness is conventionally linked with a life of folly (Prov 23:29–35). Paul further describes drunkenness in Eph 5:18 as "dissipation," reflecting a prodigal way of life that can lead to a host of other excesses.

Moreover, as Lincoln observes, the contrast between drunkenness and a life filled with the Spirit may not be quite as abrupt as it might first appear. "Both involve the self coming under the control of an external power, and the states of alcoholic and of religious intoxication were often compared" (*Ephesians* 344). Recall that at Pentecost those who observed the first followers of Jesus newly filled with the Spirit assumed that they were drunk (Acts 2:13).

The rest of this passage goes on to elucidate some of the actions that accompany the work of the Spirit in the lives of believers.[4] Singing in psalms and hymns and spiritual songs, making heartfelt melodies, and offering thanksgiving to God—all these are activities of those filled with the Spirit. They are activities of worship. That much is clear. It is not possible to dig behind such terms as "psalms," "hymns," and "spiritual songs," however, to develop a more precise picture about the structure and nature of early Christian worship.[5] These terms can be used to cover too many different types of singing and praising God.

The reflexive pronoun in v. 19 ("to each other") makes it appear that a Christian's praise has a dual object. In the course of praising God in song, Christians are also speaking to each other. What sort of speaking is this? It does not make sense to claim that in praising each other, Christians are also praising God; or that in praising God, Christians are also praising each other. Instead, believers should recognize that although our ultimate end in Christ is participation in the eternal worship of God, our sin diverts us from properly achieving this end. We need to be trained to praise God as we ought. As Rom 8:26–27 indicates,

---

4. Verses 19–20 contain three participles, all of which depend on the main verb "be filled."

5. Pliny the Younger (*Ep.* 10.96) relates that the early Christians sang songs to Christ as to a god. Unfortunately, we do not know much more than this about early Christian worship. The form-critical work on so-called early Christian hymns has foundered on the problems inherent in the presuppositions of form criticism. As a result such work has not yielded reliable information. See Fowl, *Story of Christ*, ch. 2.

believers cannot address God properly apart from the Spirit's intervention. Presumably, however, Christians filled with the Spirit (5:18) may play an educative role in training each other in the proper praise of God. Thus in praising God in a public communal way, Christians are also indirectly addressing each other, encouraging and instructing each other in what will be their eternal practice, and thus building up the church. Paul develops just this notion more fully in 1 Cor 14:1–33.

In 5:4 Paul indicates that the Ephesians are to engage in thanksgiving as an alternative to a variety of destructive ways of speaking. Here in 5:20 that idea reappears as a manifestation of being filled with the Spirit. The nature of this thanksgiving is both comprehensive, "at all times, for all things," and particular in that it is offered "in the name of our Lord Jesus Christ." In this way Paul reminds the Ephesians that "all things are summed up in Christ"; Christ is the mystery in which God's desires for the world are made known (3:1–13); Christ is the one who reconciles Jews and Gentiles to God, making them into one body, of which he himself is both head and cornerstone (2:16–22). In this way, all thanksgiving properly offered to God has its source in Christ.

Ephesians began with a powerful expression of praise, which reminded believers that the ultimate purpose of God's redemption of the world is so that the world can fulfill its proper vocation of praising God. Here toward the end of the epistle, Paul again turns his attention to the praise of God. In this case, praise of God is tied up with the role of the Spirit in the lives of believers. Working in and through believers, the Spirit both reforms and redirects their praise and worship to God. In the light of the overall concern of this passage with "walking wisely," it becomes clear that the worship of the Christian community in Ephesus is the context where the Ephesian believers will best learn how to "walk wisely."

Ephesians 5:21–6:9
Walking Worthily in Households

These verses reflect a concern with the ordering of Christian households. As such, they are often referred to as the "household codes," or *Haustafeln*. Similar admonitions can be found in Hellenistic Jewish and particularly in Greco-Roman works. At the same time, it is striking that this very conventional discussion of husbands and wives, and then children and parents and slaves and masters in Eph 6, comes amid an otherwise unbroken discussion of some ways in which believers' lives manifest the presence of the Holy Spirit. Given the place of these verses in the wider context of Ephesians, one can reasonably ask about the ways in which these admonitions might relate to the lives of believers in the present who also seek to manifest the presence of the Holy Spirit. On the one hand, one cannot rule out these concerns as beyond the scope of a commentary. On the other hand, the nature of commentary will entail that such questions are best addressed here in the course of paying close attention to what is actually written in Ephesians.

As one might expect, there has been an enormous amount of secondary literature written on this passage and the close parallel found in Col 3:18–4:1. In addition, 1 Pet 2:18–3:7 has similar material, which also figures in scholarly discussions.[1] Scholars have focused much of their attention on two particular issues. The first concerns the source material for the household codes in the NT. The second issue addresses the reasons for the inclusion of this material in Ephesians, Colossians, and 1 Peter. The commentaries of Hoehner (720–29); Best (*Ephesians* 519–27) as well as Balch's monograph (1–20) all include concise summaries of the scholarly discussion from Dibelius's commentary on Colossians (1912) to the recent past.

To the extent that one can speak of a scholarly consensus on these issues, one could summarize the general agreement this way: The household codes in Ephesians are most like admonitions found elsewhere in literature devoted to household management. These discussions are found in a wide variety of Hellenistic writings by both Gentiles and some Jews. Thus scholars now hold that there is no single text or texts behind the household codes in the NT. Rather, the

---

1. One of the most significant works on these verses is Balch, *Let Wives be Submissive*.

NT texts reflect a widespread and conventional set of concerns about household management.

In the light of this conclusion, scholars have then assumed that to understand why the material appears in the NT in the first place, one must understand the purpose and function of such discussions of household management in Greco-Roman literature more generally. These discussions originate with concerns found in both Plato and Aristotle about how to best order a city-state. Since the household was considered to be the fundamental building block of the city-state, discussions about the proper ordering of the household were part of larger discussions about the proper ordering of the city. Stable households were considered to be essential elements of social concord. In this light, scholars argue that the NT, and Ephesians and Colossians in particular, adopt these admonitions about the proper ordering of the household for apologetic reasons. In order to quell concern that the early Christians were a socially disruptive and dangerous movement because they tended to blur hierarchical distinctions between men and women, Jew and Greek, slave and master (Gal 3:27–28). Later writings such as Ephesians, Colossians, and 1 Peter admonish believers to order their households in fairly conventional ways, to show the wider world that they are not a threat to the political order. This would then allow Christians to engage more directly in evangelistic work.[2]

Recent work by Daniel Darko (ch. 3), however, has raised some significant objections to this scholarly consensus. Darko recognizes that Plato, Aristotle, and later philosophers such as Epictetus and Dionysius of Halicarnassus link discussions of household management to discussions of the larger political order. Yet numerous others, such as Plutarch and Dio Chrysostom and Musonius Rufus, address issues of household order without making any larger political connections. Moreover, the vast majority of Jewish texts that address household order do so without connecting the household to the city. The point here is that in those cases in which stability of the household is connected to the political order, such connections are explicitly made. When this connection is not made, there is no reason to assume it. Ephesians displays none of the apologetic concerns that comprise the scholarly consensus regarding the household codes. Indeed, Paul's willing acceptance of and frequent reference to his imprisonment for Christ's sake shows that he has little interest in masking the potentially disruptive costs and results of Christianity. Furthermore, in the light of 5:3–20, it is clear that Paul does not want the Ephesians to live according to the moral conventions of the world around them. Thus there is no reason to assume that when Paul addresses the ordering of Christian households in Ephesus, he has any interest in showing that Christians are not a threat to the order of the city.

---

2. This view is most clearly stated in the commentaries of MacDonald (*Ephesians* 337–38) and Lincoln (*Ephesians* 356–60).

To the extent that Paul does advocate conventionally hierarchical and patriarchal households, it is more likely because "Christianity emerged in a social context where these patriarchal structures were already in place. Its choice was not whether or not to 'adopt' domestic patterns in which its members already found themselves, but whether or not to encourage behavior within these structures which would embody a new set of values typical of a new vision of human community" (Elliott 70). To the extent to which Christians found themselves in conventionally structured patriarchal households, Ephesians gives them guidance about how best to live in those households as followers of Christ.

Roman law inscribed a patriarchal view of the household. In reality, actual households were highly varied in their composition. Sometimes households were headed by women. Often the household included children, slaves, unmarried relatives, and often freedmen and freedwomen or other renters of commercial or residential property (see Wallace-Hadrill). There is no reason to think that Christians should take either Roman law or conventions about patriarchy as the only way God intends people to live. In writing Ephesians, Paul does, however, take these as social realities within which believers in Ephesus and elsewhere found themselves. His instructions in Ephesians reflect his wisdom about how those who are in Christ should live within such social structures and arrangements. Even if they were so inclined, it would be difficult if not impossible for contemporary North American Christians to follow many of the instructions offered in this passage without first re-creating the social structures and conventions common across the Greco-Roman world. Presumably, when faced with very different social contexts, Christians should extend the same Christ-focused practical wisdom to prescribe quite different ways of living faithfully in those new contexts. Both the nature of Scripture and practical reasoning mean that such an enterprise will require Christian communities to engage each other in discussion, argument, and debate. Moreover, even after much discussion, Christians can do this badly. They can invoke a gap between Paul's world and ours simply to avoid things they would rather not do. Even when willing to subject themselves to the Spirit's transforming work, Christians may apply their practical wisdom in ways that do not result in faithful life and worship. Yet even in such instances, God delights in forgiving us. The application of Christ-focused practical wisdom can go wrong in these and many other ways, but that fact does not mean that a wooden application of these instructions is a better alternative.[3]

Formally, the passage begins by addressing wives (5:21–24). It then moves to discuss husbands (5:25–33). Chapter 6 begins with an address to children (vv. 1–4), and the section concludes by addressing slaves (vv. 5–8) and their masters (v. 9).

---

3. For a fuller accounting of the theoretical issues involved here, see Fowl, *Engaging Scripture*.

5:21 Submit[a] to one another out of reverence[b] for Christ. 22 Wives, submit[c] to your husbands as to the Lord,[d] 23 because the husband is the head of the wife as Christ is the head of the church; he[e] himself is the Savior of the body. 24 Just as the church submits to Christ, so also wives submit to their husbands in all things.

25 Husbands, love your wives just as Christ loved the church and gave himself up on her behalf 26 so that she might be holy, having cleansed[f] her by washing of water in the word,[g] 27 so that he might present the church to himself, glorious, without blemish or wrinkle[h] or any such thing, but so that she might be holy and blameless. 28 In the same way[i] husbands ought to love their wives as their own bodies. He who loves his own wife loves himself. 29 For no one ever hated his own flesh[j] but nurtures and cherishes[k] it just as Christ does for the church, 30 because we are members of his body.[l] 31 "For this reason a man will leave his father and mother and be joined to his wife, and the two will become one flesh."[m] 32 This is a great mystery, and I am applying it[n] to Christ and the church. 33 In any case,[o] each of you should love your wife as yourself, and a wife should respect her husband.

6:1 Children, obey your parents in the Lord,[p] for this is right.[q] 2 "Honor your father and your mother," which is the first commandment with a promise, 3 "that it may go well with you and you may live long on the earth."[r]

4 Fathers,[s] do not make your children angry. Rather, bring them up in the training and admonition[t] of the Lord.

5 Slaves, obey your earthly[u] masters as you would obey Christ,[v] with fear and trembling and singleness of heart, 6 not to catch someone's eye or as people-pleasers,[w] but as slaves of Christ, doing the will of God wholeheartedly,[x] 7 with goodwill, rendering service as to the Lord and not to people, 8 knowing that whatever good each person does, each will receive this good back from the Lord, whether slave or free.

9 Masters,[y] do the same to them, abandoning threats, knowing that both you and they have one Lord[z] in heaven, and with him there is no partiality.[aa]

a. There is a long scholarly discussion about whether v. 21 begins a new section or concludes the section that began at 5:15. This is discussed in the comments below. The verb translated as "submit" is a participle in Greek. It continues the string of participles that all depend on "be filled" in 5:18. Therefore it could also be translated as "submitting." This would be particularly appropriate if one takes this verse as the conclusion of 5:15–20. For reasons noted below, v. 21 will be treated as the introduction to this entire section.

b. The term translated "reverence" in this verse could also be translated as "fear." The English word "fear" often connotes terror or panic, such as when the resurrected

Christ appears to the disciples (Luke 24:36–38). In this context in Ephesians, the Greek word *phobos* implies the disposition to obey and attend to one of higher authority (cf. Rom 13:7; Phil 2:12).

c. A variety of textual variants supply some form of the Greek verb *hypotassō* (submit) to this verse. Yet 𝔓⁴⁶ and B are the earliest and best MSS that omit the verb. Omitting the verb ties v. 22 more closely to v. 21, which has a verb in the form of a participle. Although there are many interesting ways of adjudicating the text-critical arguments (see Hoehner 730 n. 2; Metzger 541), there is no doubt that the verb "submit" was either written in the original v. 22 or unmistakably understood from v. 21.

d. Recognizing how 1 Pet 3:6 mentions that Sarah called Abraham "lord," some argue that the final clause of this verse is really a reference to husbands (i.e., "wives submit to your husbands as to a lord"). But a variety of reasons tell against such a translation (see Hoehner 736). The most telling is that "lord" is singular and "husbands" is plural. Further, the subsequent analogy to Christ and the church makes it clear that Christ is the "Lord" spoken of here.

e. This phrase is a reference to Christ alone and not also to husbands. Any attempt to read this phrase in the light of 1 Cor 7:16 founders on the fact that the discussion in 1 Cor 7:16 is about marriages between believers and unbelievers, which cannot be the case here. Moreover, the use of the reflexive pronoun "himself" makes it clear Christ is the sole focus of attention. He is the one who saves the church.

f. In this verse the Greek verb *hagiasē*, "make holy," and the participle, *katharisas*, "to cleanse," are both in the aorist tense. This may lead one to think that they are chronologically contemporaneous. Logically, however, the cleansing must precede being made holy (Abbott 168; followed by Hoehner 752). The translation here follows the NRSV and others by recognizing the logical relationship between cleansing and being made holy.

g. Although there are several views about what the Greek phrase translated as "by the washing of water in the word" might mean, this is probably the most accurate translation. The Greek seems to indicate the means by which the cleansing of the church occurs. See the comments below for various interpretive options.

h. The two Greek terms translated here as "blemish" and "wrinkle" (*spilos* and *rhytis*) are relatively rare in the NT (*spilos* is used metaphorically in 2 Pet 2:13 to refer to moral failings; *rhytis* does not occur elsewhere in the NT). Each word, though, is well attested outside the NT, where they refer to blemishes and wrinkles, typical imperfections of the skin due to age, weather, and so forth.

i. The Greek conjunction *houtōs*, which begins this verse, is somewhat ambiguous. It is possible to treat the syntax in a manner similar to v. 33, where the conjunction *houtōs* (so) seems to direct the thought forward ("In any case, each of you should love his own wife as himself"; e.g., Schnackenburg 252). Most commentators, however (e.g., Hoehner 763; Best, *Ephesians* 547–48; Lincoln, *Ephesians* 378), argue that *houtōs kai* in v. 28 points backward, concluding the discussion that began in v. 25 with *kathōs kai* (just as). Verse 25 introduces a comparison with Christ, "just as Christ loved . . ." Verse 28 concludes the thought with *houtōs kai*, "In the same way husbands ought to love . . ." Readers of Greek will notice that this argument presumes that the term *kai* should be part of the text, as it is in the majority of MSS, even though it does not always appear in the same place.

j. The English term "flesh" indicates that Paul is using a different Greek word (*sarx*) from the term translated throughout here as "body" (*sōma*).

k. The two Greek words translated above as "nurture" and "cherish" (*ektrephei* and *thalpei*) have a wide range of uses. For example, *ektrephete* appears in 6:4 to refer to the proper upbringing of children. In 1 Thess 2:7 Paul uses *thalpē* to refer to the care that a nurse offers to children. Most significantly, however, these two words appear in a marriage contract to signify a husband's obligation to his wife, including the obligation to clothe her (MM 283).

l. At the end of this verse, some manuscripts (ℵ², D, F, G, et al.) add a version of the following: "out of his flesh and out of his bones." This is a rough quotation of the LXX of Gen 2:23. Although this reading has some significant textual witnesses, it appears to have been added later, in the light of the quotation of Gen 2:24 in v. 31. Among modern commentators, Hoehner (771) gives the strongest reasons for including the phrase, yet he does so with great hesitation.

m. This quote of Gen 2:24 follows the LXX with only two minor variations. First, the LXX uses the word *heneken* instead of *anti*, as appears here. Also, the LXX adds the possessive pronoun "his" (*autou*) after father and mother; this text omits it.

n. Besides this verse, the Greek phrase *egō de legō* only occurs in Matt 5:22, 28, 32, 34, 39, 44. These are the so-called antitheses of the Sermon on the Mount, where Jesus quotes a law and then adds, "But I say," thereby offering a new interpretation of the law. This has led some scholars to assume that Paul must also be countering a received interpretation of Gen 2:24 (Sampley 51–61). Although there are clearly different inter-pretations of Gen 2:24 within the NT (cf. Matt 19:5; Mark 10:7–8), there is no explicit evidence that Paul is trying to counter these (or other) interpretations. Rather, it is clear that he is applying this verse to display something about the relationship between Christ and the church. Hence the translation "I am applying it . . ."

o. The Greek adverb *plēn* is used here to conclude this paragraph and bring the argu-ment back to its main point. Thus it is translated "In any case." The verb *phobētai* is translated as respect rather than "fear" (cf. NRSV). See discussion below.

p. Some MSS omit "in the Lord" (B, D*, F, G, et al.). The phrase has widespread attestation, however (𝔓⁴⁶, ℵ, A, D¹, et al.). If it had been copied from Col 3:20, it would make more sense for it to appear after the phrase "for this is right." See Hoehner 785 n.1.

q. Although the Greek word *dikaios* is often translated as "just" or "righteous" in the NT, in this context it refers to something that is "proper" or "right." See comments below.

r. The text quoted here is closer to the LXX of Exod 20:12 than to the similar passage in Deut 5:16. The Ephesians text, however, leaves out the final clause of Exod 20:12, which identifies the "land" as "the good land that the Lord your God is giving to you." In dropping this clause, Paul turns a promise about long life in a specific place into a promise about long life in whatever place a believer happens to be.

s. The Greek word *pateres* (fathers) used here in the plural can sometimes refer to parents more generally. This seems unlikely here, however, since the Greek word *goneis* is used in 6:1 and "mother" is mentioned in 6:2. Hence the omission of "mothers" here in 6:4 seems to be intentional.

t. Three Greek terms are used in the second half of the verse to refer to the upbring-ing of children. The verb *ektrephō* also is used in 5:29 (as *ektrephei*) to refer to the way someone cares for and provides for the physical needs of one's body. Here the notion has to do with the raising of children, and so the English "upbringing" is probably better as a translation. The two Greek nouns *paideia* and *nouthesia* are used together in Philo's *Deus* 54, where anthropomorphic terms for God are used for the "training and admonition" of humans. Although sometimes these two nouns (or a cognate verb) appear individually in the NT to refer to chastisement or discipline (cf. 1 Cor 11:32; 2 Tim 3:16; Titus 2:12; 3:10), this verse is more interested in the formation of children than in their chastisement.

u. The Greek phrase *kata sarka* is translated here as "earthly." Sometimes this phrase appears as part of a contrast between flesh and spirit and is translated as "according to the flesh" (e.g., Rom 8:4; Gal 4:29). In this case the contrast is between two masters, Christ and earthly masters.

v. In Greek, the phrase comparing obedience to masters with obedience to Christ (*hōs tō Christō*, lit., "as to Christ") comes at the very end of the verse. The translation above moves this phrase earlier in the sentence to make the comparison clearer in English.

w. The Greek term *ophthalmodoulia* appears in the NT only here and in the similar passage in Col 3:22. The term might be literally rendered as "eyeservice" (so Hoehner 808). In both Colossians and Ephesians, this term is paired with *anthrōpareskoi* (pleasing to people) to signify a contrast with work that is done with an inner dedication and the proper attitude. In this light, it seems best to translate *ophthalmodoulia* as "eye-catching." That is, it signifies service done simply to catch the eye of one's master, without the proper attitude or dedication (Best, *Ephesians* 577; Lincoln, *Ephesians* 420).

x. The Greek phrase *ek psychēs* (lit., "from the soul") signifies something that stems from one's innermost being. We might say "from the heart," or as above, "wholeheartedly" (see also Best, *Ephesians* 578; Hoehner 809.)

y. Although the Greek of this verse is relatively straightforward, it is open to several variations in translation. The Greek is a single sentence, and it has been translated that way here. The NRSV, e.g., renders this verse as two English sentences, and it could easily be three. The NRSV starts a new sentence where the Greek has a participial phrase, *anientes tēn apeilēn*. One could certainly take the participle with an imperatival force, translating the clause as a new sentence beginning "Stop threatening them." The disadvantage of this translation is that it obscures the idea that "abandoning threats" is the primary way in which Paul wants slave owners to "do the same" to their slaves.

z. Second, some English versions (e.g., NASB, NRSV, NEB) use "Master" to translate the word *kyrios* in the clause "both of you have the same Master in heaven." What this preserves in English is the fact that the same word, *kyrios* in Greek, is used to refer to both slave owners and Christ. This fact is noted in the comments below. By using "Lord" to translate this clause in 6:9, one loses the wordplay but retains the point of the wordplay, which is to contrast and relativize the status of slave owners (earthly masters) with the one true Lord.

aa. Finally, the Greek word *prosōpolēmpsia* comes from the Hebraistic expression *prosōpon lambanein*. Literally, this means "to receive a face" (see the LXX of Lev 19:15; Deut 10:17; Sir 4:22, 27). We might use the phrase "to judge at face value" to convey a similar notion. When the term *prosōpolēmpsia* (or a cognate) is applied to God (Rom 2:11; 1 Pet 1:17) or to Christ, as in this case, it means that God does not show partiality.

[21–24] One significant issue for anyone reading these verses concerns the role of 5:21. Should it be taken as introducing the discussion of wives and husbands in vv. 22–33, or should it close off the string of participles that begin at 5:19? Even the two standard editions of the Greek NT have come down on different sides of this issue.[4]

On the one hand, it makes sense to see the participle, "submitting," in 5:21 as one further explication of the ways in which being filled with the Holy Spirit manifests itself in the lives of believers. The use of the more global term "one another" in v. 21 fits well with "speaking to each other" and "always giving thanks for everything" in vv. 19 and 20. Thus the more specific and focused demands of 5:22–6:9 could be taken as a distinct unit. Further, if 5:21 is taken to begin a new section, then the participle "submitting" must be taken to have the force of an imperative. This would be different from the way in which the previous three participles seem to work.

On the other hand, there is no main verb in 5:22. The "submit" of "Wives submit to your husbands" must be dependent upon the verb "submit" in 5:21. Just as the prior three participles in 5:19–20 further specify the shape of a Spirit-filled life, so 5:22–6:9 further specifies the nature of mutual submission in the body of Christ.[5] Although this would indicate that the participle in 5:21 takes on an overt imperatival force, one could also claim that the participles in 5:19–20 have strong imperatival implications.

Each way of resolving this issue has problems. For the organizational purposes of this commentary, 5:21 is treated as part of a unit that runs until 5:33. In the light of the various considerations noted above, however, it is crucial that readers interpret 5:21 as pointing both backward and forward. It serves to conclude a section that presents some of the ways in which believers are to manifest the life of the Spirit, and it also serves as an overarching admonition for the relationships between wives and husbands, children and parents, and slaves and masters in the church.[6] In fact, almost all commentators, no matter how they divide the passage, treat the verse this way.

Thus believers filled with the Spirit will submit to one another. Obviously, person A cannot submit to person B at the exact same time that person B is submitting to person A. Instead, the mutual submission admonished here relativizes conventional authority structures for people who lived in a society where

---

4. The NA[26] (1979) has a period and paragraph break after 5:20. This is retained in NA[27] (1993). The UBS[3] (1975) puts the break after 5:21. But the UBS[3] Corrected ed. (1983), UBS[4] (1993) puts the break after 5:20.

5. The repetition of the word "fear" (*phobos*) in 5:21 and "respect" (*phobētai*) in 5:33 might also argue for a connection between 5:21 and vv. 22–33—as suggested by Lincoln, *Ephesians* 52.

6. Dawes (19) calls v. 21 a "Janus sentence," one that looks both ways.

status and authority were rigidly marked and strictly observed.[7] The epistle's call for some relativity of authority within the Spirit-filled body requires a disposition of humility similar to that described in Phil 2:3–4, where others are considered to be of higher status, and people attend to the interests of others rather than their own.

Moreover, mutual submission is done "in reverence for Christ." That is, believers' obedience to Christ will lead them to submit to one another. Whatever authority and status an individual might have in the world is relativized by believers' common service to one Lord, Christ. In this common service they are both able to and called to submit to each other.

Having said all this, one must also admit that vv. 22–24 operate within a fairly conventional model of a Greco-Roman household, in which the husband would have been the locus of ultimate authority. Within the confines of that particular social arrangement, Paul employs a christological set of motivations and justifications. In v. 21 believers are called to submit to one another "out of reverence for Christ." Then in v. 22 wives are called to submit to their husbands "as to the Lord." This is not to put husbands in the same place as Christ. Rather, these terse references to Christ characterize the nature of that submission: willingly and out of love. Wives can reflect on the reason for the submission: "out of reverence for Christ" (5:21). This admonition can also remind all believers that the one who must ultimately be obeyed is the Lord.

Paul explicates these christological points further by calling wives to submit to their husbands "because the husband is the head of the wife as Christ is head of the church." Indeed, v. 24 further clarifies this by saying that "just as the church submits to Christ, so wives should submit to their husbands in all things."

What might it mean for the church to submit to Christ as its head?[8] How might this illustrate the relationship between wives and husbands? Christ's unquestioned preeminence relative to the church certainly can underwrite a wife's submission to her husband. In a first-century context, however, it is not clear that such a comparison really says much. The paterfamilias would have already been considered the head of the household. One may find more illumination of believers' relationships with each other by exploring the connection between Christ and the church further.

Twice in Ephesians Paul speaks of Christ as the head of the church. In 1:22 the resurrection reveals what has always been the case, that Christ is preeminent over all things and that all things will ultimately be placed in their proper relationship to Christ, who is their head and the head of the church. In 4:15

---

7. Calvin (204) also notes this relativizing tendency with regard to kings and governors, each of whom must learn submission.

8. Dawes is one of the few who ask this sort of question; see esp. his ch. 4.

Christ's role as head of the church emphasizes his preeminence as the one who is the source, organizing principle, and ultimate goal of the church's life. In these cases as well as other passages illustrating the relationship between Christ and the church in Ephesians (e.g., 4:1–6), Christ rather than the church is the primary actor. Thus it seems that this analogy has more to say to husbands than to wives. In addition, the church's submission to Christ depends upon recognizing what God has revealed in Christ and upon maintaining a proper relationship with Christ, the head, through the power of the Spirit. The church's submission to Christ would further involve coming to recognize the good work that Christ desires to do in and through the church, learning to desire that good work, and participating in that work over time until it is brought to its proper end. It would in particular involve allowing the gifts that Christ has given the church to operate and flourish so that "we all come to the unity of the faith and knowledge of the Son of God, to the complete person, the measure of the stature of the fullness of Christ" (4:13). Ultimately, then, the church's submission to Christ results in the church's coming to love and desire for itself that which Christ loves and desires for the church, that is, union with Christ and each other. On the one hand, we can hardly imagine a better model for husbands and wives. On the other hand, this notion of the church's submission to Christ would set a model for all believers, not simply husbands and wives.

[25–33] Although the instruction here is to husbands to love their wives, a large portion of the first part of the passage, vv. 25–27, is devoted to describing Christ's love for the church. There are a few examples of Greco-Roman household codes where husbands are advised to love their wives, but none of these codes use the verb *agapaō* or the noun *agapē*.[9] Moreover, Paul makes it clear that the sort of love he is talking about here is first and foremost the love displayed by Christ for the church.

The first characteristic of Christ's love for the church involves his freely willed self-offering on behalf of the church. In this respect v. 25 echoes 5:2, where believers are told to "walk in love just as Christ loved us and handed himself over for us." Thus husbands are to love their wives with the self-emptying love that Christ paradigmatically displays for believers. Given the ways in which this self-emptying love is described in passages such as Phil 2:6–8, it is certainly possible to think of displaying this love to another as a specific form of submitting to one another out of reverence for Christ (5:21).

The next two verses explicate the aims of Christ's self-offering on behalf of the church. The first aim is to sanctify the church, to render her holy. Paul has already indicated that God has chosen believers in Christ to be "holy and

9. See Ps.-Phoc. 195–97; Plutarch, *Mor.* 143A; also Dixon, who shows that many Roman marriages were characterized by romantic love.

blameless before him in love" (1:4). This language, which Deuteronomy first uses to characterize God's purposes in calling Israel (Deut 7:6–8), was extended in Eph 1:4 to speak of God's purposes for believers in Christ and now is used in 5:26 to speak of Christ's purposes for the church. Believers are called to holiness as part of their participation in Christ, and the church as a whole is called to that same holiness.

Obviously, believers individually and the church more generally are not holy on their own. As 5:26 explains, Christ accomplishes a cleansing of the church "by the washing of water in the word." There are two particular ways of understanding this image of washing. Within the Christian tradition the most obvious is as a reference to baptism. Most ancient commentators and the bulk of modern commentators all see this as a reference to baptism. One should note, however, that the NT says very little about Christian baptism. Titus 3:5 mentions washing in a larger discussion of redemption without explicitly linking washing to baptism. And 1 Pet 3:21 says that Christian baptism is not the sort of washing that removes physical dirt from the body, but the epistle does not go on to make the explicit case that it is precisely a spiritual cleansing that renders one holy. Thus the text is not as clear in its reference to baptism as one might like. Nevertheless, sacramental accounts of baptism as a washing that brings about the cleansing of sin certainly are compatible with Eph 5:26. Moreover, the argument that baptism is something that individuals undertake and not the church as a whole misses that point that both Rom 6:1–11 and Col 2:10–13 speak of baptism as the act that brings one into the church and thus could be seen as being constitutive of the church. This is also supported by Eph 4:3–7, where "one baptism" helps to comprise the unity of the body of Christ.

Can one assert with absolute certainty that the first readers of Ephesians would have understood this washing as a reference to baptism? Probably not. Yet it is the most likely option. Moreover, it is the most theologically rich way to read this text. If one reads the notion of being washed in water as a reference to baptism, then the additional phrase "in the word" might be taken to modify the washing in water. In that case it can be either a reference to the candidate's confession of faith or more likely to a baptismal formula pronounced at the baptism (e.g., Schnackenburg 250; Lincoln, *Ephesians* 376; Best, *Ephesians* 544). If one takes "in the word" to be an additional modification of "having cleansed," then "in the word" is probably a more general reference to the proclamation of the gospel (e.g., Heil, *Ephesians* 246; Hoehner 755) or postbaptismal teaching or edification (Muddiman 265).

In addition to a reference to baptism, one can see in this text a reference back to Ezek 16.[10] There God speaks of Israel first as an abandoned child that God rescues (16:6–7), then as a forsaken women whom God marries, washing her

---

10. Lincoln (*Ephesians* 375) makes this connection.

with water and anointing her with oil (16:9), beautifying her and offering her all sorts of good gifts (16:10–14). Much of the rest of Ezek 16 relates Israel's surprising infidelity to her divine husband, and the subsequent judgment she incurs as a result. Nevertheless, God remembers God's own pledge of fidelity to Israel and brings about her redemption, recalling and yet forgiving the sins of her past (16:59–63).

The nuptial imagery here is particularly relevant for Eph 5:25–27. Moreover, it can provide some ways of addressing the obvious discrepancy between the church that Christ renders holy and blameless, without blemish or wrinkle, and the very flawed and sinful manifestations of Christ's body that the Ephesians and all subsequent Christians know. The church would do well to read her "marriage" to Christ through Ezek 16. In this light, Christ desires holiness for the church and pledges himself to ensure that holiness. Holiness is Christ's gift to and desire for the church. Holiness is not the church's self-acquired character. At the same time, just as God does not overlook Israel's infidelity, Christ does not overlook the church's failings. Indeed, these failings may well generate the sort of judgment that Israel faced. Nevertheless, the Christ who pledges himself to the church will establish the church's holiness, recalling yet forgiving her sins.

The idea of Christ's presenting the church to himself in 5:27 reminds believers that Christ is the one who establishes and ensures the church's holiness. The church does not present itself to Christ as a potential bride might present herself to a suitor for inspection. The church does not seek to acquire its own holiness. Rather, the church is to "grow up together in all things into him who is the head, into Christ" (4:15).[11]

At 5:28 Paul extends the discussion of the relationship between Christ and the church as the basis for his admonition to husbands to love their wives as their own bodies. Clearly there are certain respects in which husbands cannot exactly replicate the relationship between Christ and the church. For example, husbands cannot present their wives to themselves as holy and blameless, without blemish or wrinkle. Nevertheless, the self-giving, other-regarding love that Christ displays for the church is the same love that husbands are to display for their wives. Indeed, the clause instructing husbands to love their wives as their own bodies picks up the claim that the church is Christ's body in 5:23 and later in 5:30. The analogies between Christ-and-the-church and husbands-and-wives are not exact in every respect, but the admonition here in 5:28 indicates that this analogy is to be taken in all seriousness as the standard against which a husband's love for his wife is measured.

---

11. Paul can speak of himself as a sort of marriage broker in 2 Cor 11:1–6. In 2 Corinthians, however, the issues seem more about a particular congregation's relationship to Paul and Paul's relationship to other apostles.

The comment that concludes v. 28, "He who loves his own wife loves himself," appears to be a transitional comment. It both indicates that the first part of v. 28 is not primarily an admonition to self-love and introduces the subsequent discussion of love of one's own body in the light of Christ's love of his body, the church.

Initially, though, Paul begins v. 29 with an everyday observation: "No one ever hated his own flesh." Certainly most contemporary readers will know of exceptions to this truism. Nevertheless, Paul's point here is to present the normal care one extends to one's own body as an extension of the care and nurture Christ lavishes on his body, the church. It appears that the primary point of connection here is not between the specific practices of care and nurture of our human bodies and Christ's practices of care for the church. Rather, the point seems to be to indicate that Christ's care and nurture of his body, the church, is as natural, normal, and uncoerced as humans' care for their own bodies. Christ's care of the church is not so much a duty grudgingly performed as a joyful act of love. Further, as members of his body, believers participate in and enjoy that freely offered nurture and care. This care that Christ lavishes freely on his body is the model of the nurture and care that husbands should display toward their own "flesh," a flesh that is actually a shared flesh, composed of husband and wife. Paul makes this point through the quotation of Gen 2:24 in 5:31.

The logic of 5:28–31 runs something like this: Husbands should love their wives as they love their own bodies. The point of mentioning the love of one's own body is not to advocate self-absorption. Rather, the point emphasizes that love of one's own body is uncoerced, joyfully and unself-consciously offered. This is evident because no one hates his own body. Rather, he happily cares for and nurtures it. Christ's love for his body, the church, is just like this. All believers participate in this freely offered care because we are all members of his body. Thus husbands are to offer this same freely offered nurture and care to their wives because husbands and wives are actually one flesh, as Gen 2:24 reminds us, and no one hates his own flesh.

Thus far, although Paul has moved back and forth between instructions for husbands and reflections on Christ's love of the church, the christological has served as the model for the marital. In 5:32 this is reversed as Paul reveals a "great mystery." Throughout Ephesians, Paul has used the Greek term *mystērion* (mystery) to refer to God's drama of salvation, which results in all things being brought to their proper end in Christ, including a church composed of Jews and Gentiles united in one body (see 1:9–10; 3:1–11; 6:18–20).[12] This mystery was something hidden. With the coming of Christ, however, the true nature and movements of God's drama of salvation have been revealed to the world.

12. See Dawes 190; Sampley 95.

In this light, Paul can further highlight this mystery in terms of Gen 2:24. The union between husband and wife into one flesh displays and anticipates the union between Christ and the church.

Readers should not infer from this that Paul seeks to combat other specific interpretations of Gen 2:24.[13] Rather, he offers the Ephesians this additional christological reflection in the course of a larger discussion of husbands and wives. Indeed, rather than develop this notion of ecclesial union with Christ more fully, Paul returns to the matter at hand in v. 33, where he reasserts that husbands are to love their wives as themselves and wives are to "respect" their husbands. In this final clause Paul uses the Greek verb *phobētai*, which recalls the use of the noun *phobos* in v. 21. In v. 21 all believers are called to submit to each other out of "reverence" for Christ. Here wives are admonished to "respect" their husbands.

As with 5:21 the English term "fear," though certainly an accurate rendering of the Greek, can convey an image of terror that is not in view here. Rather, this term designates the appropriate attitude one should have to a superior. In the highly stratified and status-conscious world of the NT, superiors were due respect, obedience, submission, and deference. This was simply the just thing to do. It rendered to superiors what they deserved. The degree to which one was obliged to submit to one's superiors depended on the gap between them. Paul, like his Jewish and pagan contemporaries, assumed that men were naturally superior to women in nature's hierarchy, and thus wives should display the appropriate dispositions of respect to their husbands. Thus, as we will find throughout the household codes, Paul tends to leave conventional lines of authority intact while urging behavior among various groups in the household that will enhance their Christ-focused "unity of the Spirit in the bond of peace" (4:3). Moreover, in certain cases Paul will extend such familial lines of authority to relations within the body of Christ (e.g., 1 Cor 4:15; 2 Cor 6:11–12; 12:14; Phil 2:22). At the same time, passages such as Gal 3:27–29, the rather extensive relativizing of status terms in the Corinthian Letters, and Paul's ambivalence to "pillars" of the church in Galatians (as in 1:17; 2:6–14)—all indicate that he is also willing to transgress what those in his world would have seen as natural hierarchical distinctions.

[6:1–4] Paul now moves on to admonish children to obey both parents "in the Lord." The notion that children were to obey parents is deeply written into both Judaism and Greco-Roman moral philosophy.[14] Moreover, the fact that children are directly addressed here indicates that they are of a sufficient age to understand and act upon the epistle as it is read aloud in the congregation. The

13. Contra Sampley 96–101.
14. See Josephus, *C. Ap.* 2.206; Philo, *Decal.* 165–67; Dionysius of Halicarnassus, *Ant. rom.* 2.26.

phrase "in the Lord" modifies the verb "obey" and not the noun "parents." In this way, the manner and motive of the obedience are located in their Christian identity. This will parallel the manner of obedience that Paul commends to slaves in 6:5–9.

The subsequent clauses add some further specification to children's obedience to parents. First, we are told it is "right." That is, children's obeying parents is just and proper, because this is what is due to parents. The second reason for obeying parents is related through a citation of Exod 20:12 LXX. This citation is offered without introduction and presumes that readers will detect that it comes from the Decalogue. Moreover, using the quotation implies that "honoring," which in its OT context entails a wide range of practices beyond simple obedience, is tied closely to obeying.

Paul goes on to relate that this is the "first commandment with a promise." This claim is puzzling in that honoring parents comes in the fifth commandment (Exod 20:12), and it appears that the second commandment (20:4–6) contains a promise: punishment to those who disobey and steadfast love to those who obey.[15] Thus it is unclear how this could be the first commandment with a promise.

This situation has spawned a variety of explanations. These include dividing the law into two parts, with the fifth commandment being actually the first to deal with duties toward other humans after the first four address duties to God (Gnilka 297). This view relies on a comment by Philo in *Spec.* 2.261 but ignores his comment in *Decal.* 121, treating the fifth commandment as the last one concerned with duties toward God. Others argue that "first" is not numerically first, but first in terms of most difficult or most important (cf. "first" in Matt 22:34–40; Mark 12:28–31; so Schlier 281). Although there is some rabbinic evidence that saw the fifth commandment this way (*Deut. Rab.* 6), it seems unlikely that the Christians in Ephesus would have been aware of this rabbinic tradition and would not have been aware that Jesus gives a different answer when asked about the "first" commandment.

Of the variety of solutions to this problem, Lincoln's (*Ephesians* 404) is the best. He questions the claim that Exod 20:4–6 actually contains a promise. Rather, it contains a set of descriptions of God, from which one is meant to draw conclusions about the consequences of various actions. Once this is taken into consideration, then one can genuinely treat the commandment to honor father and mother as the first with a promise.[16]

---

15. Calvin (213) argues that this promise is universal and not attached to any specific commandment.

16. Lincoln's solution, however, has its own problem. According to Best (*Ephesians* 567), although one might argue that Exod 20:4–6 does not contain a promise, Exod 15:26 uses the word "commandment" and contain promises. Moreover, Exod 12:13–17 connects commandments and promises. One would have to respond that Paul does not appear to be using "commandment" in this more general sense. That is hardly conclusive, however.

The actual promise is more significant than how one takes its priority. The promise in Exodus is directed to prosperity in the promised land. In Ephesians the notion of well-being and long life is not tied to any particular place, but to all places. When taken in this way rather than as a condition of remaining in the promised land, this promise becomes more of a prudential rule of thumb. If this promise is taken as more than a prudential rule of thumb, it can certainly raise theological and ethical problems for Christians today. The promise that things will go well and one will live long is insufficient motivation for Christians who are pondering most types of action.[17] Paul's repeated references to his chains remind the Ephesians that fidelity to the gospel may cost believers their lives or their freedom. Engaging the principalities and powers, as 6:10–17 advocates, requires spiritual weaponry, but it also recognizes that the principalities and powers can work material harm on believers. Moreover, the prospect of material harm cannot override the necessity for engaging those powers. Thus long life in itself is not an ultimate goal for Christians. It appears to be the likely outcome of obedience to parents, but it cannot trump the demands of fidelity, of walking in a manner worthy of one's calling.[18]

Children are called to obey their parents. In 6:4 Paul only addresses fathers. Fathers are to avoid angering their children.[19] The father in a Greco-Roman household would have held absolute authority to do with his children as he saw fit. There would have been countless ways in which fathers could have enraged their children. Further, given that the "children" addressed here could range in age from the quite young to the young adult, driving a child to anger will involve very different things. Nevertheless, Paul has already warned the Ephesians about anger, discussing when it is appropriate and what its dangers are (4:26–27). At the very least, taking this admonition to heart will require fathers to take their children's perspectives into account.

The second half of this verse directs fathers to a more constructive activity. Here fathers are instructed to bring up their children in the "training and

17. Calvin (212) says that Paul uses this as seasoning, "to render the submission he enjoins on children more pleasant and agreeable."

18. In addition, this emphasis on a long life seems at odds with an outlook that anticipates the imminent return of Christ. This then is taken as evidence that Ephesians is not Pauline (Lincoln, *Ephesians* 406). With this, as with most of the issues used to adjudicate authorship, much hangs on one's account of the historical Paul and how much continuity and discontinuity one is willing to allow this character. In passages such as 1 Cor 7, Paul speaks as if Christ will return very soon. In Philippians, Paul has no doubt that the day of Christ will come (1:6), but he does not indicate how soon he thinks it will come. Indeed, he seems more concerned for the faithfulness of the Philippians over the long haul, should that be necessary. In Romans, Paul relates plans for a long journey to Spain. Once one raises the issue of development in Paul's thinking about this or any other matter, then the matter of how much discontinuity is possible becomes almost impossible to judge with any confidence.

19. Plutarch (*Mor.* 2.8F–9A) and Ps.-Phoc. 207 make similar observations.

admonition of the Lord." Such training and admonition would be undertaken with a particular goal in mind. Within the pagan household the training of the children, especially sons, would be directed to the end of preparing them to fulfill their proper role in the household and in the community at large. In Ephesians, fathers are admonished to form their children to fulfill their proper ends as people of the Lord. That is, the formation of children in the household should be in the light of their identity as Christians, not primarily as members of a specific family or citizens of a particular city.[20] The primary role of the phrase "of the Lord" is properly to locate the primary loyalty of Christians and the importance of making that known in the formation of children and all others.

[5–9] This section closes with a set of admonitions to slaves and masters. For Americans, it is important to understand that Greco-Roman slavery was very different from the slavery practiced in the United States. In Paul's world, slavery was a widespread phenomenon. One could become a slave because of economic misfortune, capture in war, kidnapping, or simply being born into slavery. Within a household, work was divided according to gender rather than one's status as free or slave. Thus slaves and free members of a household worked side by side. In urban contexts, slaves could become doctors and tutors. They could handle money and the financial affairs of households. They could earn money and sometimes purchase their freedom. They could marry, and female slaves could be freed in order to marry their masters. This should not blunt the fact that many slaves were worked to death in mines and were often subject to horrible conditions. Moreover, female slaves were available for the sexual use of their masters.[21] Although there were many forms of Greco-Roman slavery, all slaves shared the common situation of being under the control of their master.

Paul addresses slaves directly here (also in 1 Cor 7:21; Col 3:22). Paul takes them to be full members of the Ephesian church. Moreover, although their actions are often governed by the will of another, the nature of his admonitions indicates that Paul takes them to be in full control of their inner dispositions. Thus, calling slaves to obey their "earthly masters" is not really the issue here. In this they had little choice. Rather, Paul focuses on the nature and quality of that obedience. Not surprisingly, this obedience is modeled on the type of obedience that believers display toward Christ.[22]

More precisely, slaves are to obey in "fear and trembling." There are two other passages where Paul uses the phrase "fear and trembling" to describe

20. This appears to be the best way to understand the force of the genitive *kyriou* in 6:4. See Lincoln's similar comments (*Ephesians* 408).

21. See essays by Martin, Osiek, and Saller for excellent introductions to a variety of issues related to ancient slavery and early Christianity.

22. Although Paul goes on to address slave owners directly in 6:9, we should not assume that all of the Christian slaves in the Ephesian congregation are owned by other members of the church.

obedience. In 2 Cor 7:15 it describes the disposition of the Corinthian Christians toward Titus, who was acting as an emissary of Paul. Paul also uses the phrase in Phil 2:12 to characterize the type of obedience he has come to expect from the Philippian Christians. In each of these cases "fear and trembling" has little to do with terror and panic. Rather, it describes the proper disposition that a person of inferior status should display toward the wishes of a superior; it reflects the willingness to recognize another's authority. In addition, slaves are to obey with singleness of heart. This reflects a simplicity of will, a will without distraction, guile, or mixed motivation.[23]

These dispositions are also dispositions that all believers are to display toward Christ, their Lord and Master. Indeed, vv. 6 and 7 repeatedly contrast service that is less than wholehearted with the service that believers owe to the Lord. This is the attitude that slaves are to display to their earthly masters. Although they are only "earthly" masters, the obedience owed to them is modeled on obedience rendered to the one, true Lord.

Paul calls these masters *kyrioi*, the same Greek word used to describe Jesus the Lord (*kyrios*). There can be no confusion between the two here, however, because these masters are *kyrioi* "according to the flesh," or "earthly" (v. 5). As Lincoln (*Ephesians* 420) suggests, Paul may implicitly be playing off the two ways of using this term in order to relativize the status of Christian slave owners in 6:5–8, a point he makes more explicit in 6:9.[24]

Before moving to address slave owners, however, Paul inserts a brief comment about the recompense all (both slave and free) will receive from the Lord of all. This promise reminds slaves that even if their work does not catch the eye of their owners, it is seen by Christ, and they will be compensated at some future point. It also works to contrast the fidelity of Christ, the Lord (*kyrios*), with any "earthly master" who might promise freedom in return for good work and fail to deliver.[25]

This section concludes with a brief address to slave owners. Continuing to call them *kyrioi* (masters), Paul admonishes masters "to do the same" to their slaves. Doing "the same" may refer back to "serving wholeheartedly" in v. 7. In this way Paul would be turning the tables on the master-slave relationship by having both parties serve each other. This would certainly fit with the call to mutual submission that started this passage in 5:21 (Chrysostom, *Hom. Eph.* 32). It seems more likely, however, that Paul is urging slave owners to extend the same disposition of integrity and singleness of heart that they owe to Christ to their slaves as well (Hoehner 813; Thomas Aq. 233; Lincoln, *Ephesians* 423).

---

23. See the uses of the Greek term *haplotēs* in *T. Isaac* 6.1–4.

24. In 1 Tim 6:1 and Titus 2:9 Paul uses the word *despotēs* to refer to slave owners.

25. Tacitus (*Ann.* 14.42) relates just such an incident. As Best (*Ephesians* 575) observes, this promise shows that the eschatology of Ephesians is not wholly realized.

In practice this seems, in the first instance, to entail abandoning threats. One must assume that this does not mean abandoning threats of punishment or abuse and simply moving straight to the action. Rather, abandoning threats must entail the abandoning of punishment and abuse in the face of the failures of one's slaves. The reason for this is that even though one might be a *kyrios kata sarka* (earthly master), even these *kyrioi* are subject to the one Lord of heaven and earth, Jesus Christ. Slave owners are to abandon threats (and punishment) in the face of a slave's failure because Christian slave owners understand that this is the way Christ has treated both them and their slaves. Moreover, this Lord is an impartial judge. Although the world may grant the slave owner a higher status than the slave, Christ does not recognize status in these terms (see Bassler 178).

When faced with these household codes, Christians in America find themselves in an awkward position. It may be useful to begin by reflecting on the source and nature of this awkwardness. First, Americans live with their own very complicated and often underacknowledged legacy of slavery and of the racism that underwrote slavery and continues today. Further, we live in a world where both virtual and actual slavery still exist, and Christians quite rightly want to insist that this is wrong and should not be allowed even though both the OT and the NT take the presence of various forms of slavery as a given. In addition, domestic violence is prevalent, particularly violence against women and children. This should always be unacceptable to Christians, even though sometimes churches invoke passages such as Eph 5:21–6:9 to underwrite such violence through advocating the comprehensive submission of wives to husbands. Most of us no longer believe in biologically inscribed hierarchies such as those Paul and his contemporaries assumed. Moreover, even though Christians in America often have both the freedom and the power to bring about certain changes in social arrangements both large and small, that would have been inconceivable to Paul and the Ephesians.

Nevertheless, for Christians, Ephesians (along with Colossians, 1 Peter, and the Pastoral Epistles) is part of Scripture.[26] Christians must treat them as such. Such a claim does not prescribe any specific pattern of interpreting or embodying these texts. Neither does such a claim rule out bringing texts—such as Gal 3:27–29; 1 Cor 12:12–31 (both of which might relativize or reconfigure notions of status); or 1 Cor 7 (which reminds Christians that singleness is an equally acceptable form of life)—into the discussion. It simply recognizes that there may be occasions when these texts need to be addressed. This recognition becomes even more complicated in the light of significant changes in the composition of the worldwide church. Over 60 percent of the world's Christians

---

26. Issues of authorship, even if they are resolvable, are not relevant to this discussion. To argue that the Ephesians is not Pauline is simply not relevant to this point. Paul is not canonical; Ephesians is.

now live outside of the United States and Europe, and this percentage is growing. These Christians often live in situations where the social arrangements share far more with those of the Christians in Ephesus than they do with Christians in America. Interpretive and ecclesial conflict over passages such as Eph 5:21–6:9 seem inevitable and indeed are already emerging.

Such conflict in itself is not a problem; it is even to be expected. Disagreement over the interpretation and embodiment of Scripture is not a failure in itself. Further, faithfully resolving such disagreements requires significant investments of time, patience, and love. In addition, one of the hardest parts about such disputes involves establishing a common framework and vocabulary. Apart from this, Christians will find that they cannot even come to agreement on how to describe a conflict, much less to resolve it.

In this respect, Ephesians may provide some resources in addition to its various conundrums. In Ephesians, and particularly in 5:21–33, Paul interprets household relationships in thoroughly christological terms. Many commentators suggest that the practical result of this may well have been a rather conventional household arrangement. Even if this is so, and it is not clear that it is so, the most important thing Paul offers the Ephesians is the example of seeing and interpreting the world through christologically ground lenses, rather than lenses ground by Roman social custom and convention. If the Ephesians and all Christians learn this skill of seeing and interpreting their world through Christ-focused lenses, even as various social and material and political circumstances change, they will be able to continue to "walk in a manner worthy of [their] calling" (4:1). Moreover, they will be able to recognize some alternative practices of other Christians in different circumstances as examples of "walking worthily"; they will have a framework and language for recognizing both their own and others' failures to "walk worthily" and to repent accordingly; they will also have a basis for faithfully resolving arguments and disputes about how to "walk worthily" in specific contexts. In this way, Paul's theological practice displayed in 5:21–6:9 provides resources for contemporary Christians across the globe as they debate and argue with each other about how to interpret and embody these particular texts.

Ephesians 6:10–20
Strong in the Lord

This passage is often referred to as the climax of the paraenetic section of the epistle, which begins at 4:1. Some use the technical rhetorical designation *peroratio* to indicate this. The claim is that this passage summarizes and brings to a head the key elements of the body of the letter, offering encouragement to the readers to go and do that which the writer desires them to do. Although many scholars agree that this is the aim of the paragraph, they do not all agree in identifying it as a *peroratio* (e.g., Lincoln uses *peroratio*; Best disagrees).[1] This particular judgment may well depend on how narrowly one conceives of the *peroratio* as a rhetorical genre. Thomas Aquinas (234) is probably equally on the mark when he says that 6:10–20 is a discussion of the power by which believers "carry out the precepts of destroying the old man of sin and encouraging the newness of grace."

Regardless of whether one considers 6:10–20 to be a *peroratio* or not, one should recognize some ways in which this passage is both like and not like what comes before it. Like much of the material from 4:1 to 6:9, this passage addresses issues of the character and moral practices that Paul wants to see cultivated in the Ephesians. In various ways 6:10–20 continues the discussion of walking in a manner worthy of Christ's call.

Nevertheless, the tone and focus of 6:10–20 is quite different from 4:1–6:9. From 4:1 onward, Paul has used the image of "walking" in a particular way to carry out his argument. He presents the Christian life as a communal journey of believers from where they once were, to where they now are, and on to their ultimate end in God. The ways in which they conduct themselves in the course of this journey will have a significant impact on the course and outcome of this journey as well as on believers' abilities to draw others in as fellow travelers. Because this journey passes through places already shaped and influenced by

---

1. Lincoln ("Ephesians 6:10 as *Peroratio*") offers a fuller account of this passage as a *peroratio* than one finds in his commentary. Reinhard explores a variety of ways in which this passage summarizes the whole of the letter, rather than just the paraenetic section. This is primarily done by connecting various pieces of the armor of God with similar terms that occur in both parts of the letter. I do not find this persuasive, but I do agree that this passage is not about personal piety.

the surrounding pagan cultures, the Ephesians will need wisdom from the Holy Spirit to engage these cultures and to negotiate their paths through them in a manner that will enhance rather than frustrate their journey.

In contrast to this, the dominant image in 6:10–20 is standing firm against an array of diabolical enemies.[2] Defense and resistance are the primary images here. Since a Christ-focused, Spirit-inspired wisdom is essential to walking in a manner worthy of the Ephesians' calling in 4:1–6:9, then 6:10–20 requires courage and steadfastness. Without question, Paul is quite willing to offer judgments about the corruption and decadence of the cultures in which the Ephesians find themselves. He can even speak of them as if they are under the influence of corrupting spiritual powers. In 6:10–20, however, Paul is quite adamant that believers in Ephesus are engaged in a battle against spiritual foes.

These two images, "walking" and "standing firm," are not incompatible. They can be different ways of approaching particular aspects of the Christian life. Unfortunately for modern readers, there is little in the epistle that offers enough concrete information about the original context of this letter to help us discern how Paul expected the Ephesians concretely to practice "standing firm."

In addition to offering a conclusion of some sort to the arguments of 4:1–6:9, one also finds connections between 6:10–20 and earlier parts of the epistle. In 6:12 Paul locates the various spiritual forces arrayed against believers in "the heavenlies." This is the same place where God has blessed believers "with every spiritual blessing in Christ" (1:3). It is also where believers have been made alive and seated with Christ (2:5–6). In 6:10 Paul calls on believers to be empowered (presumably by God) with God's great power. This is precisely what Paul has prayed for the Ephesians in 1:19–23 and reiterated in a prayer in 3:16–21.

Most significantly, in 3:7–13 Paul speaks about the church and its relationship to various spiritual powers. In this passage Paul continues his earlier discussion of his mission to reveal the mystery of God's drama of salvation in Christ, in which Jews and Gentiles are joined into one body in Christ (3:1–6). In the light of this mission, Paul goes on in 3:7–13 to declare that the church plays a particular role in revealing God's drama of salvation to spiritual powers taken to be hostile to God's economy. Since this is the only other point in the letter where Paul speaks of the church's relationship to the powers, it seems reasonable to seek to interpret 6:10–20 in the light of 3:7–13.

There is one further important point to make about this passage. It is very easy to read this discussion of the armor of God and then to assume that this is

---

2. The image of standing or standing firm is fairly common in Paul, such as 1 Thess 3:8, "Continue to stand firm in the Lord"; 2 Thess 2:15, "Stand firm and hold fast to the traditions that you were taught"; in 1 Cor 10:12 some think they are standing but may soon fall; 15:1 speaks of the gospel in which the Corinthians stand; 16:13, "Keep alert, stand firm in your faith"; in Phil 1:27 believers "are standing firm in one spirit."

a set of instructions to individual believers to take up the armor of God. That is not really the way the text reads. Rather, the command to take up the armor of God is a summons to the community as a whole. Taking up the armor of God is a communal practice integrally tied to the unity of the church and the church's witness to the powers. In this respect, 6:10–20 continues the emphasis on the common life of the church that began in 4:1.

6:10 Finally,[a] be strengthened in the Lord and[b] in the power of his might. 11 Put on the armor of God so that you will be able to stand against the schemes of the devil; 12 because our[c] struggle[d] is not against blood and flesh but against rulers, against powers, against cosmic forces of this darkness, against the spiritual forces of evil in the heavenly realms. Therefore take up the whole armor of God so that you will be able to stand fast on the day of evil, and having done everything, to stand. 14 Stand, therefore, having fastened[e] the belt of truth around your waist and having put on the breastplate of righteousness, 15 having fitted your feet with the readiness of the gospel of peace; 16 in addition to all this,[f] take up[g] the shield of faith, with which you may extinguish all the flaming arrows of the evil one. 17 Take the helmet of salvation and the sword of the Spirit, which is the word of God. 18 Through every prayer and petition, pray always in the Spirit with this end in mind: Always be watchful in all perseverance[h] and petition for all the saints. 19 Pray also for me that when I open my mouth, the right words[i] will be given to me so that with all boldness I may make known the mystery of the gospel,[j] 20 on behalf of which I am an ambassador in chains, so that I may speak boldly about the gospel[k] as I ought to do.

a. It is more usual to find the nominative *to loipon* (2 Cor 13:11; Phil 3:1; 4:8; 1 Thess 4:1; 2 Thess 3:1) rather than the genitive *tou loipou*, which is here (also in Gal 6:17, where it is often translated "from now on"). It is most likely that the current text—supported by $\mathfrak{P}^{46}$, ℵ*, A, B, et al.—was corrected to the more common form by ℵ², D, F, Ψ, et al. The addition of "my brothers" would also be accounted for by the attempt to make this text conform to Phil 3:1; 4:8; and 1 Thess 4:1. The best MSS omit "my brothers."

b. In addition, the Greek reflects the pleonastic style typical of the rest of the epistle. Literally, the clause reads "be strengthened in the Lord in the power of his strength." The passive voice of the imperative "be strengthened" implies that the subject who empowers here is God.

c. There is a textual variant with regard to the pronoun preceding "struggle." Some MSS have "your" ($\mathfrak{P}^{46}$, B, D*, F, G, Ψ, et al.); other MSS have "our" (ℵ, A, D², et al.). The manuscript witnesses are not decisive here. Given that the entire passage is in the second-person plural, it is more likely that "our" is original and was corrected early on for the sake of consistency (Hoehner 824; Metzger 542).

d. The word translated "struggle" (*palē*) originally referred to types of wrestling. By the time of Ephesians, however, it was also used more generally of types of combat.

Given the emphasis on armor, it is rather clear that more than wrestling is involved here. Gudorf, however, argues that some fully armed soldiers were accomplished wrestlers, capable of hand-to-hand combat. He argues that the term should be translated as "wrestle."

e. The Greek verb *perizōsamenoi* could also be translated with the more archaic English word "gird."

f. The Greek phrase *en pasin* might be rendered into English as "above all" (as in RSV), which gives the impression that the shield of faith is the most important of all the pieces of God's armor. The context does not support such a hierarchy. Rather, all of the pieces are important and to be worn.

g. Although the Greek here continues a series of participles that started in v. 14, the translation above uses a finite verb ("take up") to render the passage more readable in English.

h. The noun "perseverance" (*proskarterēsis*) is quite rare. The verbal form of this word occurs more regularly (e.g., Num 13:20; Theodotion: Tob 5:8; Sus 6) with the same idea of extreme persistence.

i. In Greek these verses are part of a single sentence that begins at v. 18. They have been divided into several English sentences here. Paul's request in v. 19 might literally be rendered, "that I might be given a word when I open my mouth." Some translations use "message" (NRSV) or "utterance" (Hoehner 860). Although these are formally correct, the context here makes it clear that Paul does not simply want words to come out of his mouth. Rather, he wants the right words to come out, as in the translation above.

j. Some MSS omit the word "gospel" at the end of v. 19. The textual evidence for including the phrase, however, is quite strong (א, A, D, Ψ, et al.) Moreover, the context would probably lead one to assume that the "mystery" referred to here is the mystery of the gospel, whether the term were there or not (contra Best, *Ephesians* 608).

k. In v. 20 the Greek simply has a pronoun instead of "the gospel," which the translation above has used. There is no doubt that the antecedent of the pronoun is "the gospel."

[10–13] As a way of completing his epistle, Paul in this final substantive section shifts from admonitions about walking in a manner worthy of the gospel to a discussion of the strength, power, and defenses needed to stand and resist the spiritual forces arrayed against the church.

Paul begins by urging the Ephesians to be strengthened in the Lord. The use of the passive voice here reminds the Ephesians that although this strength is necessary in order to withstand the forces of evil, it is not something the Ephesians can really do for themselves.[3] One way of understanding this notion of being strengthened in the Lord is in the light of John 15. There Jesus teaches his followers that abiding in him, "the vine," is the only way to maintain the

---

3. This is contra Yoder Neufeld (*Divine Warrior*, 109–16), who argues that the verb should be read as a middle, elucidating the command to become imitators of God in 5:1. But 5:2 elucidates this command in quite different ways. Moreover, Yoder Neufeld's approach to Ephesians depends on a reconstructed tradition history that makes far too much of a relatively small amount of shared vocabulary.

possibility of bearing fruit in an otherwise hostile environment. Abiding in the Lord is the way in which believers may come to be strengthened by the Lord. The issue here does not seem to be one of preferring weakness to strength or even of misperceiving the true nature of strength and weakness, as in 1 Corinthians. Rather, the issue seems to focus on where one finds strength. The struggle is to seek strength in God rather than in other apparent sources of power and security (see Isa 40:12–31). On the one hand, this would seem to be a fairly straightforward task. On the other hand, the story of the people of God in the OT is one of constantly seeking power and protection from things, people, and nations that are not God. Moreover, when the supreme nature of God's power and strength is manifested in being nailed to a cross, it becomes clear that this is a puzzling and even scandalous strength, in which it might be difficult and even terrifying to abide.

To stand against the deceits of the devil, Paul continues, believers must put on the armor of God. This notion reiterates the theme of v. 10 that only God and God's armor provides a suitable defense for believers. This verse also declares that the Ephesians' struggle is against spiritual and demonic forces that are not merely indifferent to their presence, but also are actively seeking to deceive them.[4]

To defend themselves, believers are to put on the "whole armor of God." The term "armor" refers to the equipment of a foot soldier. In 4:24 Paul admonishes believers to put on a new self, created in the likeness of God, in true righteousness and holiness. Putting on this new self is crucial to walking in a manner worthy of one's calling. Now in 6:10–11, putting on the armor of God is equally important to being able to stand firm in the Lord and against the devil.[5]

Throughout this passage, with its rich description of military hardware, it is significant that believers are not called to make war on the devil or any other spiritual power. Although once a battle is joined it is difficult to distinguish between offensive and defensive measures, it appears that believers' fundamental posture in this case is defensive.[6] The devil is the one who makes war on the church (Rev 12:17; 1 Pet 5:8). In these two passages the devil seems to make explicit frontal assaults on believers. In Ephesians the attacks are cast as schemes or plots. The implication here is that the devil will rely on subterfuge

---

4. The same Greek word, *methodeia,* also appears in 4:14, to refer to deceptive schemes.

5. Lincoln (*Ephesians* 442) makes the connection between these two verses about "putting on."

6. Yoder Neufeld (*Divine Warrior,* 109–31) argues that these verses advocate both defensive and offensive measures. This claim depends on allowing a reconstructed tradition of the "divine warrior" to govern the interpretation of Eph 6:10–20. Although there are clear verbal connections between this passage and Isa 59 (among other passages in Isaiah), Yoder Neufeld's thesis constructs a tradition history based on very little direct evidence. The sword of the Spirit in 6:17 is really the only part of the armor that could be used offensively as a weapon. It would be used for fighting at close quarters when offense and defense would seem hard to distinguish.

rather than trying to match God power for power. If this is the case, the assaults of the devil will tend to look more like seductions than military offensives. As will become evident, this shapes the nature of the church's armor. In addition, the church will need a form of wisdom similar to that called for in 4:1–6:9.

Before discussing the precise nature of the church's armor, Paul goes to some length to identify the spiritual nature the church's opponents in v. 12. The term "struggle" here often refers to a wrestling match, though it can refer to a more general struggle. Yet as Lincoln (*Ephesians* 444) observes, focusing on whether Paul imagines a wrestling match or a pitched battle misses the point of the verse, which is to contrast the spiritual nature of the opponents with "blood and flesh."[7] The type of weapons appropriate to such a struggle are spiritual. Nevertheless, one must imagine that such powers will manfiest themselves in the material world and that Christians will engage these powers in the material world.

Paul then lists various spiritual powers: rulers, powers, cosmic forces of this darkness, the spiritual forces of evil in the heavenly realms. Paul has already spoken of various rulers and "powers" in 1:21 and 3:10; he has already used "darkness" in 5:8 to speak of the character of the Ephesians' lives prior to Christ. The final phrase, "spiritual forces of evil in the heavenly realms," is meant to cover all sorts and conditions of spiritual beings. Paul's point here is not to produce a precise list of the species that inhabit the heavenly realms, but to signify the vast multiplicity of demonic forces allied against the church.

Paul has already stated that a unified church of Jews and Gentiles in Christ has a particular mission relative to these spiritual forces in the heavenly realms. The boundless riches of Christ found and sustain a church of Jews and Gentiles reconciled to God and to each other. The presence of this church makes God's gracious wisdom known to these spiritual forces (3:7–13). Here in chapter 6 Paul may be making more explicit that at which he only hints in chapter 3. That is, these spiritual forces reject and/or resist God's plan and wisdom, to which the church bears witness. Thus they attack the church in hopes of undermining the economy of salvation. If this is so, it would reinforce the notion that the central component of the church's witness to the powers depends on common life that maintains "the unity of the Spirit in the bond of peace" (4:3).

Although Paul does not spell out the cause and aim of the hostility of these spiritual powers in quite this way, such an account makes sense in the light of

---

7. The more common order is "flesh and blood," as in Matt 16:17; Gal 1:16 RSV; 1 Cor 15:50. "Blood and flesh" appears also in Heb 2:14 AT. In all of these cases the point is to stress the human, transitory, and finite aspect of flesh and blood. Thomas Aq. (236) notes that Gal 5:17 makes it clear that flesh does struggle against the Spirit. Hence, Paul must mean either that the struggle is not *only* against flesh and blood, or that the *real* struggle is with the power behind mere flesh and blood.

Paul's claims in 3:7–13; it fits particularly well with the need to be equipped with the "gospel of peace," and accounts for Paul's particular desires in 6:18–20.

After describing the nature of the church's struggle, in v. 13 Paul resumes his admonition for the Ephesians to put on "the whole armor of God." Believers are to prepare themselves in this way so that they can withstand "on the evil day." This phrase "the evil day" is obscure. It is unclear what Paul means in using it and precisely what sort of time he imagines "the evil day" to be. Scholarly opinion about this odd phrase varies quite a bit. Paul refers to the present time as "evil days" in 5:16. Although "the evil day" is similar to 5:16, Paul uses a definite article to denote one day rather than simply repeat the claim of 5:16. In this respect Paul is probably referring to some point in the future when God will judge the world. For those who are unrighteous, this will be an evil day (e.g., Amos 5:18–20; 6:3; 1 Thess 5:2–4; *T. Dan* 5.4–13).[8] To take both of these pieces of data seriously, one must argue that Paul imagines that believers are currently in a time marked by great evil, within which they must resist the schemes of Satan. This time of evil will ultimately reach a climactic point at which God will intervene and judge the world. This day will be one of great evil for those who are not prepared.[9]

[14–17] Before going on to describe various pieces of this armor, Paul reiterates the command to stand firm. He then begins by urging the church to gird itself with truth. Here Paul does not seem to be speaking of the great war belts that would have been worn outside the armor, which play such a key role in epics such as Homer's *Iliad* and Virgil's *Aeneid*. Rather, the article in question would have been more like a leather apron worn under the armor, protecting the upper thighs while allowing freedom of movement. Paul seems to be drawing directly on the LXX of Isa 11:5, where the Messianic figure is girded with righteousness and truth. He has already emphasized the importance of "speaking the truth in love" (4:15), avoiding falsehood, and speaking the truth with each other (4:25). In 5:9 truth, as well as righteousness, is one of the fruits of light that believers are to manifest now that they are no longer darkness. Truthfulness in particular is a crucial component of the common life of the church, which will render the church's witness to the spiritual powers regarding the mystery of salvation effective. This particular point should call readers back to 1:13, where Paul declares that Christ is the source of the "word of truth, the gospel of your salvation."

---

8. Parallels with the Qumran *War Scroll* (e.g., 1QM 1.10–13), such as Lincoln (*Ephesians* 446) sees, are overdrawn in one crucial respect: In the war of the Sons of Light against the Sons of Darkness, those on the side of light take the initiative and actively make war on the Sons of Darkness. The posture of believers in Ephesians is defensive, standing firm. In 1:20–23 Paul has already indicated that any offensive action has already been taken by Christ.

9. In essence this view is reflected in Arnold 113–15; Best, *Ephesians* 596–97; Hoehner 834; Lincoln, *Ephesians* 446.

In Eph 4–5 Paul has already indicated that failures of truth will have significant consequences for the church's ability to walk in a manner worthy of its calling. Here in chapter 6 Paul treats truthfulness as one of the church's defenses as it seeks to present the mystery of salvation to spiritual powers seeking to frustrate God's economy. In this way one can begin to see that there is a connection between those virtues and practices necessary to walk in a manner worthy of the church's calling and the armor of God needed to withstand attack from spiritual forces opposed to the church's witness to the mystery of salvation.

The next piece of God's armor is the breastplate of righteousness. The term "breastplate of righteousness" appears in the LXX of Isa 59:17 and Wis 5:18. There is also a similar image in Isa 11:5.[10] The breastplate covers and protects a soldier's vital organs. In addition, righteousness and truth are linked in 4:24 as characteristics of the new person that believers are called to put on. Further, in 5:9 righteousness and truth are linked as two of the three fruits of light that believers are to manifest. Thus, if one must decide whether the breastplate of righteousness is the righteousness that comes from faith in God, or the just and righteous actions of believers (and it is not clear that only one of these is in view), then the connections with 4:24 and 5:9 would probably favor the just and righteous actions of believers (Heil, *Ephesians* 284). More significantly, the use of truthfulness and justice as components of God's armor and as practices of a community that walks in a manner worthy of its calling reinforces the notion that the common life of the church is a crucial component in its witness to the spiritual powers in the heavenlies.

As this passage moves on, it becomes clear that the next piece of the armor of God is most clearly defined by where it goes on the body. We know that this piece of equipment goes on the feet. Whether this is a reference to sandals or a soldier's hobnailed boot or some other thing is unclear. This lack of precision regarding the nature of the footwear seems to support Lincoln's view (*Ephesians* 448) that fitting one's feet "with the readiness of the gospel of peace" alludes in part to Isa 52:7, "How beautiful upon the mountains are the feet of the messenger who announces peace."

The unusual description of this piece of armor as the "readiness of the gospel of peace" indicates that more than simple proclamation of the gospel is in view here. It is less clear, however, what more is implied in this phrase. Certainly the notion of readiness conforms to the passage's overall emphasis of defense and standing firm. Further, in making Jew and Gentile into one body through the cross, Christ makes peace, reconciling these two groups to God (2:14–16).

---

10. This shared vocabulary, along with the phrase "breastplate of faith and love" in 1 Thess 5:8, is not sufficient evidence (contra Yoder Neufeld, *Divine Warrior* 135) that Paul and the author of Ephesians are directly engaging a tradition of interpretation of the divine-warrior motif. Such a case can only be made when one speculates well beyond the actual evidence.

Indeed, to speak of Christ's proclamation of peace both to those near and those far, which thereby opens access to the Father through the Spirit (2:17–18), is a succinct summary of the mystery of salvation that God has revealed to Paul, which Paul has made known to the Ephesians and other Gentiles, and which the church makes known to the powers (3:1–12).

If one continues to read this passage in the light of the church's witness to the powers, then one may also tie this verse into 4:3, where Paul admonishes believers to "maintain the unity of the Spirit in the bond of peace." Manifesting the unity established and desired by Christ would be the "readiness of the gospel of peace," and that is one component of the church's witness to the powers regarding God's economy of salvation. Of course, failure of unity and thus failure to manifest the readiness of the gospel of peace would then frustrate the church's witness to the powers.

Believers are then called to take up the "shield of faith" (v. 16). This is to be used to quench the flaming arrows of the evil one.[11] The phrase used for "shield" here (*thyreos*) refers to an oblong shield about four feet by two feet, constructed from wooden planks and covered with animal hides. As Livy (*Hist.* 21.8.12) describes the practice, shooting flaming arrows into shields caused inexperienced or fearful shield-bearers to lower the shield, thus exposing him to attack by spear. The shield itself apparently was sufficient to extinguish the arrow if one maintained one's composure.

As part of God's armor, this shield is identified as the shield of faith. Faith here could refer to the content of what is believed, as in 4:5. It might also be a reference to the act of believing (1:13; 2:8), along with the vigor of one's belief (1:15). Neither of these two alternatives can really exist apart from the other. Faith must be faith in something; knowledge of a set of doctrines apart from conviction about the truthfulness of those doctrines does not really count as faith. Instead, Paul's image here indicates that persistent, attentive fidelity to the gospel of peace is an essential component in resisting the arrows of the evil one.

The final two parts of God's armor appear in 6:17. These are "the helmet of salvation and the sword of the Spirit, which is the word of God." The phrase "helmet of salvation" is probably taken directly from the LXX of Isa 59:17.[12] In Isa 59 Yahweh takes up the helmet of salvation in the course of avenging the righteous against the unrighteous. In 1 Thess 5:8 Paul uses the phrase "for a helmet the hope of salvation." In 1 Thess 5 the Paul seems to think of believers fighting through obstacles to attain salvation (cf. 5:9). In Ephesians the church is called to witness among the powers in the heavenlies to God's mystery of

---

11. On practice of shooting flaming arrows, see Herodotus, *Hist.* 8.52; Thucydides, *War* 2.75.4; Livy, *Hist.* 21.8.

12. This is supported by the use of the neuter adjective *sōtērion* instead of the feminine noun *sōtēria*, as in 1:13 (so Yoder Neufeld, *Divine Warrior* 141; Hoehner 850).

salvation. The helmet is both protection, but also a means of identifying a soldier (as in *Iliad* 16.326–330). In this respect the call to take up the helmet of salvation in Eph 6:17 refers to the protection that God's salvation affords believers, but it also openly identifies the church as the community where the mystery of salvation is made known to all.

Finally, the church is to avail itself of the "sword of the Spirit, which is the word of God." The Greek term *machaira*, translated here as "sword," refers to a weapon with a blade about two inches wide and about two feet long. This is in contrast to the larger broadsword that a soldier might also use.[13] The sword described in this verse would have been used in close combat. This is the only weapon that Paul urges the Ephesians to pick up. As Best notes, no description of "the whole armor of God" would really be complete without the sword, and it may be unwise to read too much into the role of the sword in what is fundamentally a defensive description (Best, *Ephesians* 603). In addition, it is a weapon for fighting at close quarters; in such a context, it would be difficult or impossible to distinguish the aggressor from the defender.

Since God is the one who provides this armor, the Spirit in this verse does not refer to the source of the sword, but to the power that makes it effective (Lincoln, *Ephesians* 451; Schnackenburg 279). The sword of the Spirit is further identified as the "word of the God." Paul uses the Greek term *rhēma* rather than *logos* to refer to the word of God. This is the same phrase used in 5:26. There it refers either to a general proclamation of the gospel or more specifically to a baptismal formula.[14] If the term was used in this more specific sense, it was due to the context of 5:26. Here in 6:17 it is much more likely that the term reflects the mystery of salvation that Paul has articulated in chapters 2–3, to which the church is to bear witness before the powers.

[18–20] In v. 18 the focus shifts away from the pieces of God's armor. The discussion of prayer in vv. 18–20 might be considered a separate paragraph except for the fact that these verses lack a main verb. These verses are therefore dependent upon the series of commands that govern the discussion of the armor of God: "be strengthened" (v. 10), "put on" (v. 11), "stand " (v. 14). The prayer discussed here, therefore, is not another piece of armor (contra Wink 88). Rather, prayer is presented as a comprehensive activity that covers and supports every aspect of the church's witness to the powers.[15]

---

13. See Hoehner 851–52 for a useful discussion of the relevant vocabulary and weaponry in the Roman army.

14. Fee (729) states, "Paul is not identifying the 'sword' with the book, but with the proclamation of Christ, which in our case is indeed to be found in the book."

15. Most commentators grammatically tie vv. 18–20 to the command to "stand " in 6:14 (e.g., Best, *Ephesians* 604; Lincoln, *Ephesians* 451; Hoehner 854; et al.). Although this is grammatically appropriate, the repeated use of "all" in v. 18 gives the clear impression that prayer is supposed to underwrite the entirety of the church's witness to the powers.

Every prayer, offered always in the Spirit, should work to keep the Ephesians alert in all perseverance and prayer for all the saints. The notion of keeping watchful and praying will remind readers of the Gospels of Jesus' admonition to his followers when he presents them with a set of signs for his return. In several textual versions of Mark 13:33, Jesus tells his disciples to "watch and pray," using the same Greek verbs as in Eph 6:18, because they do not know when these things will happen. In Luke 21:36 Jesus again uses similar vocabulary to advise the disciples to "watch and pray" that they may be strengthened. Although different verbs are used, Jesus in Gethsemane also admonishes his disciples to watch and pray that they may be able to resist the "time of trial" (Mark 14:38 par.). Thus, given the nature of the struggle that Paul has outlined in 6:12, it would be odd if he did not advocate a similar pattern of prayer and watchfulness for the Ephesians.

Paul's admonition further reminds believers that the struggle against the powers is one that "all the saints" are engaged in. This struggle is not simply an activity of local congregations, but also of the church catholic. Paul presumes that as the Ephesians watchfully persevere in prayer, such prayer in the Spirit will help to forge their connection to "all the saints."

Verses 19–20 bring this section to a fitting close. In chapter 3 Paul wraps up his presentation of the drama of salvation, explaining both his role in making the mystery of God's salvation known to the church and the church's role in manifesting this mystery to the powers. He closes chapter 3 with a prayer for the Ephesians that they, along with all the saints, may have the power to comprehend this mystery and to know the love of Christ, which surpasses knowledge. Now in chapter 6, Paul has explained the nature of the church's struggle with the powers and the armor they will need in order to fulfill their mission. He now closes with a request that they pray for him. Just as Paul prayed that God would grant the Ephesians what they would need to fulfill their mission, Paul now asks the Ephesians to pray that God would grant him what he needs to fulfill his mission (cf. Matt 10:19–20//Mark 13:11//Luke 12:11).[16]

As he sees it, Paul needs to be infused with boldness from God so that he might rightly proclaim the "mystery of the gospel." Paul goes on to identify himself as an "ambassador in chains" for the sake of this mystery of the gospel. This term for being an ambassador (*presbeuō*) can be used of an imperial legate. Paul also uses the same term in 2 Cor 5:20 to refer to himself and his coworkers as ambassadors of Christ. The term conveys both a person of high office and someone who will faithfully pursue the wishes and plans of the one he represents.

---

16. Commentators often note the parallels between Eph 6:18–20 and Col 4:3–4. In the case of Ephesians, this is generally taken to be a pseudonymous device. Commentators generally do not recognize the connections between Eph 3 and Eph 6 noted above. Whether this is evidence of Pauline authorship or not is unclear. It does seem to indicate that Eph 6:18–20 is more than a pseudonymous device.

The great scandal here is that Paul is an ambassador in chains, on behalf of the mystery of the gospel. One can read this as a mark of Paul's fidelity to his mission. That is, the world, and the powers in particular, is so hostile to God's economy of salvation that it rightly sees Paul as a faithful minister of that economy and focuses its hostility on Paul. In addition, this image reminds the Ephesians that their witness to the powers is not incompatible with being in chains and that witness cannot be thwarted by their imprisonment.

If one reads 6:10–20 in the light of Paul's previous discussion about the church's relationship to the powers in 3:1–12, it allows one to connect the admonitions of 6:10–20 with much of the prior argument of Ephesians. The admonition to put on the armor of God gains new force when it is seen in light of the church's witness to the powers, which itself is tied to Paul's explication of the mystery of salvation that runs through Eph 2–3. Moreover, the practices and habits of walking worthily that begin from the discussion of unity in Eph 4 are then tied to the church's abilities faithfully to witness to the spiritual forces opposed to God's economy of salvation.

Perhaps most significant for contemporary Christians, Paul closes Ephesians with a further emphasis on the church's role as witness to God's mystery of salvation. A divided body of Christ is all too vulnerable to being manipulated and co-opted by forces hostile to God's economy of salvation. Ultimately God will ensure that God's desires for the world are brought to fruition. In this respect, God does not need the church. Alternatively, however, the church will need to stand before the Lord "on the evil day," give an account of its witness to a world that was in desperate need of reconciliation, and admit how its own divisions and disunity threatened to falsify the reconciliation accomplished in the death and resurrection of Christ.

Ephesians 6:21–24
Final Words

This section of Ephesians concludes the letter in fairly typical ways. Verses 21–22 show a remarkable correspondence to Col 4:7–8. Readers can refer to the introduction to see how this correspondence might be evaluated.[1] Paul tells the Ephesians that he is sending Tychicus to them to keep them informed about Paul's circumstances and how he is doing in those circumstances. Paul concludes the letter with a benediction of peace upon the church.

6:21 So[a] that you might also[b] know about my circumstances and how I am doing, I am sending[c] Tychicus, the beloved brother and faithful servant in the Lord. He will make everything known to you. 22 I am sending him to you for this purpose: so that you might know about our circumstances and that your hearts might be comforted.

23 Peace to you, brothers and sisters,[d] and love with faith from God the Father and the Lord Jesus Christ. 24 Grace be with all who have an undying love of the Lord Jesus Christ.

a. There is some textual variation regarding the word order at the beginning of v. 21. The word order here does not affect the meaning. As is often the case in Ephesians, vv. 21–22 comprise a single Greek sentence. The translation above has rendered this single Greek sentence as three English sentences.

b. The term translated "also" in v. 21 is a bit anomalous. It may refer to others beyond the Ephesians to whom Tychicus may have been sent (Hoehner 869, but reluctantly). The Colossians would be the most likely "other." It may refer to a shift from more doctrinal and moral information to sharing about Paul's personal circumstances. Thomas Aquinas (246) and Schnackenburg (288) each offer variations on this possibility. The most likely explanation, however, is that the Greek *kai* is simply a loose formulation, as in 1:15 and 2:1, and does not really refer to anything in particular (Lincoln, *Ephesians* 465; Best, *Ephesians* 615).

c. In the translation above the Greek aorist *epempsa* (I have sent) is rendered as "I am sending." The use of the aorist here is often called the epistolary aorist. By the time

1. See also Best, "Who Used Whom?"

the letter is heard by its recipients, the "sending" has already occurred. Of course, at the time of writing the sending could not have occurred.

d. The Greek simply has "brothers." "Brothers and sisters" retains the inclusive nature of the Greek *adelphos* without blunting the important familial imagery. The addition of "you" in the translation is to make explicit in English what Paul seems to assume.

[21–22] Here Paul promises to send his coworker Tychicus to the Ephesians to relate information to them about Paul.[2] In addition to the parallel verse in Col 4:7, Tychicus appears in Acts 20:4 in a list of Paul's traveling companions. He is identified along with Trophimus as coming from Asia. He also appears in 2 Tim 4:12 and Titus 3:12. The reference in 2 Timothy says that Paul has sent Tychicus to Ephesus. In Titus, Tychicus again appears as someone Paul might send to Titus. The picture that emerges is of a trusted emissary; someone close to Paul whom Paul trusts to convey reliable information and whose pastoral skills in speaking to congregations about Paul will offer "comfort."

In this electronic age in which we pass around ever more trivial information ever faster, it is easy to forget how difficult it would be for an apostle in prison to give and receive news. Emissaries such as Tychicus played an important role in keeping a network of communities both in touch with each other and in touch with Paul.

[23–24] The epistle began with Paul's wishing grace and peace to the Ephesians (1:2). This is a common salutation in Paul's Letters (cf. Rom 1:7; 1 Cor 1:3; 2 Cor 1:2; Gal 1:3; Phil 1:2; 2 Thess 1:2; Phlm 3). In 6:23–24 that wish of grace and peace is repeated. Here at the end, however, peace and grace should be understood in the light of the things Paul has said in the body of the letter about God's gracious economy of salvation and Christ's work of peacemaking among Jews and Gentiles.

Unlike other Pauline Letters, the Ephesians are addressed in the third person (brothers and sisters) rather than the second-person "you." As one might expect, this becomes evidence in the discussion of Pauline authorship. That issue aside, this form of address does inject a distance between writer and reader. At the very least it may indicate that this letter is intended for a wider audience such as we find in 1 Pet 5:9 ("your brotherhood in all the world").[3]

Given that Paul has reemphasized the church's mission to witness to the powers about the mystery of salvation, a mystery that is focused on Christ's becoming our peace by uniting Jew and Gentile into one body, the wish of "peace" here is most fitting. The church's embodiment of this peace must be a crucial component in its mission (cf. 4:3). Paul also wishes love with faith from God the Father and the Lord Jesus Christ. This love that comes from God

2. See the discussion of Tychicus and Col 4 in the introduction.
3. So Lincoln, *Ephesians* 465; Schnackenburg 290.

is seen as key to maintaining the unity of the Spirit in the bond of peace, which is crucial for walking in a manner worthy of the gospel (4:1–7).

Finally, God's grace has established the church, bringing the Ephesians (and all believers) into this mystery of salvation (3:9). The grace that Paul wishes on all those who have an undying love for the Lord is to sustain them in the life and work that God has given them to do.

INDEX OF ANCIENT SOURCES

INDEX OF SUBJECTS AND AUTHORS

CPSIA information can be obtained
at www.ICGtesting.com
Printed in the USA
LVHW042258090723
751960LV00002B/291

9 780664 239442